Peter E. Murphy

Tourism

A community approach

METHUEN

New York and London

First published in 1985 by Methuen, Inc.
29 West 35th Street, New York, NY 10001

Published in Great Britain by Methuen & Co. Ltd
11 New Fetter Lane, London EC4P 4EE

© 1985 Peter E. Murphy

Typeset by Keyset Composition
Printed in Great Britain at the
University Press, Cambridge

Library of Congress Cataloging in Publication Data
Murphy, Peter E.
    Tourism: a community approach.
    Bibliography: p.
    Includes index.
    1. Tourist trade.   I. Title.
G155.M86   1985   380.1′459104   85–13884
ISBN 0 416 39790 5
        0 416 35930 2 (pbk.)

British Library Cataloguing in Publication Data
Murphy, Peter E.
    Tourism: a community approach.
    1. Tourist trade
    I. Title
    338.4′791   G155.A1
ISBN 0 416 39790 5
        0 416 35930 2 Pbk

To Susan, Margaret, and Ann,
for their constant encouragement and patience

Contents

List of figures   ix
List of tables   xi
Acknowledgements   xiii
Preface   xv

Section 1   Tourism and its significance   1

    1   Scope and nature of tourism   3
    2   Evolution of tourism   17
    3   Issues in tourism   30

Section 2   The environment and accessibility   39

    4   Environmental–accessibility issues   41
    5   Environmental and accessibility strategies   60

Section 3   Economics and business   77

    6   Economic cycles and benefits   79
    7   Economic response strategies   104

Section 4   Society and culture   117

    8   Hospitality and authenticity issues   119
    9   Social and cultural strategies   134

Section 5   Planning and management   153

    10   Tourism planning goals and methods   155
    11   Tourism as a community industry   166

Afterword   177
References   179
Name index   191
Subject index   196

List of figures

1 Relationships between recreation and tourism 9
2 Components of the tourism market 10
3 Two views of the USS *Massachusetts* anchored at Fall River, a declining industrial center of New England 15
4 T-shirt recording unfortunate result of territorial disputes between man and wildlife in Banff National Park 31
5 Languedoc–Roussillon regional development incorporating Tourist Units 35
6 Major components for a community-oriented tourism strategy 37
7 Banff Township in mid-summer, complete with hotels, restaurants, stores, and crowds 42
8 Climbers on Stanage Edge, Peak District National Park 43
9 Cross-section of coastal dunes 44
10 Erosion at Land's End, England 47
11 Destination area's perspective of a vacation experience 55
12 Man's perceptual map of his home town, surrounding regions, and far places 56
13 Daniel Wallingford's view of a "typical" New Yorker's mental map of the USA 58
14 The relative emphasis on preservation and use in individual zones of the zoning system for National Parks 63
15 Plan of Farnborough resort complex, Queensland, Australia 67
16 Yosemite Valley's Shuttle Bus system 72
17 Goyt Valley traffic experiment 73
18 Park and ride scheme in St Ives, Cornwall 74
19 Traffic planning within the Tower of London Jewel House 75
20 Renovations during the off-season 82
21 Off-season recuperation for Nanaimo's palms 83
22 Theoretical growth curve for a new product 85
23 Spatial impact of varying degrees of transport flexibility 88
24 Economic impact of tourist spending on a community 91
25 Tourism regions and eligible–ineligible areas for TIDSA in British Columbia 96
26 Aesthetic despoliation of coastal areas by uncontrolled trailer camps 113
27 Diagram of a tourist region 121
28 Causation theory of visitor–resident irritants 124
29 Attitudinal/behavioral attributes of inter-cultural perception 125
30 Distribution of decision-making group views toward local tourism 127
31 Exposure to the democratic parliamentary process 129
32 Cherokee Indian displays near Great Smoky Mountains National Park 136

List of figures

33	Kimberley's Bavarian-style clock and town center	139
34	Baltimore's tourism-oriented Inner Harbor	141
35	Regional dispersion strategies in London	143
36	Staged attractions of Fort Steele (pioneer days) and *Queen Mary* (technological exhibit)	147
37	The Vacation Village calendar	150
38	Evolution of approaches to tourism planning	160
39	Standard master plan process	161
40	PASOLP method of tourism planning	162
41	Illustration of systems planning method using the PASOLP approach	164
42	Ecological model of tourism planning	168
43	Task model for "Tourism Victoria"	178

List of tables

1	Tourist typologies	6
2	Changing mobility	20
3	Growth factors in the evolution of tourism	22
4	Travel industry growth trend factors, 1929–2029	28
5	Planned participation of residents and tourists in the Yellowknife region of the Northwest Territories	48
6	Visitation levels of selected North American National Parks	50
7	Seasonal distribution of London's visitor arrivals	79
8	Accommodation load factors	80
9	International travel to and from the United States in 1980	85
10	Visitor expenditures by accommodation category	90
11	Tourism multiplier calculations for various economies	92
12	Tourist income multipliers for accommodation sectors of Anglesey	93
13	Results of input–output model for Anglesey accommodation sectors, 1970	94
14	Income from selected industries in and around Exmoor National Park	98
15	Costs per visitor-day of public services rendered directly to visitors to Hawaii, 1968	99
16	Heeley's calculation of Norfolk's Fire Brigade tourism costs, 1974–5	100
17	Summary statement of net local authority infrastructure expenditure attributable to tourism in Norfolk, 1975–6	101
18	Net cost of tourism to local authorities in Norfolk, 1975–6	102
19	Seasonal distribution of conventions	105
20	Revenue–expenditure ratios for non-resident tourists to San Diego, California	107
21	Percentage of farms offering tourist accommodation, 1979–81 (estimates)	108
22	Percentage distribution of recreational subdivisions of 1000 acres or more	114
23	Local attitudes toward tourism in Torquay, Windsor, and York (1977)	123
24	Negative tourism impacts identified in resident surveys	123
25	Stepwise discriminant analysis of local groups toward tourism	126
26	Types of touristic situations	128
27	Number of hotels abroad associated with leading transnational corporations, 1978	132
28	TIDSA and related multi-sector agreements in Canada	158
29	Systems components in urban spatial structure and a destination area	175

Acknowledgements

This book has been produced with the help of several people in the Department of Geography at the University of Victoria. In particular, I wish to thank Ole Heggen and Ken Josephson for the illustrations, and Debbie Penner for typing the manuscript. Finally, I would like to acknowledge the feedback and encouragement received from my students, and the financial support of a Canada Council research grant.

The author and the publishers would like to thank the following individuals, journal editors, organizations and publishers for permission to reproduce copyright material that appears on the pages below:

Z. T. Mieczkowski and the *Canadian Geographer* for Figure 1   *9*

Department of Geography, University of Victoria, British Columbia, for Figure 2, with G. Montgomery for Table 28, and with J. Lundgren for Figure 23   *10, 158 and 88*

C. J. Metelka for a prose extract   *11*

J. W. Darlington for prose extracts   *18 and 19*

H. Kahn and *Travel Trade News* for Tables 2 and 4   *20 and 28*

A. Haulot for a prose extract   *24*

A. Clarke and *Annals of Tourism Research*, and D. Pearce and Longman, London, for Figure 5   *35*

R. C. Mings and *Tourist Review* for prose extracts   *36*

I. L. McHarg and Doubleday, New York, for Figure 9   *44*

E. L. Jackson, D. R. Schinkel and the *Canadian Geographer* for Table 5   *48*

J. C. Hendee, R. W. Harris and the *Journal of Forestry* for a prose extract   *49*

J. Overton and the *Canadian Geographer* for a prose extract   *49*

B. Goodey and the Editor, Occasional Papers, CURS, University of Birmingham, for Figure 12   *56*

P. Gould, R. White and Penguin Books, Harmondsworth, for a prose extract   *56–7*

F. V. Thierfeldt for Figure 13   *58*

B. K. Downie and *The Operational Geographer* for Figure 14   *63*

Bligh, Jessup, Bretnall Architects and the *Annals of Tourism Research* for Figure 15   *67*

The Yosemite National History Association for Figure 16   *72*

The Countryside Commission for Figure 17   *73*

The Greater London Council for Table 7   *79*

R. W. Butler and the *Canadian Geographer* for a prose extract   *86*

R. D. Kreutzwiser for Figure 24   *91*

B. Archer and the University of Wales Press for Tables 12 and 13   *93 and 94*

The Tourism and Recreation Research Unit, University of Edinburgh, for Table 14   *98*

D. E. Lundberg and CBI Publishing, Boston, for Table 15   *99*

J. Heeley for Tables 16, 17 and 18   *100, 101 and 102*

D. L. Tatzin and the Travel and Tourism Research Association for Table 20   *107*

L. A. Dernoi and *Tourism Management* for Table 21   *108*

J. T. Coppock and Pergamon Press, Oxford, for prose extracts   *112*

H. B. Stroud and the Association of American Geographers for Table 22 and prose extracts   *114 and 115*

Acknowledgements

V. L. Smith and the *Annals of Tourism Research* for Figure 27 *121*

E. M. Bjorklund, R. W. Butler and Trent University for Figure 29 *125*

The *Journal of Travel Research* for Table 25 and Figure 30 *126 and 127*

L. Norris and the *Vancouver Sun* for Figure 31 *129*

E. Cohen and the *Annals of Tourism Research* for Table 26 *128*

J. H. Dunning, M. McQueen and the *Annals of Tourism Research* for Table 27 *132*

J. W. Jordan and the *Annals of Tourism Research* for Figure 37 and prose extracts *150, 149, 150 and 151*

J.P. Gravel and Dowden, Hutchinson & Ross, Strouds-burg, PA, for Figure 38 *160*

M. Baud-Bovey and F. Lawson and the Architectural Press, London, for Figures 39, 40 and 41 *161, 162 and 164*

L. S. Bourne and Oxford University Press for Table 29 *175* (From *Internal Structure of the City: Readings on Urban Form, Growth, and Policy* by Larry S. Bourne. Copyright © 1982 by Oxford University Press, Inc. Reprinted by permission.)

Tourism Management for Figure 42, Table 29 and a prose extract *168, 175 and 166–76*

P. Blake and the *Architectural Forum* for prose extracts *169 and 170*

D. Runyan, C.T. Wu and the *Annals of Tourism Research* for a prose extract *171*

The author and publisher have made every effort to obtain permission to reproduce copyright material throughout this book. If any proper acknowledgement has not been made, or permission not received, we would invite any copyright holder to inform us of this oversight.

Preface

Anyone who decides to write a book requires both motivation and a masochistic streak. The first drives the author on, the second conditions him to the domination and demands of the project. In this case there were three prime motives to set pen to paper. First, a feeling that the growing tourism literature needed some form of synthesis to make it intelligible to the student of tourism and managers of the industry. Second, to offer an approach that would correct the inadequacies of previous survey texts. Third, in recognition that tourism in industrial nations was now reaching a crucial stage in its development, to suggest a planning method that would meet the needs of tourism and integrate them into the general planning process of western nations.

The first motive stemmed primarily from personal contact with citizens and university students, living in a popular tourist destination yet with little appreciation of what tourism meant to their community or where it could lead them. Those involved in the industry, or who were responsible for its development and planning, had little knowledge of what was happening elsewhere or understanding of the regional and long-term effects of their various proposals. Those who had investigated the growing literature on tourism were either confused by the technicalities of many papers, or were not sure where the individual studies fitted into the overall development picture. To these groups, professionals, laymen, and students, some form of integrating framework was necessary at this stage.

Some attempts to provide a synoptic summary of the literature have been made recently, but there have generally been some serious inadequacies. Foremost amongst these has been the systematic approach to the industry, which reviews its individual components in turn. While this may be justified as a categorizing and simplifying technique, it does little to reveal the importance of cross-sectional linkages and the building up of a complete tourist product and image. Past surveys have also been guilty of a lack of focus in their examination of tourism. One's view of the industry's problems and prospects vary considerably according to the perspective taken; thus confusion reigns when development decisions require consideration of external impacts and trade-off priorities need to be established. Finally, most texts have been descriptive rather than prescriptive, yet they offer plenty of evidence that tourism can create problems and requires corrective actions.

The modern tourism industry of the post Second World War era is now approaching its fortieth anniversary, and in some ways is facing its own mid-life crisis. During this 40-year period we have witnessed increased mobility and affluence leading to more extensive and extravagant travel, tastes have changed and certain areas and facilities have become outmoded. But this boom period has given way to uncertainty and readjustment as rising fuel prices, inflation, and recession have taken their toll on this discretionary activity. Despite these recent setbacks no one expects the tourism industry to disappear, but changes in its form and structure are inevitable and will need a new form of planning and management.

In response to the above considerations this book attempts to offer a more comprehensive examination of tourism development, a new perspective for its evaluation, and a suggested strategy for its continued development and evolution.

Much can be learned from the past, and the text examines those themes which emerge from the industry's history and have a bearing on its future. In order to simplify the analysis of issues it adopts a systematic approach, but with two differences. First, after examining common problems it examines strategies or policies that have been used to resolve them. Second, to reflect the holistic nature of tourism it combines the individual parts into an integrated approach of issue identification and planning.

Throughout the book the focus of attention is on tourism in the industrial nations of North America and western Europe, with an investigative perspective based on the destination community. This choice was made because industrial nations form the major tourist generating and receiving areas, with domestic tourism outstripping international travel by a four to one margin. In an era of uncertainty and individual restraint such a margin may be magnified as people holiday closer to home. Within this context those destinations that have committed themselves to tourism, or are planning to embrace this activity, are a logical base from which to assess the industry. They represent the industry's shop floor, where visitor and host meet, where its impacts are felt most keenly, and where the hopes of corporate and government planning will lie. Taking a community approach permits a more balanced assessment of the

industry and its impacts, since it involves the interests of many groups within one setting.

This balance is continued in the concluding section, which advocates the adoption of an ecological approach to tourism planning. The basis of this argument is that the natural resources of a community (both physical and human) are often the *raison d'être* for the industry and that stewardship of such resources is essential to its long-term success and survival. In addition, the ecological approach allows the various components of the industry and community to be integrated, permitting the assessment of conflict situations and trade-off opportunities.

Such an approach leads naturally into the systems planning methods that have been adopted in many industrial nations. This type of planning permits tourism to be integrated into general community goals and planning strategies, and also provides the flexibility needed to adjust to changing economic and market circumstances. Furthermore, the concepts of monitoring and management associated with systems planning fit in well with the idea that successful destination development involves people management as well as physical development.

Section 1

Tourism and its significance

Tourism has become one of the world's major industries, but its emergence since the Second World War has caught many unaware and unprepared. Its revenue and development potential were soon recognized and pursued in the expansionary post-war economy, first by individual entrepreneurs and then governments. Consequently, the early emphasis was on growth and promotion rather than management and control. Tourism was viewed as being a "natural" renewable resource industry, with visitors portrayed as coming only to admire—not consume—the landscape, customs, and monuments of a destination area. However, as tourism grew in size and scope it became apparent that this industry, like others, competed for scarce resources and capital, and that its non-consumptive attributes did not necessarily prevent the erosion or alteration of attractions.

With the advent of mass tourism has come the reckoning and a belated recognition that to become a renewable resource industry tourism requires careful planning and management. Mass tourism is more than an increased volume of visitors, it has come to mean a myriad of manufacturing and service businesses which combine to offer a travel experience through scale economies and mass-merchandising. The heady days of rapid expansion tended to overshadow growing signs of negative environmental and social impacts, but as the competition for scarce resources grew more intense and the pressures of many visitors more evident, the problems of certain destinations and stress within the system could not be denied.

It is the purpose of this section to define the nature and scope of tourism, examine its evolution, and illustrate some of the major issues to be faced in maintaining and developing this industry. The text focuses on tourism problems and possible response strategies of destination areas in developed countries. Destinations are the interface between tourists and local communities, where the negative impacts and conflicts are felt most strongly and where remedial action will be required, whether it be physical or strategic planning.

This section concludes with the contention that the opportunities presented by the industry and the difficulties arising from its rapid development can best be examined and resolved through a community approach. Tourism has been examined traditionally in a systematic and aspatial manner, which has failed to give sufficient weight to the significance of its interactions and the importance of destination character. By focusing attention on the development of a community tourism product it is felt that several past research and planning weaknesses can be rectified. A community emphasis would temper the economic concerns with environmental and social considerations. The spatial impact of national policies and individual developments can be traced throughout a nation, thanks to the multi-scale interpretation and interlinkage of the term "community." Finally, the importance of community survival, as a permanent home in which to live, work, and play, can be acknowledged in addition to the focus on its tourism potential.

1

Scope and nature of tourism

Size and importance

Tourism has grown from the pursuits of a privileged few to a mass movement of people, with the "urge to discover the unknown, to explore new and strange places, to seek changes in environment and to undergo new experiences" (Robinson 1976, xxi). During the post-war period tourism grew into a mass tourist industry. The number of international tourist arrivals rose from 25 million in 1950 to 183 million in 1970, an average growth rate of more than 10 percent (IUOTO 1970). Since 1973 the effect of fuel price increases has merely moderated the rate of expansion. According to estimates by the World Tourist Organization (WTO) international tourist arrivals in 1982 reached 280 million; but even more remarkable is the fact that these numbers reflect only the minor, and more easily measured, aspects of the tourism picture. Domestic tourism, which involves travel within one's own country, is more difficult to quantify but generally accounts for 75–80 percent of all tourism activity (Lundberg 1976, 9). According to the WTO there were over 2 billion domestic trips in 1981, representing a 240 percent increase over 1975 figures.

Such mass movements of people have been described as contemporary migration patterns. Migration can be seen as a response to stress, and Wolfe (1966) identifies three migration patterns in our society. The first, migration to the city, is a continuation of the nineteenth-century phenomenon, and, in the opinion of some, may have run its course in the developed world. The second, the journey to and from work, is a result of our large-scale urbanization and spatial separation of workplace and home. The third, recreational travel, is the newest migration and a function of the other two. It

has been stimulated by the stress and uniformity of urban life and been accommodated by the standard of living and mobility provided by the same urban-economic system. Being the newest migration, recreational travel has experienced phenomenal growth rates—rates which cannot be maintained but which led to a major change in our lifestyles. Like the other migrations before it, tourism will peak and probably decline, but it will remain a part of our lives and probably change in form and emphasis in the process.

The multi-faceted nature of tourism, its various links with the manufacturing and retail sectors, and its numerous seasonal or unofficial businesses make it extremely difficult to assess its market size. One estimate, however, suggests that worldwide travel spending reached $488 billion in 1978 (Waters 1978, 5). This represented 6 percent of the world's 1978 Gross National Product (GNP), which in turn was the equivalent of West Germany's GNP at that time. A more recent WTO estimate places the 1981 expenditure on world travel at $919 billion. The growth in tourism revenues has been substantial since the Second World War, but as in the case of visitor volumes the rate of growth has slowed since the oil crisis and inflation of the 1970s. When calculated in real terms the revenue increases have declined from the post-war region of 10 percent a year to 3 percent, but it is still growth nevertheless (OECD 1980).

Despite the short-term setbacks of the energy crises and recessions of the late 1970s and early 1980s, tourism is seen as a growth industry of the future. Toffler's *Future Shock* (1971) described the modern businessman and vacation traveler as the "new nomads" and foresaw:

a revolutionary expansion of certain industries where sole output consists not of manufactured goods, nor even of

3

ordinary services, but of pre-programmed "experiences". The experience industry could turn out to be one of the pillars of super-industrialism, the very foundation, in fact, of the post-service economy. (Toffler 1971, 208)

His more recent work, *The Third Wave* (1981), predicted the breakup of industrial society, as we know it, through a process of "demassification," breaking up large units of government and industry into more individual and flexible lifestyles. Among the changes which will relate to tourism he foresaw:

Large numbers of workers already do paid work for what averages out to only three or four days a week, or they take six months or a year off to pursue educational or recreational goals. This pattern may well grow as two-paycheck households multiply. (Toffler 1981, 277)

The appeal of this industry for the transitory period from an industrial society to whatever future awaits us is not limited to futurologists. Nations, such as Spain and Austria, have based much of their post-war development on growth in their tourism sectors. Earnings from the international tourist account contributed a significant portion of their export earnings in 1977, 22.5 percent for Spain and 21.7 percent for Austria. This compared with a European Community average of 4.7 percent (British Tourist Authority 1981, 13), and created a major source of "hard" currency for other development projects. Furthermore, in a time of growing automation and rising unemployment, tourism as a labor-intensive industry has proved to be both economically and politically appealing. As the then Prime Minister of England, James Callaghan, once described the situation:

Now new plants in manufacturing and new investment and new methods bring greater efficiency but it does not necessarily mean more jobs, and for this reason, we need to look at the service industries of which tourism is a notable example as an additional and important source of income and work. (English Tourist Board 1977, 5)

The development of mass tourism has created a powerful and influential recreational travel industry. For example, in England it is estimated that "some 1½ million jobs were generated either directly or indirectly by tourism in 1975, equivalent to about 6 percent of total employment" (English Tourist Board 1978a, 4). In Canada tourism is promoted as big business which is important to all Canadians, because it employs one out of ten workers and is the seventh largest earner of foreign exchange (CGOT 1982). In the United States

the tourism industry grosses an estimated $105 billion annually and employs over 5 million workers (Pizam and Pokela 1983). With such impressive statistics and employment opportunities it is little wonder that this industry has become a powerful political lobby. In Britain and Canada the industry has received generous development grants, and in Canada a private sector task force is cooperating with the government to produce the first national tourism plan (Powell 1978).

At the international level the United Nations has noted the economic and social significance of this growth industry. A 1979 report stated that tourism was bigger business than iron and steel or armaments, and that about 500 million workers and their families throughout the world were entitled to paid vacations. While recognizing the beneficial economic effects tourism can bring to national economies and world trade, the United Nations Manila Conference on World Tourism noted that its potential goes beyond just economic considerations. The first declaration of that Conference read:

Tourism is considered an activity essential to the life of nations because of its direct effects on the social, cultural, educational and economic sectors of national societies and their international relations. (UN 1981, 5)

Since tourism is now an integral part of modern societies, its study and analysis becomes imperative if its potential economic and social benefits are to be maximized and developed in a manner consistent with society's goals. The growth of tourism has converted many communities into destination areas, either as major resorts or as temporary stop-overs for travelers. The impact of the industry and its local issues will vary according to its magnitude and relative importance, but in every case politicians, businessmen, and residents are recognizing they cannot ignore tourism if they wish to benefit from it.

Definitions

The *raison d'être* of the industry is the tourist, so all development and planning must be predicated on the understanding of who this person is, if it is to succeed. The term "tourist" is derived from the word "tour," meaning, according to *Webster's Dictionary*, "a journey at which one returns to the starting point; a circular trip usually for business, pleasure or education during which various places are visited and for which an itinerary is usually planned." As this definition indicates, there are several motives for travel, each requiring its own facilities and having a different impact. Thus, government agencies in search of a comprehensive definition of tourist, and one which will facilitate the measurement of this activity, have resorted to the more general term of "visitor." The definition most widely recognized and used is that produced by the 1963 United Nations Conference on Travel and Tourism in Rome, which was adopted by the International Union of Official Travel Organizations (IUOTO) in 1968. It states that a visitor is:

any person visiting a country other than that in which he has his usual place of residence, for any reason other than following an occupation remunerated from within the country visited.

Thus, tourism is concerned with all travelers visiting foreign parts, whether it be for pleasure, business, or a combination of the two. The only exception is someone who is setting up a new residence in a foreign country and will be earning a salary and paying taxes in this new country. The IUOTO definition was intended for international travel but it can accommodate domestic tourism by substituting region for country.

Visitors have been subdivided further into two categories to assist the measurement of tourist traffic and the assessment of its economic impact.

(1) Tourists—who are visitors making at least one overnight stop in a country or region and staying for at least 24 hours.

(2) Excursionists—who are visitors that do not make an overnight stop, but pass through the country or region. An excursionist stays for less than 24 hours, and includes day-trippers and people on cruises.

This division has the practical value of using overnight accommodation records (registrations) as the basic source of tourist information, which can be used in conjunction with border crossing records if international movement is involved. By focusing on the accommodation sector of the industry, however, it also produces conservative estimates of the travel picture. There is no way to count overnight visits with relatives and friends and it is often impossible to obtain accurate records from small or temporary establishments like guest houses and farms.

The excursionist, or day-tripper, can be viewed as a special tourist. Such a person visits a destination for a day or spends some time there while passing through as part of a tour. In either case, he or she is a visitor, spending time and money while utilizing space and facilities in the destination area.

Types of tourist

There are as many types of tourist as there are motives for travel. Each type makes different demands of a destination, and has its own particular impacts. Business travel can range from convention and trade fair meetings to vacations that include self-advancement courses or permit the traveler to update certain areas of his profession. Leisure travel can incorporate activity packages where the tourist learns a new sports skill or craft, as well as developing a tan. The impact of tourists' demands will vary according to the demands they place on a destination's physical and human resources.

Tourist typologies can be grouped into two general categories (Table 1). *Interactional* types emphasize the manner of interaction between visitors and destination areas, whereas the *cognitive–normative* models stress the motivations behind travel. Both approaches indicate the strong links between visitor expectations–motivations and the structure of destination areas. Thus it can be seen immediately that no destination appeals to all tourists and each can develop its own segment of the tourism market.

Among the interaction models are those of Cohen (1972) and Smith (1977b). Cohen classified tourists according to the degree they seek familiar or strange settings and whether or not they were willing to be institutionalized (organized) in their travel. Smith's more detailed breakdown incorporates recent market developments such as the unorganized "hippie treks" to Nepal and the social implications of a highly structured charter business. Smith, like Cohen, views explorers and elite travelers as having little impact upon indigenous cultures. Their small number requires little in the way of special accommodation, and their desire to gain insight into local customs is aided by a sympathetic attitude to the local way of life. In contrast, the charter tourists travel in their own environmental bubble, viewing everything from the security of their pre-paid and price-guaranteed package tour. To accommodate the large numbers and organizational structure of charters a community must become commercial in its dealings with tourists, and often needs to import foreign capital and expertise.

In contrast to the interaction models which focus on the market characteristics and symptoms of travel, the

Tourism and its significance

Table 1 Tourist typologies

	Experience	Demands	Destination impacts
Interactional models *Cohen (1972):*			
Non-institutionalized traveler	Drifter	Search for exotic and strange environment	Little because of small numbers
	Explorer	Arrange own trip and try to get off the beaten track	Local facilities sufficient and contact with residents high
Institutionalized traveler	Individual mass tourist	Arrangements made through tourist agency to popular destinations	Growing commercialization and specialization as demand grows
	Organized mass tourist	Search for familiar, travel in the security of own "environmental bubble" and guided tour	Development of "artificial" facilities, growth of foreign investment, reduced local control
Smith (1977b):	Explorer	Quest for discovery and desire to interact with hosts	Easy to accommodate in terms of numbers, acceptance of local norms
	Elite	Tour of unusual places, using pre-arranged native facilities	Small in number and easily adapted into surrounding environments
	Off-beat	Get away from the crowds	Minor because willing to put up with simple accommodation and service
	Unusual	Occasional side trips to explore more isolated area or undertake more risky activity	Temporary destinations can be simple but support base needs to have full range of services
	Incipient mass	Travel as individuals or small groups; seeking combination of amenities and authenticity	Numbers increasing as destination becomes popular; growing demand for services and facilities
	Mass	Middle-class income and values leads to development of a "tourist bubble"	Tourism now a major industry, little interaction with local people beyond commercial links
	Charter	Search for relaxation and good times in a new but familiar environment	Massive arrivals; to avoid complaints hotels and facilities standardized to western tastes
Cognitive–normative models *Plog (1972):*	Allocentric	Adventuresome and individual exploration	Small in number, board with local residents
	Mid-centric	Individual travel to areas with facilities and growing reputation	Increased commercialization of visitor–host relationship
	Psychocentric	Organized package holiday to "popular" destinations	Large-scale business, with facilities similar to visitors' home area
Cohen (1979a): Modern pilgrimage	Existential	Leave world of everyday life and practicality to escape to "elective center" for spiritual sustenance	Few participants who are absorbed into community, little impact on local life
	Experimental	Quest for alternative lifestyle and to engage in authentic life of others	Assimilated into destination areas because of small numbers and desires
	Experiential	Look for meaning in life of others, enjoyment of authenticity	Some impact as destination provides accommodation and facilities to "show" local culture
Search for pleasure	Diversionary	Escape from boredom and routine of everyday existence; therapy which makes alienation endurable	Mass tourism with large demand for recreation and leisure facilities; large impact because of numbers and commercialization
	Recreational	Trip as entertainment, relaxation to restore physical and mental powers	Artificial pleasure environment created; major impact on local lifestyles

cognitive–normative models attempt to reveal the causes of travel. Plog (1972) and Cohen (1979a) both look at the sociological concept of "center," which considers that every society possesses a center representing the charismatic nexus of its supreme, ultimate moral values. Plog develops a polar continuum consisting of those who differ from the normal (centric) values of society and follow their independent vacation desires (allocentrics), and those who conform to society's norms and values and thus become part of the mass market of tourism (psychocentrics).

Plog suggests that tourist destinations are attractive to different types of visitors as they evolve from untouched discoveries to popular resorts. A community can enter the tourism business with the arrival of a small number of adventurous allocentrics, but their impact would be small because no special facilities would be desired or required for this type of traveler. As the area becomes more accessible, better serviced and more widely known an increasing number of mid-centrics would visit. They in turn give way to large numbers of psychocentrics as the destination becomes a popular resort dependent on foreign investment and labor. The new visitors are made to feel at home, with a full range of facilities and attractions that may now be divorced from the natural geographic and social attractions which first attracted the allocentrics.

Cohen elaborates on this theme making further reference to people's "spiritual center, whether religious or cultural—the center which for the individual symbolizes ultimate meanings" (Cohen 1979b, 181). Those traveling on vacation believe there is some experience available elsewhere which cannot be found at home and which makes the travel worthwhile. The spiritual center of this quest may be purely hedonistic, such as in the case of diversionary and recreational travel, or it may be a new type of pilgrimage, with travelers seeking answers through experiential, experimental, or existential forms of travel. Cohen notes that these three levels of tourism represent different depths of meaning for the individual, but unlike traditional pilgrimages they involve movement away from the center of the tourist's culture toward an "elective center," which he has chosen or converted to.

Destination areas

To satisfy the variety of motives outlined above and to accommodate overnight or passing-through visitors, a physical setting is required. "Tourism as an industry occurs at 'destination areas'—areas with different natural and/or man-made features, which attract non-local visitors (or tourists) for [a variety of] activities" (Georgulas 1970, 442). This definition by Georgulas possesses two key aspects which distinguish a destination area; it must contain "features that will attract" and it must appeal to "non-local visitors."

Tourism is a voluntary activity; therefore a destination area must have attractions which appeal to at least one type of tourist. These attractions can be as varied as the tourist types, but they are generally divided into two categories, natural or man-made. Natural attractions include such features as sunshine or scenic landscapes, while man-made features can be primary attractions like Disneyland and the Edinburgh Festival, or support facilities like hotels and restaurants. A third category, which is now receiving more attention, would be a destination area's hospitality record. The manner in which visitors are received, and the quality of service provided, forms a major component of a destination's tourist image.

To be a destination an area must attract non-local visitors, people who have traveled some distance from their home town to see the attractions or use the facilities. This is an important feature because it differentiates recreational travel, where travel is an important and possibly the most important component of the experience, from outdoor recreation, where the activity is the prime objective and travel to a recreational site is of secondary importance or even an inconvenience. Furthermore, the emphasis on non-local visitors is a major economic consideration. Money spent by non-local visitors to an area becomes basic income, or earned income, for that community. If the money was spent by local people it would be redistributed income and thus not so beneficial to the destination area.

To determine whether an area can be classified as a tourist destination has traditionally required criteria to distinguish whether recreational traffic is local and not touristic, or non-local and therefore touristic. Burton (1971) identified five periods of recreational time which may help to distinguish local from non-local recreational travel. The five were: (i) very short (up to one hour), (ii) short (a few hours), (iii) a full day, (iv) several days (usually a weekend), and (v) a week or more (usually the annual vacation). Using this classification, those periods extending beyond a single full day would produce a full-fledged tourist because of the need for overnight stops, and it would provide sufficient opportunities for travel on a regional or national basis. Thanks to our increased mobility, however, it is possible to move beyond the physical limits of a home town in a matter of hours, thus making travel on a regional or non-local basis feasible in time periods (ii) and (iii).

Attempts to operationalize such a classification system have produced a rough guide by which to differentiate between local and non-local recreational travel. Wall (1972) in a study of recreational car trips in England classified a traveler as a "pleasure tripper" if he traveled 5 miles or more from his point of origin. Therefore, any village, stately home, or country park beyond this range can be considered a tourist destination if it was included in a day's outing or afternoon drive. Likewise, Clawson and Knetsch (1966, 38) in their classification of North American recreation areas have identified "intermediate areas" which they described as being "used for all-day outings and on weekends." Such areas include state parks, reservoirs and lakes which can be reached within two hours or so of driving. They possess no, or limited, accommodation yet they are definite destination areas for nearby urban centers. Such empirical classifications indicate that any community or area outside of a local recreational and economic hinterland can be considered a destination area.

In North America where freeways and emptier roads allow greater mobility, Wall's 5-mile radius to delimit destination areas needs to be extended considerably. Statistics Canada (1981, 30) uses 80 kilometers (50 miles) as its break point between local and non-local recreational travel. British Columbia (1979, 1) defines domestic tourism as "the travel, activities and services used by any British Columbia resident beyond a 40 kilometer (25 miles) radius from home for the purpose of personal enjoyment and travel."

In addition to concerns over the non-resident tourist and his generation of basic income, there is a growing awareness of the importance of resident tourists, those who are making new uses of their local settings. In economic terms it can be just as vital to keep more residents vacationing at home, rather than see them and their money disappear on external trips. Concern over the travel budget account is most frequently expressed at the national level, but since this is the sum of individual community accounts some areas have become anxious about their own deficits. Interest in attracting residents to vacation in their own town or area goes beyond economic considerations, however, to include a growing sense of pride in local heritage and amenities. The growing emphasis on a community's quality of life has encouraged many areas to invest in conservation and facilities that can create a viable, if occasional, tourist destination for residents.

Travel

A common theme in all definitions of tourism is travel, and Peters (1969, 2) went so far as to declare "the tourist industry is an industry concerned with movement." As we have seen, the journey must take a traveler beyond his home turf and because of this unfamiliarity it becomes an important part of the travel experience. "Getting there is half the fun" when people travel through different areas on their way to a destination. This fact has been recognized by tourism agencies in their attempts to develop scenic and circular routes that will stimulate the senses and curiosity of the traveler.

Travel and time are interwoven and it is necessary to be aware of both in order to appreciate their significance to tourism. Hartmann (1981), in a paper entitled "Tourism, travel, and timing," notes:

Whether we decide to travel by package tours where we trust in a fixed route and a pre-arranged time frame, or if we time our stay and change of place completely [by] ourselves, we need to know the principles of timing or at least to appreciate them.

Since tourism involves travel it requires greater blocks of discretionary time than much recreational activity. Thus, Burton's first recreational time period which accounts for much of our urban-oriented recreation has been discounted in the tourism context. The major blocks of discretionary time are the weekends and annual vacations, which account for the peaking of tourist travel in these periods and the problems of seasonality in the industry. Time also affects the demands for travel and structure of the industry. As people grow older their travel demands change. Young adults and elderly couples are considered a prime travel market because they have relatively large amounts of discretionary time and income. Between these two states the cost of buying a home and raising a family tends to reduce the discretionary aspects of a family budget. Likewise, the tourist industry can age and get out of step with technological innovations and consumer tastes. Lundgren (1983) illustrates this travel-time link in his temporal analysis of the Laurentians, north of Montreal, one of Canada's oldest tourist destinations.

Tourism

Tourism is a sum of the above elements, resulting from the *travel* of non-residents (*tourists*, including excursionists) to *destination areas*, as long as their sojourn does not become a permanent residence. It is a combination of recreation and business. Mieczkowski (1981) notes that while most tourism is recreational in nature, some tourism, such as business, professional, and personal travel is not associated with recreation (Figure 1). Recreation falls entirely within leisure since it is an experience during free or discretionary time which leads to some form of revitalization of the body and mind. Part of this recreational activity takes place outside of the local community and as a result travel becomes an important component, leading this form of recreation to be classified as tourism. Tourism's orb extends beyond recreation to become associated with

business trips and family reunions; and beyond leisure itself into personal and business motives for travel, such as health and professional development.

To move from the conceptual level to reality requires a system; therefore tourism is frequently referred to as a business or industry (Wahab 1975, 8; Lundberg 1976, 1; McIntosh 1977, 3). The tourism process combines a demand (tourist), suppliers (tourist industry), and a product (attractions), which Chau (1977) has summarized as the subject, means and object of tourism.

Most economists and compilers of industrial classifications argue that a tourism industry does not exist because it does not produce a distinct product (Chadwick 1981). One problem is that certain industries which sell a large proportion of their output to tourists, such as transport, accommodation, and entertainment, are not exclusively tourism industries, for they sell these services to local residents as well. Kaiser and Helber (1978, 3) maintain that it is not "properly" an industry, but more a cross-section of a regional or national economy. This does not however prevent them using the "industry" nomenclature throughout their book. Opposing this view, Mawhinney and Bagnall (1976, 383)

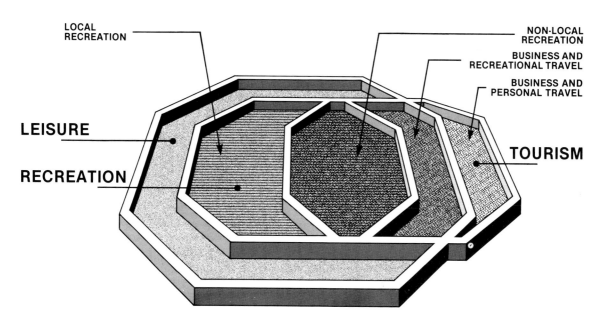

Figure 1 Relationships between recreation and tourism
Source: Mieczkowski (1981)

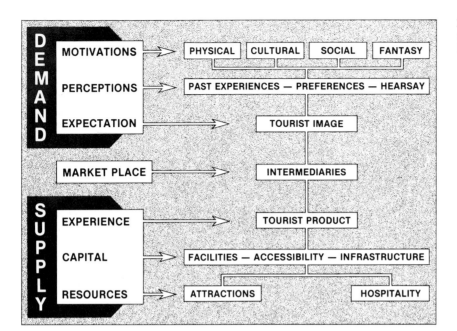

Figure 2 Components of the tourism market
Source: Murphy (1983)

take the position that tourism is an industry, similar to other industries like agriculture and mining in that it is dependent on the continued availability of those resources upon which it is based. In other words, it is a resource industry, one which sells to local and non-local markets but one whose success and future depend on careful management.

Whether one classifies tourism as an industry or not, one cannot ignore the resource base which is its *raison d'être*, or the delivery system which permits people to utilize those resources, if tourism is to be understood and managed for the benefit of society. Modern tourism must develop and protect its attractions, whether they be natural or man-made, and become a hospitality industry to make visitor experiences as enjoyable as possible. The tourism industry is highly fragmented with many types of businesses and many levels of industrialization, but they all have a common purpose and that is to help a visitor enjoy his trip. The travel experience is this industry's product, but unlike other industries it is the consumer who travels and not the product. Figure 2 demonstrates the supply and demand characteristics of tourism and how the industry attempts to bring these market forces together.

The industry's structure

Demand factors

Some understanding of basic demand motivations is necessary if the industry and planner are to fulfill tourists' desires. Four basic travel motivators have been identified by the industry (Figure 2). *Physical or physiological* motivators, such as relaxation and medical treatment are major reasons for a vacation, and the quality of food, drink, and comfort frequently represents an important criterion in assessing the travel experience. *Cultural* motivators have long been associated with the desire to learn about foreign countries and customs. *Social* motivators include visits with relatives and friends, meeting business associates at conferences, and pursuing activities associated with status and prestige. Combinations of cultural and social motives could be seen in the early tours of China, where influential people vied not only to see this previously closed society but also for the prestige of being one of the first to report on this great unknown. *Fantasy* motivators form an important element of travel demand and illustrate its individualistic nature. Dann (1976, 19) notes "holidays are essentially experiences in fantasy."

A good deal of this fantasy takes place before the trip itself:

a certain picture is built up of a world that marks an escape from present reality, and environment for acting out psychic needs, and the playing of certain roles which cannot be fulfilled at home, and it is this which forms part and parcel of tourist motivation. (Dann 1976, 22)

He goes on to identify two types of fantasy, the "anomic" where the average city dweller desires to transcend the monotony of everyday life, and "ego-enhancement" which provides psychological boosts through such activities as gambling holidays or sexual adventures—real or imagined.

To convert such motivation into a trip requires knowledge about the conditions and opportunities that exist within our reach. Unfortunately, as consumers and geographers we are flawed, we have fragmentary information and distorted images (mental maps) of the real world (Gould and White 1974). These images are our perceptions. Studies have shown that some regions have very favorable images while others have relatively negative ones, and that the differentiation is fairly consistent (Mayo 1973). The dominant attributes people use to sort out these mental images are often related to cost, climate, scenery, personal safety, and sanitation, and thus can have an important bearing on their choice of destination (Anderson and Colberg 1973; Crompton 1979).

Perception of holiday options and various destination areas is conditioned by three important elements (Figure 2). Individual preferences, reflecting an individual's personality, will direct the search for specific forms of gratification. They will dictate whether a person wishes to indulge in the gastronomic delights of a cruise or pit his skill and stamina against some mountain. Perceptions will be colored by past vacation experiences, with a satisfactory experience tempting repetition and possibly encouraging more adventurous pursuits. These two elements reflect the two schools of thought concerning image causation (Kotler 1975). One school suggests that images are largely person-determined whereas the other approach suggests that people's mental image is largely destination-determined.

The third element in image creation is hearsay, information from friends and relatives, the media, or travel agents. A study by Henderson and Voiland (1975, 91) revealed "communication or second-hand sources seem to play the strongest role when a person assesses an area's recreational utility." This conclusion supports the general communication and marketing models regarding a two-step flow of communication. According to this theory, ideas flow from radio and print to opinion leaders and from them to the more conservative sections of the population (Lazarsfeld *et al.* 1944; Cox 1964). Within the opinion leadership are two groups, the innovators and influentials. Much of the promotion for new destinations or experiences is directed at the adventurous and innovative market, and word of their pioneering experiences is channeled to the influential opinion leaders with the hope that they will adopt this new vacation and spread the concept by example to the masses. As we will see later this two-step theory of communication fits in very well with the general evolutionary pattern of resorts.

Motivation and perceived options build an *image* of each tourist destination (Figure 2). This image may be defined as the sum of beliefs, ideas, and impressions that a person has regarding a destination. It is a personal composite view of a destination's tourism potential, and where prices are comparable it is often the decisive factor in a tourist's selection process. The images are not necessarily the same for each visitor and this makes it difficult to allocate resources and plan for future land use in destination areas. To overcome this problem many areas attempt to appeal to a specific group through extensive and expensive promotion, presenting themselves as a family-oriented resort, a place for rugged outdoor enthusiasts, or a swinging locale for night people.

One problem which emerges with this system of image building is the time-lag between initial purchase, based on a projected image, and the actual experience. Tourism is unique, for as Metelka points out:

the would-be customer must decide to expend his valued resources of time and money BEFORE he actually consumes the product or service. Blatantly stated, a person decides to visit Tahiti and purchases the transport seat, the hotel and many other items long before he arrives in Tahiti. This dichotomy between time of decision/purchase and time of use has permitted if not encouraged promotional practices which some regard as dishonest. (Metelka 1977, 4)

Thus the time-lag makes misrepresentation easier, and the creation of a false image can spoil a vacation not only for the visitor but also for those around him, as they try to accommodate and humor a person who feels he has been sold "a pig in a poke."

Tourism and its significance

The potential for diverse perceptions can create a critical situation if it extends to differences between the residents and the industry. Metelka notes:

A second functional dichotomy exists between the residents of tourism destination areas and the would-be customers in the market place. Past and present marketing practices reflect the fact that destination area residents are overwhelmingly unaware of how their homeland is described in promotional material. (Metelka 1977, 4)

The image builders are often marketing or advertising experts who select and arrange "facts" about the destination that will entice would-be visitors. These promotional messages are beamed to other states and countries, and therefore the resident is in no position to correct mistakes or misrepresentations because he is not the intended viewer or purchaser. This lack of inherent control for the industry's marketing can lead to advertisements of questionable taste and of a self-destructive nature. Metelka gives some examples:

the Seychelles have been dubbed "The Promiscuous Isles."

In Honolulu, an aerial sightseeing firm prints brochures in English and Japanese asking tourists to imagine: "It's December 7th and you are there! Fly over Pearl Harbor, follow the same flight plan as the attacking Japanese planes."

Elegant, erotic, exotic! This is how the brochure describes a new jungle resort for the jet set, Habitation Le Clere, a spread of luxurious villas surrounded by areas of poverty.

"Ibiza: The invaded paradise." Living here is cheap . . . and was, until recently at least blissfully tranquil. But lately, Ibiza's slumberous calm has been jarred by the shockwaves of notoriety. (Metelka 1977)

As Metelka asks when he presents these and other examples, as a destination area resident, how would your opinions regarding local tourism be affected by these words?

Supply factors

Such a question is pertinent to an industry which regards itself as a host industry and is dependent on local goodwill, but it also needs to develop the resources and product which will substantiate the image. With such diversity of tourist demands and interests destinations need to focus on a particular market subset, one they can satisfy in terms of resources and facilities. When the supply side of the tourism market is considered the twin foundations of the industry are its destination area *attractions* and *hospitality* (Figure 2).

Tourism is a resource industry, one which is dependent on nature's endowment and society's heritage. Visitors are attracted to areas of outstanding beauty and this beauty can take many forms. In some areas it is the climate which is the major attraction, as can be seen with the sunbelt and Mediterranean resorts. In others it is landforms such as the Grand Canyon, the Rockies, or Alps, or specific terrain within these areas which may facilitate certain activities like the skiing in Vail, Colorado, or mountaineering around the Matterhorn. Water has always appealed as a source of relaxation whether it be associated with a seaside beach, a waterfall, or lake and river fishing. Flora and fauna provide idyllic settings and as such enhance a visit, such as the host of daffodils in the English Lake District at Easter; or provide a specific purpose to the visit, as with walks through alpine meadows or observing game in national parks and game reserves. Wherever an accessible area possesses several of these natural attributes it becomes a major attraction and in many cases has been designated a national park, so as to conserve these resources for future generations.

In addition to nature's resources, people are attracted by the cultural attributes of society and its heritage. Centers of learning (Oxford, Heidelberg), of culture (Stratford-upon-Avon, Athens), and of entertainment (London, New York) have long been magnets for travelers. Likewise, the splendor and history attached to various buildings and locations have created major attractions. Numerous castles (Windsor, Caernarvon), palaces (Versailles, Blenheim), stately homes (Woburn Abbey, Mount Vernon), ruins (Colosseum, Parthenon), and battlefields (Gettysburg, Pearl Harbor) feature prominently in the tourist literature. As the significance of heritage and its conservation has spread, whole city districts have been preserved because of their architectural merit, historical significance, and potential tourist value. "Venice is an extreme example of a tourist-dominated city," where the original city on the islands has become a tourist Mecca and the scene of an international restoration rescue, while its mainland twins of Marghera and Mestre provide the bulk of the region's industry and housing, and local life (Appleyard 1979, 15).

As important as the natural and cultural resources, which combine to form the major attractions, is the welcome which is accorded to a visitor. Public goodwill is an essential ingredient of any trip, for if the host community is antagonistic to visitors, no amount of attractions will compensate for the rudeness or hostility. It is for this reason that various governments feel obligated to remind residents of the value of tourism to local economies and encourage local people to be hospitable and friendly toward the visitor.

There are three facets to note about tourism's resource base. First, it is a combination of physical and human resources which form the basis of the industry. Nowhere is this more important than in the case where the major attraction is a public amenity, either publicly owned or subsidized by the public purse. Under these circumstances the industry's foundation is a public good (a beach, a plaza, a park, or museum), and as such the industry should be cognizant of its special relationship with the local community. It has a responsibility to foster what is in fact a community resource, and has no right to enclose or destroy it for its own purposes. Second, the physical resources often possess a seasonal element that encourages variations in visitation patterns. The most obvious is the climatic variation experienced in northern latitudes which encourages most people to consider vacations during the sunny summer weather. This climatic variation also affects the flora and fauna and attractiveness of various locations, providing each with a periodic climax. Thus, many of its attractions ensure that tourism will remain a seasonal activity, and any attempts to extend the seasonal life of a destination will need to consider supplementary activities. Finally, tourism has frequently been described as a search for the four S's — surf, sand, sun, and sex. If this sarcastic description of the industry has any truth in it, it is that prime attractions can be found in many areas of the world. This makes the industry very competitive and flexible, for it can often find substitute resources and locations if an original destination turns sour because of growing residential hostility or changing fashions and economic circumstances. As Peters (1969) has noted, the optimum situation for a destination is to offer "an asset so outstanding and unique that the tourist industry can largely depend on, and be prompted by, this feature." Since this stituation occurs rarely the industry and communities often attempt to supplement the natural tourist resources of an area with other facilities and man-made attractions.

To develop the tourist resources, making them more accessible and comfortable to experience, requires considerable *capital investment*, in some cases so

considerable it is beyond the capability of the individual businessman and private sector (Figure 2). A major expense, and prime area of government support, is in the provision of water supplies, public utilities, sewage systems, and highways. These are the pre-requisites for extensive development and are known as "infrastructure." These facilities are usually available in urban areas but must be created specifically for the industry in rural or isolated areas. Examples of government assistance in providing such basic services are very clear in new isolated resorts, such as federal–provincial support for the Whistler Mountain ski resort north of Vancouver, or in mega-projects such as the French government's support of the Languedoc recreation–tourism complex. But such assistance also occurs within the city, for its existing infrastructure frequently requires adjustment to accommodate new tourism facilities. For example, the building of a major hotel can necessitate changes to local water and sewer lines, the building of a convention or trade center usually requires direct financial aid and complementary adjustments to local traffic flows and parking. In most cases government assistance appears inevitable if extensive development of tourism resources is to occur, and such assistance is offered in the hope that future employment and taxes will justify the public expense.

To make a destination area more appealing and diversified in the competitive tourism market the industry often creates support facilities and artificial attractions. The objective is to create a more enjoyable and comfortable visit and thereby earn more revenue by inducing visitors to stay longer. An old maxim in tourism is "the longer they stay the more they spend," thus the industry continues to pursue the objective of enticing visitors to stay.

Ideally, the support facilities and attractions will supplement and complement the natural resources of the area. Hotels and motels should blend with the local architecture and landscape. Stores should emphasize local customs and handicrafts and, where possible, visitors should have access to local markets where informality and daily bustle add an air of authenticity and local flavor. Likewise, attractions are hopefully in keeping with the natural resources and customs of the area, providing complementary educational and enter-tainment themes. For example, coastal cities are developing marine exhibits to show sea-life, historic centers develop museums and tours, industrial centers are stressing industrial heritage as in the case of

Tourism and its significance

Stoke-on-Trent's renovated potteries and Dayton, Ohio's National Air Museum. Unfortunately, as we will see, such ideals are not always met and uncoordinated development can result in monotonous homogeneity and garish low-quality tourist traps, which clash with the destination's ambience.

In some cases the quality of the facilities and created attractions has been high enough, however, to rival the original tourist resources as a major destination attraction. Famous examples of this are Disneyland, California, and Disney World, Florida. They attract millions of visitors to what were previously agricultural areas, with Disneyland recording nearly 11 million visitors in 1978 and Disney World attracting over 14 million visitors in 1978—only 6 years after being opened. In the process, these Disney parks have set the standards by which all other thematic parks are judged.

Artificial attractions take many forms. A de-commissioned battleship, the USS *Massachusetts*, was introduced to the non-tourist area of Fall River, Massachusetts, to help boost and diversify the local economy (Figure 3). It has more than fulfilled those expectations, for the ship has over 200,000 visitors a year and generates over $2 million into the local economy annually (Lundberg 1976, 40). Such success has encouraged similar ventures in Long Beach, California (*Queen Mary*), and London (HMS *Belfast*), and now competition for retiring famous vessels has become intense. *Newsweek* (1980) reported a battle between the US Naval Academy in Annapolis, Maryland, and the submarine base in Groton, Connecticut, over who would have the honor of putting the world's first nuclear submarine, the USS *Nautilus*, on display.

Facilities designed to improve accessibility are a key capital investment for destination areas since the industry is based on travel. Investment in various forms of transport is considered desirable in order to remain competitive and flexible with ever-changing transport technology. Each new form of transport changes the accessibility equation for tourist destinations, especially those in peripheral regions. For example, Rudney considers:

Like most other tourist regions, the Côte d'Azure attained its "take-off" point when a means of fast comfortable transportation was introduced. In this case it was the railroad.... By 1889, the train trip from Paris to Nice took a mere 18 hours, where once it had taken 13 days by coach. (Rudney 1980, 215)

Similarly, development of the freeway system has brought certain scenic peripheral areas closer to urban–industrial centers, in terms of time, with dramatic increases in visitor volumes being the result. In the United States, Interstates 75 and 81 bring people from the Midwest and Atlantic states within a few hours of Gatlinburg and the Great Smoky Mountains National Park. As a result, this park receives over 8 million visits a year, more than three times the number of any other national park in the United States (Coppock and Rogers 1975).

Although transport links are seldom built solely for tourism purposes, the tourism market potential plays a major role in upgrading existing facilities and creating new ones. Competition for international tourists has encouraged various governments to build new airports or operate national airlines. Development of Hawaii's airport enabled it to take advantage of new generations of jet aircraft and their associated economies (Farrell 1982, 23). In some cases the importance of a tourist link becomes so important that governments will protect it with special legislation. British Columbia's government, for example, has promised to incorporate the ferry connection between Vancouver Island and the mainland into an Essential Services Act, to ensure it is not disrupted by labor disputes. A major factor in bringing this about is the importance of tourism to the Island in general and to Victoria, the Island's provincial capital, in particular.

The resources and created facilities of a destination combine to produce an amalgam of activities and functions called a *tourist product*. Due to the inter-related nature of the industry and its dependence on public facilities and goodwill, destination areas attempt to create a package or basket of goods for the visitor to perceive and experience. Naturally, the more co-ordinated the individual items, the more noticeable and effective the package. Thus, destinations attempt to present a theme that will attract attention and appeal to tourist images. Prominent successes in product formation include Las Vegas and Monte Carlo, which have become associated with gambling, entertainment, and luxury, or Disneyland which is synonymous with quality family entertainment.

The creation of a product that is noticeable and marketable in a competitive business world would appear to be a simple task for most industries, but for one made up of numerous individual businesses and entrepreneurial spirits, it is a major challenge. In a free enterprise system there is little control over market

Figure 3 Two views of the USS *Massachusetts* anchored at Fall River, a declining industrial center of New England

entry or quality. As Disneyland in Anaheim experienced, there is no way of influencing the quality and type of neighboring facility; there a carefully planned and developed attraction is surrounded by a jungle of neon lights, garish architecture, and snarled traffic. Not only is it difficult to develop a harmonious product within a destination, but it is even more difficult, with the competition for visitors, to get various destinations to combine their development and promotion into an effective regional product. Yet regional cooperation is required as the public becomes more mobile and is no longer content to spend its entire vacation in one place. Therefore, the need for government coordination and promotion has become more essential in drawing businessmen and destinations together in order to form regional product units, where the whole has more appeal than the sum of individual parts. This approach can be seen at the national level in England where the English Tourist Board has divided the country up into 12 regions, and, at the state/provincial level, with British Columbia's strategy of developing and promoting nine geophysical-tourism regions.

Market place

To be successful, an industry must sell its product in the market place. Since tourism's product is immobile and its potential customers need to build and compare destination images before they travel, some form of intermediary is required. This is the function of the travel agent, who must successfully match a tourist image and tourist product if the travel experience is to have any chance of success. Four phases in this process have been identified. First, the development of a tourist product and promotion of an image is the role of tour wholesalers. Three of the biggest companies are Thomas Cook, Amex, and Intertourist, and they send out representatives to find new destinations or combinations that can be put together as a saleable package. Second, the actual selling of individual vacations is the responsibility of the store front travel agent. These people act as advisors and consultants, and a sense of geography is vital if they are to match their customers' wishes with suitable customs and climate. Third, the travel agent either arranges accommodation directly or leaves it to the destination area to provide such services and supplementary information concerning local attractions and events. In this way it is hoped that most tastes and budgets can be satisfied. The final objective is to have a satisfied customer, who is likely to make a return trip and act as a goodwill ambassador, for this is the most effective way of nurturing the industry and fulfilling the goals of tourism.

Community approach

The product and image that intermediaries package and sell is a destination experience, and as such creates an industry that is highly dependent on the goodwill and cooperation of host communities. Many destination area attractions are public property or public goods, and the hospitality needed for a memorable visit must come from members of the public as well as employees of the industry. Increasingly, development of new facilities requires public investment in infrastructure and shared facilities; and many festivals or events that evolved to fill local needs are being commercialized and promoted as tourist events. It is the citizen who must live with the cumulative outcome of such developments and needs to have greater input into how his community is packaged and sold as a tourist product on the world market.

2

Evolution of tourism

Development trends

To understand tourism's growth and development requires analysis of its past, for the seeds of change can be used not only to explain the present but as pointers to the future. Travel is a long-established tradition. Its origins can be found in pre-industrial society, but over time the opportunities to travel have increased, changing the picture from one of individual travel to mass tourism.

In the pre-industrial era pleasure travel was limited to the wealthy and privileged. The earliest travelers were the explorers but, like many today, they frequently combined business interests with the exploration. Marco Polo is an excellent example of such a pioneer, as are numerous explorer–traders of the New World. The most popular form of domestic travel was the pilgrimage, which became a social and recreational event in addition to a religious commitment. Indeed, contemporary observations by Chaucer would indicate that self-fulfillment took on a higher priority than self-denial. Another symbol of these early stirrings of tourism is the security against vandalism undertaken at various shrines. In St Albans Abbey there is an observation balcony overlooking the Shrine of St Alban where the monks could watch the pilgrims and ensure they did not abscond with any souvenirs.

More extensive reminders of the early days of tourism lie in the spas and seaside resorts whose origins were linked to the pursuit of health, but which eventually became centers of amusement and recreation. In Europe, locations favored with hot springs or mineral waters were strongly recommended for their therapeutic value by the early medical profession. Since it was mainly the rich and powerful who could seek such advice and follow it, spas like Bath and Carlsbad became magnets for society and merchants. As a result the natural resource of the community was supplemented by accommodation and entertainment facilities that became attractions in their own right, as can be seen in the Regency terraces and public buildings in Bath. Furthermore, the prospect of attracting business by developing local natural resources led to the earliest examples of city council investment in tourist attractions. Brighton city council, for example, erected promenades and piers to facilitate exposure to the sea air and compensate for its lack of sandy beaches.

A notable legacy for today's tourism from the pre-industrial era is the Grand Tour. During the seventeenth century "increasing numbers of potential diplomats, men becoming rich through England's growing foreign trade and scholars in search of European learning, began to legitimize gallants' jaunts which thus imperceptibly merged into the educative and political institution known as the Grand Tour" (Fairburn 1951, 118). The route prescribed for this tour by John Gailhard in his book, *The Compleat Gentleman*, was a three-year exploration of the capitals, politics, culture, and society of western Europe. The proposed itinerary was an outbound trip to Paris and Italy, with stops in Genoa, Milan, Florence, Rome, and Venice, followed by a return trip through Switzerland, Germany, and the Low Countries. The motives for the Grand Tour have a lot in common with present-day university students who frequently "take a year off" to travel, between leaving school and starting their first job, while the development of a specified route is reflected in our modern package tours.

The industrial revolution brought about major

changes in the scale and type of tourism development. The increases in productivity, regular employment, and growing urbanization gave more people the motivation and opportunity to go on holiday. In contrast to the earlier dominance by the wealthy, tourism began to embrace a broader social spectrum, and as in other areas of social behavior, class distinctions became apparent. The emerging middle class combined higher incomes and growing education into annual holidays. To escape from their responsibilities and the congested urban environment they sought relaxation and renewal in areas of natural beauty and, in turn, created the beginning of the modern holiday industry. In some cases established resorts with prestige and notoriety expanded and developed to capture this new market. In others, new locations became popular destinations. The working class also experienced higher wages and more regular work, but their hours were longer and their proportion of discretionary wealth smaller. Consequently, working-class involvement in tourism was more gradual, and began in the form of day-trip outings. But due to their number this had a significant impact on the industry and saw the creation of working-class resorts close to major industrial centers.

The force behind the upsurge in productivity and higher incomes was the development of steam power. This innovation not only stimulated the industrial revolution, but it provided the increased mobility needed by the burgeoning tourism business. Steamers on the major rivers provided reliable and inexpensive transportation that led to popular day-trip cruises and the growth of coastal resorts near large industrial towns. The London to Margate route was carrying over 100,000 visitors by 1830 (Robinson 1976, 14). Steamers were carrying hundreds of thousands of Liverpool residents across the Mersey to New Brighton, Rhyl, and Llandudno, and had initiated the Isle of Man holiday industry (Cosgrove and Jackson 1972, 37). The railroads were, however, the major agent of change, and as they began to develop their passenger market, access to a rail system became the prime development consideration in the tourism market. A rail link between the industrial city and sea or mountains was a major asset to tourism in general and to the selected communities in particular.

Examples of this rail–tourism symbiosis can be seen on both sides of the Atlantic. The small fishing village of Whitby, Yorkshire, was transformed into a Victorian resort serving industrial West Yorkshire due to the

creation of a rail link with York. The construction of a railroad northward from Montreal to the Laurentian hills during the 1890s made this scenic recreation area accessible for mass tourism for the first time. In the process it changed the recreational and touristic preferences of Montrealers, which until that time had been manifested by riverine tourism and vacation travel east and west along the St Lawrence valley (Lundgren 1983). Tourism in the Catskill Mountains started in 1824 with the construction of a large resort hotel on the crest of an escarpment, known as the "Wall of Manitou" overlooking the Hudson Valley. The majority of patrons during the early years were members of the social elite of New York and Philadelphia, who willingly spent 8 hours traveling up the Hudson by steamboat and then endured a 4-hour, 12-mile stagecoach ride in order to experience the splendor of nature while enjoying the hospitality of a first-class hotel (Darlington 1981). The rugged physical terrain and limited economic base deterred any railroad construction in the Catskills until 1868 when work started on the Ulster and Delaware Railroad:

Although promoted as a freight carrier, the railroad management soon realized that the bulk of the company's revenue was to come from seasonal passenger traffic. New hotel construction began along the route in 1870, two years before the line's completion. By the end of 1870 many resort hotels, often situated within a short carriage ride of a station, sprang up along the route. (Darlington 1981, 8)

The improved accessibility brought about dramatic increases not only in accommodation but also in visitor numbers. It has been estimated that between 4000 and 5000 visitors traveled to the Catskill region by 1870, but by 1890 the Ulster and Delaware line was carrying "in excess of 175,000 passengers, the bulk of whom were summer visitors. This was an increase of 17 fold in twenty years" (Best 1972, 162).

The railroads created not only more business by providing reliable and inexpensive transportation for the first time, but also more competition as various companies and resorts vied for this new business. The new resorts were based primarily on natural resources that appealed to the urbanite wishing to break free from the crowds and pollution of the city. Due to the scale of development and increased competition such amenities needed to be augmented by man-made facilities. Private companies invested heavily in hotels, resort development, and entertainment facilities, but tourism's growth also encouraged municipal investment in parades, parks, piers, and baths. Notable municipal ventures included Atlantic City's "boardwalk" and Blackpool's "tower."

The scale and mobility introduced by the railroad transformed tourism from a small business catering to the elite into the start of a mass market, where consumers found a growing and complex number of options. The novelty of a holiday plus the confusion of a rapidly expanding travel industry provided an opportunity for the professional consultant, and this era saw the emergence of the travel organizer. The first and most famous of these was Thomas Cook. His first excursion train trip was between Leicester and Loughborough on July 5 1841, with 570 passengers at a round-trip fare of one shilling. By 1851 Cook was arranging transport and lodging for 165,000 visitors to London's World Exposition at Crystal Palace. In 1866 he organized his first American tour and in 1874 introduced "circular notes" which were accepted by banks, hotels, shops, and restaurants. These were in effect the first traveler's checks. Amongst all these achievements Burkart and Medlik contend that his true significance

lies in the origination of the excursion or holiday as a single transaction or package, rather than his establishment of a retail agency. His concept perfectly complemented the growth of the railways and later passenger shipping, and brought organized travel to an increasingly large section of the public. (Burkart and Medlik 1974, 15)

The dynamic nature of the market place in terms of technical innovation and the increasing numbers of people who could afford and accept the idea of vacations brought changes to the resorts. Many inaccessible resort areas that had been exclusive through their association with the elite became more cosmopolitan and proletarian as the railroads offered better service and local entrepreneurs responded to the new business opportunities. The Catskills, mentioned earlier, experienced such a change:

The social character of the Catskill vacationers also changed with the expansion of the resort area. Businessmen and professionals emulated the established elite by sending their families to the mountains for extended vacations while they themselves remained behind in New York City. As the new arrivals began to outnumber the "Old Guard," the latter began to abandon the Catskills for more socially and geographically restricted resorts outside the area. Thus between 1870 and 1900 the region stabilized as the haunt of the upper middle ranks of the protestant establishment. (Darlington 1981, 9)

This new stability was only a temporary state, however, and by the outbreak of the Second World War the Catskill resort region was accepting

minority groups which had heretofore been excluded from the region [and] began to occupy the vacuum created by the exiting upper middle classes. ... Realizing that most of the newcomers were neither wealthy nor accustomed to living conditions as fine as the resort hotels provided, the hotel owners lowered their rates and reduced room size.... The social transition in the region was soon apparent as Germans, Italians, Americans, and Cubans all laid claim to one or more of the resort communities. The most significant group to gain a foothold were, however, the Jews. (Darlington 1981, 10)

Tourism continued to develop in close association with the railroad until the Second World War, after which the technological advances of wartime were transferred to peaceful pursuits and governments faced demands for a new order. The post-war era, like those preceding it, presented a continuation of trends plus some innovations, but in total it has been the most dramatic period of growth so far recorded.

The greatest change after the Second World War was increased mobility. The development of jet engines made it possible to fly large numbers of people great distances at high speed. Furthermore, as aircraft design evolved, airlines were able to do so with increased comfort, because they could fly above the weather, and at very economical rates. A trip undertaken by the author in the late 1960s from the United States to England worked out at 2c a mile, including meals and entertainment. Herman Kahn provides another illustration of the airlines' growing speed and efficiency in a comparison of a trans-American flight between 1929 and 1979 (Table 2). In 1933 a New York to San Francisco flight took 21½ hours (if it was on time, flying against the prevailing westerly winds) and the round trip cost $320 or $1,900 in 1979 dollars. That same flight in 1979 took 5½ hours and was more likely to be on time, but, most important, cost only $234, despite the upsurge of oil prices. These improvements in air transport not only encouraged greater transcontinental travel but were instrumental in the explosion of intercontinental travel in the 1960s and 1970s. The earth literally shrank for the tourist, bringing distant exotic islands closer and replacing week-long sea voyages with a few hours of armchair comfort.

Increased mobility was not confined to air travel; after the war the western world became a consumer society and the major goal for many was an automobile. The

Table 2 Changing mobility

Approximate maximum travel speeds

Characteristics	1929			1949			1969			1979			1989 (estimates)			2009 (estimates)	2029 (estimates)
	100–125 mph			250–300 mph			500–600 mph			500–1300 mph			500–2000 mph			500–3000 mph	500–6000 mph
	Auto	Rail	Air	Auto	Rail	Air	Auto	Rail	Air	Auto	Rail	Air	Auto	Rail	Air	Air	Air
Time: Travel time from NY to:																	
Washington, DC (200 mi.)	9 hrs	5 hrs	3 hrs	6 hrs	4 hrs	3 hrs	4 hrs	4 hrs	1½ hrs	4½ hrs	3½ hrs	1 hr	3 hrs	2 hrs	1 hr	1 hour	½ hour
Chicago (700 mi.)	25 hrs	16 hrs	9 hrs	15 hrs	14 hrs	5 hrs	13 hrs	13 hrs	3 hrs	15 hrs	13 hrs	2 hrs	12 hrs	12 hrs	2 hrs	1 hour	1 hour
Los Angeles (2500 mi.)	120 hrs	70 hrs	25 hrs	80 hrs	65 hrs	12 hrs	60 hrs	55 hrs	5 hrs	70 hrs	—	5 hrs	50 hrs	—	4 hrs	2 hours	1 hour
London (3500 mi.)	5 days (ship)					18 hrs			7 hrs			4 hrs			4 hrs	3 hours	2 hours
Sydney (10,000 mi.)	2 weeks (ship)					2 days			1 day			1 day			15 hrs	8 hours	3 hours
Fares: Minimum travel fares from NY (1979 US dollars)	San Francisco 28c/mi.			San Francisco 19c/mi. London 31c/mi. Sydney 25c/mi. (1947 figures)			San Francisco 8c/mi. London 8c/mi. Sydney 8c/mi.			San Francisco 5c/mi. London 4.5c/mi. Sydney 8c/mi.			About 5c/mi.			0–5c/mi.	0–5c/mi.
Destinations and accessibility	Only nearby destinations are practical			Continental travel possible for many tourists; overseas travel limited			Continental travel for most; overseas travel for many			Overseas travel possible for most people; new range of destinations opening up			Frequent weekend commutations over hundreds and even thousands of miles			Very extensive worldwide travel; all destinations accessible	Cheap, fast, and convenient

Source: Kahn (1979, 4–5)

automobile diffused tourism more than any other form of transport. It brought back the true meaning of the word "touring" for it provided flexible and personal transportation which freed people from the schedules and fixed routes of public transport. Resorts could no longer depend on the traditional two-week vacation, but became temporary stop-overs on family automobile tours. It enabled people to travel wherever there was a road, while new recreation vehicles (four-wheel drives and snowmobiles) do not even face this restriction. Any amenity or community can now become a tourist attraction if it can be reached by the automobile or one of its derivatives. For many the purchase of such an expensive item can be justified only through maximum use, including that of pleasure driving and vacations. Consequently, we find that "outside the home, the dominant form of outdoor recreation in terms of both the total time involved and the frequency with which it is undertaken, is pleasure driving" (Patmore 1972, 36).

Although the dramatic changes in mobility after the Second World War may have had the most visible impact, other forces were at work which permitted the growth and proletarianization of tourism. More people found they had the leisure time and discretionary income that are necessary prerequisites for a vacation. Thanks to labor negotiations and social legislation the length of official and paid holidays has been steadily increasing. Governments have created more vacation time by incorporating isolated public holidays into the now familiar "long weekends" throughout the year. In addition, the post-war economic recovery provided a major increase in real income, which many people converted into increased recreation and travel. By the 1970s two vacations a year were not uncommon. The enlarged market potential did not escape the notice of travel companies who established tours and created familiar environments for the uninitiated traveler. In this way many working-class people were tempted to break with tradition and replace the local resort holiday with a package vacation on distant shores. These travelers were offered a "guarantee" of sun plus accommodation and entertainment that would not be too different from the familiar resort back home. Furthermore, thanks to the economies of scale and vertical linkages of such mass-marketing these trips to the Mediterranean or Caribbean shores could be offered at very competitive rates.

The big question now is what direction will tourism take in the future? Over the last few years there have

been dramatic increases in world energy prices with resulting repercussions on individual mobility and national economies. Between 1972 and 1982 world oil prices increased from $1.25 to $34 a barrel, and the operating costs for an automobile have risen by 158 percent since 1973, according to a Hertz report. In addition, the rising price of oil has been blamed, in part, for the combined inflation and recession of the 1970s, which became known as "stagflation." People found inflation cutting into their discretionary income and the cost of travel rising abruptly, while recession was challenging the notion of job security or leaving a member of the family unemployed.

The prospects for tourism may appear bleak but if we look at the record for the 1970s we find the industry has been resilient and even managed to grow. The industry's phenomenal growth rates of the 1960s have disappeared but there is still growth, even after adjusting for inflation. Like many other consumer industries, tourism may be entering a more stabilized period of operation, following the boom years of expansionary development. Stability, however, does not mean static. The industry is more diversified and flexible than ever before and should be able to respond to changing visitor needs and preferences.

Growth factors

The reasons for tourism's resilience in the face of adverse conditions lie in its evolution and the hold it has taken on our lives. Table 3 outlines the major trends encountered in our historical review and groups them under three general headings—motivation, ability, and mobility. These three factors account for past growth and can be used to identify future growth trends.

Motivation to travel is necessary for the development of tourism since if there was no interest in travel or need to travel the tourist industry could not exist. Maslow (1954), in his book *Motivation and Personality*, identifies a hierarchy of human needs, the uppermost of which is self-actualization and self-realization. The concept is that after our basic psychological needs, security and social acceptance have been realized, we turn to self-fulfillment. The dramatic advances in living standards since the Second World War have enabled more people to indulge in personal preferences, and one of these, according to Taylor (1983), has been to travel. Taylor refers to the observations of Yankelovich

Tourism and its significance

Table 3 Growth factors in the evolution of tourism

Era	Motivation	Ability	Mobility
Pre-industrial	Exploration and business Pilgrimage–religion Education Health	Few travelers, those involved were wealthy, influential or received permission	Slow and treacherous
Industrial	Positive impact of education, print, and radio Escape from city Colonial empires	Higher incomes More leisure time Organized tours	Lower transport costs Reliable public transportation
Consumer society	Positive impact of visual communication Consumer society Escape from work routine	Shorter work week More discretionary income Mass marketing Package tours	Growth of personal transportation Faster and more efficient transport
Future	Vacations a right and necessity Combined with business and learning	Self-catering Smaller families Two wage earners per household Demographic trends favor travel groups	Alternative fuels More efficient transportation Greater use of public transport and package deals

and Lefkowitz (1980) who consider Americans no longer limit their priorities to money and status. They feel three other ideas have been appropriated by the majority of Americans:

(1) First, the growing conviction that what is regarded as a "nose-to-the-grindstone" way of life is too high a price to pay for material success.

(2) Second, the feeling that Americans have devoted too much time and attention to the task of how to make a living and not enough to the question of how to live.

(3) Last, the belief that what counts most in life is that "I keep growing" as an individual, "that I have an opportunity to fulfill my potential," and "that I have a moral obligation to do so."

As Yankelovich and Lefkowitz observe, "this is a startling new conception of moral obligations." The departure from a rigid work ethic toward a more complete lifestyle is seen by Sarbin as

the quest for self-fulfillment and the sense of frustration at not being able to achieve it in many aspects of our lives (jobs) causes people to shift the search into the private parts of their lives— into their leisure pursuits where they can express some individuality. And indeed, travel is one of the beneficiaries of that search for self-fulfillment and self-expression. (Sarbin 1978)

Such observations and predictions would indicate that even with temporary declines in our living standards, modern man's motivation has changed sufficiently to ensure a place for leisure and travel in future lifestyles.

As the world has developed into an industrial and post-industrial society, the means to learn about travel opportunities has increased while the stress and pressure of modern life has transformed the vacation into a new form of therapy. A survey conducted by *Psychology Today* (Rubenstein 1980) showed the two major reasons for taking vacations among its readers were rest and relaxation (63 percent) and escape from routine (52 percent). While the survey's sample is not truly representative of the United States population because it involved a high proportion of young postgraduates, its analysis of leisure priorities is informative because this group of influential consumers has a major impact on the tourist market. A factor analysis indicated that relieving the tension of responsible and stressful jobs was the most popular motive for travel. This was followed, in descending order of importance, by intellectual enrichment, family togetherness, exotic adventure, self-discovery, and escape. Thus, one can see a wide variety of travel motives exists in today's society and many of them can be considered basic needs. For example, family togetherness incorporated not just the needs of extended families to have periodical reunions, but also reflected the needs within a single household to have the opportunity to get together and rediscover each other.

During its heady post-war expansion the tourist industry largely ignored tourist motives and expectations because it was too busy serving the growth to become overly concerned with those who were disappointed with their travel experience. The recent slowdown in business and increased competition for tourist revenues, however, has created more interest in market research and the needs of the tourist. More countries and states are investigating the motives of travelers and potential tourists. For example, Tourism Canada has explored the perceptions and motives behind French, British, and Japanese interest in Canada, and has duly adjusted its marketing to suit the individual tastes of these contrasting markets (Taylor 1983). One champion of such research into motivation and preferences is Pearce. He feels that tourist expectations have been taken for granted in the past, but that "one can obtain a social psychological profile of tourists which links roles, motivation and social and environmental preferences" (Pearce 1982, 146). If this can be achieved, destinations would be in a better position to identify their particular market, determine its travel expectations, and decide how best to accommodate and satisfy those expectations.

Motivation considerations should now extend beyond individual consensus to include corporate, agency and government policy decisions. Each of these groups has become increasingly involved in providing vacation opportunities, with their motivation varying from productivity to therapy and preventative medicine. It all results in some form of "social tourism," a term which in itself indicates how far tourism has penetrated our value system.

Social tourism can be described as "the relationships and phenomena in the field of tourism resulting from participation in travel by economically weak or otherwise disadvantaged elements of society" (Hunzinger, "Social tourism, its nature and problems," quoted in ETB and TUC 1976, 5). It involves the provision of vacations for people who can afford them only with the aid of a third party. Although the aim of social tourism is unitarian in philosophy—to extend the benefits of vacations to a broader segment of society—it is expressed in a variety of forms.

Trade unions in industrialized nations have long sought and won paid vacation time for their members, and by example, have won similar rights for most industrial and service workers. In Europe and Japan some companies help pay for a substantial portion of vacation costs. Most workers in West Germany receive *Urlaubsgeld* (holiday money), a bonus that can equal 45 percent of their regular vacation pay. In France, the state-owned Renault company contributes to the operation of thirty family vacation villages for its workers (*Time* 1981).

Social agencies such as the YMCA, Boy Scouts, and church groups support many summer camps which offer subsidized vacations to the young, poor or handicapped. In the United States there is evidence of "social tourism with a twist," according to Lundberg (1976, 170). He notes that social tourism is designed to subsidize vacations or facilities for the working class, but points out that recent resort development in certain state parks is really social tourism for the middle class. These resort park projects offer country club quality and settings at a subsidized price, and have proved to be very popular attractions.

In Europe the emphasis is on families, and many central and local governments are committed to develop and operate facilities for low-income or otherwise disadvantaged families. A good illustration of this is Villages-Vacances-Familiales (VVF) in France. This association, created in 1959 by national and regional government bodies, operated 78 family vacation centers with a total capacity of 40,600 beds in 1974. There are two types of center, either a village providing full board or self-catering accommodation, or campsites established near villages so campers can take advantage of local facilities. In Switzerland a Travel Saving Fund (REKA) has been established which permits residents to systematically save for their holidays, offering them a discount on domestic vacations or international travel using local agencies or tour companies. Furthermore, the capital so invested has permitted REKA to construct its own holiday centers, which are oriented to family needs. "Today REKA owns six holiday centres with 254 family units and 1,434 guest beds. . . . In order not to exclude any families from the possibility of REKA holidays, a graded rental discount of 10% to 50% is granted to families with lower incomes" (Teuscher 1983, 219).

Government involvement in social tourism is not

simply an altruistic matter—for some the motive is cultural and political. Moulin (1983) reports that Quebec's interest in social tourism has been aided by the rise of the Parti Quebecois and its separatist philosophy. It wishes to foster tourism in Quebec by Quebec residents, to help reduce its travel deficit and maintain its cultural identity within a predominantly English-speaking continent.

Social tourism has become a recognized component and legitimate objective for modern tourism. By extending the physical and psychological benefits of rest and travel to less fortunate people, it can be looked upon as a form of preventative medicine. By emphasizing national and regional resources and cultural heritage it can be viewed as a means of cementing the economic, social and political ties of a country. To encourage the adoption of this concept, the International Bureau of Social Tourism (BITS) has been created, with the goal of promoting social tourism at the international level. Its success can be seen in one of the declarations of the United Nations World Tourism Conference, held in Manila in October 1980. This declaration affirmed that:

Modern tourism was born out of the application of social policies which led to industrial workers obtaining annual paid holidays, and at the same time found its expression through the recognition of the basic human right to rest and leisure.

In his eloquent summary of this Conference and its adoption of the social tourism principles, Haulot notes:

Social tourism should be considered for what it is—not a "low-level" form of tourism which is some way second-class, but, above all, the expression of the desire of millions of people to enjoy for themselves the natural beauty of the world and to experience the exhilaration that discovery and rest can bring to each person. This can be achieved in practice by undertaking large-scale and benevolent regulatory action. Such action also finds justification in that its individual and collective objectives are consistent with the view that all measures taken by modern society should ensure more justice, more dignity and improved enjoyment of life for all citizens. (Haulot 1981, 212)

The *ability* to travel is necessary if people are to fulfill their desires, and this essentially requires time and money. Tourism, as distinct from other forms of leisure pursuits, requires blocks of time in order to make the journey and stay worthwhile. Tourism also calls for more money than most other forms of recreation because of the cost of travel, accommodation, meals, and souvenirs.

Thus tourism and particularly vacations are a major commitment.

The ability to travel depends on a combination of personal circumstances and the tourism industry's initiatives to expand its market. As Table 3 indicates, there has been a steady increase in discretionary income and leisure time, but recently both of these forces have come under increasing pressure from inflation. As rising prices for basic needs have eroded personal and family discretionary incomes, one response has been to sacrifice some leisure time by taking on a second job, or undertaking one's own maintenance and repair work. However, the industry has continually attempted to lower the price of vacations and expand the number of options, so that a moderate decrease in discretionary income and leisure time does not mean the end of vacation travel.

A driving force behind many industry innovations has been value, and nowhere is this more evident than in the growth of organized tours, which now offer a myriad of options to suit all tastes and pocketbooks. The modern package tour provides value for money through economies of scale and vertical linkage. If a coach, airplane, or hotel can be assured full capacity then the cost per traveler declines drastically, as the overheads are spread over large numbers of visitors. Add to this the advantages of one company owning the travel agency, the transport system and the accommodation, and tremendous savings can be made by channeling the visitor from one branch to another and ensuring high business volume throughout the system. The savings of such an arrangement can, to some extent, be passed on to the traveler and thus provide an attractive and competitive package. Examples of this trend can be seen in the growth of travel wholesale giants like Amex and Cooks, national networks such as Intertourist, and mutual arrangements like the "fly and cruise" packages.

In addition to the large-scale solution many individual entrepreneurs and travelers have made personal adjustments to lower the price of vacations. Foremost amongst these is the trend to self-catering. This term is used to describe travelers who provide some of their own services, such as accommodation and meals. It is a far cry from the traditional concept of a vacation, where one is pampered and gets away from the usual household chores, but by washing one's own dishes and providing one's own bed considerable savings can be achieved.

Self-catering takes on many forms, but the most evident has been the growth in camping and recreation vehicles. There have always been camping enthusiasts of course, people who wished to get away from the crowds and close to nature. These people generally used tents, had few luxuries and favored isolated campsites. Over the past 20 years or so, however, more people have become campers because of its economic appeal and in the process changed the camping scene. Very often these campers prefer to bring the comforts of home on their vacation, so they purchase or rent trailers and recreation vehicles. There has been a major growth of private campgrounds designed to provide convenient access to the highway and tourist attractions while offering reasonable rates by operating at high densities.

The ultimate development along these lines are the new franchise campgrounds that operate like motel chains, providing a standard format at each camp and offering reservation systems. Kampgrounds of America (KOA) for example, has an extensive franchise of campsites and can offer rates that are a third to a quarter the cost of a hotel room. Each has a standard design which includes a redwood-colored central complex containing a general store, washroom, and laundry facilities, a games room with pinball and electronic games, plus a swimming pool which is heated where necessary. These campgrounds provide sites for the tent, and that post-war phenomenon, the recreational vehicle. This vehicle is no longer a simple caravan or trailer to be pulled behind a car but has become a sophisticated mobile home, either towed or self-propelled. It requires water and electricity hook-ups, sewage disposal units, and pull-through sites so the driver does not have to back up.

The newest form of self-catering is the time-share concept, where people may purchase a short time period in a condominium or apartment-hotel that is located in a resort area. "Whether it's a hedge against inflation or just a guaranteed getaway, throngs of Americans are now buying vacation homes by the slice" (*Newsweek* 1979, 104). The time-share system is a derivative of the European holiday flat or villa, which was leased by its owner during the tourist season. This system has evolved in North America into two systems of time-sharing. The more popular is "interval owner-ship" where consumers purchase a certain time period in a resort condominium, say a two-week Christmas period on Maui, Hawaii, which can be used personally

or sub-let. The second type is called a "vacation license" or "right to use" which in effect is a long lease. The buyer gets the right to use an apartment, or class of apartment, for a designated number of years before it reverts back to the developer. To make these purchase or lease arrangements more flexible, exchange networks, such as Resort Condominiums International, have been created. These enable time-sharers to swap locations and times, and therefore permit an investment in one location to be used as a passport into similar developments around the world.

The third growth factor in tourism's evolution presented in Table 3 is personal *mobility*, which is a crucial element for an activity involving travel. Mobility expanded dramatically with the introduction of steam-power, but both the steamboats and railroads were public transport which meant travelers had to travel according to a company schedule and route pattern. The result was an explosion of tourism development along selected routes and at popular destinations in the recreation hinterland of urban–industrial centers. True personal mobility had to await development and widespread adoption of the automobile. When this was achieved after the Second World War the restraints of schedules and routes were thrown off and people began to tour in the true sense of the word. The resulting drop in static holidays saw a decline in many traditional resorts and the spread of tourism activity as people sought out new experiences and unspoiled areas. The development of air travel extended such searching to distant places and tourism became truly international, although this component still remained far behind domestic, or national, travel.

The expansion of personal mobility received a setback with the energy crisis of 1973 and the continuing price spiral for all forms of fuel. The days of cheap energy ended with the creation of the OPEC cartel, for its price hikes had an immediate impact on tourism as prices doubled and supplies became unreliable. Of these two consequences, the latter was more troublesome because uncertainty of supply was a big deterrent to long distance travel—no one relished the thought of being stranded in a foreign country or at empty gas stations. In terms of the price increases, however, both the public and the industry were able to make adjustments to meet the new situation.

The resilience of the industry has pleased and puzzled many observers, and a whole series of reasons have been put forward to explain its recovery from the energy crisis shockwaves. The most probable explanation for the industry's continued growth during the 1970s is that travel was so inexpensive in the early part of the decade there was plenty of slack in the system, so adjustments could be made without tearing it apart. For example, airlines began to reduce the number of flights and collaborated on schedules to produce higher payloads per flight. These and other economies enabled them to mitigate the impact of the early oil price increases.

Individual adjustment and resourcefulness were provided an opportunity to distinguish themselves in such times of crisis. The tourist industry adjusted by promoting more extensive use of tours so that per capita travel and accommodation costs were reduced. One of the prime growth sectors during the 1970s was the increase in sea cruises, which, when combined with air travel to the port of embarkation and bus tours at various stop-overs, meant a traveler spent his entire vacation aboard some form of public transport. Private individuals adjusted by traveling out of season, using package tours and charter arrangements for the first time, or traveling closer to home. Corsi and Harvey (1979), for example, in a survey of shifts in vacation travel between 1973 and 1975 found that households in southeast Wisconsin were willing to experiment with various vacation adjustments. These included greater use of public transport and more local vacations.

People have been able to nullify the higher costs of travel to a greater extent than imagined by making more efficient use of an existing asset—the family automobile. The automobile has a strong hold on people because it offers privacy, status, speed, convenience, and comfort unparalleled in any other form of transport. Added to that the cost of owning and operating an automobile, which was estimated to be 43.28 cents a mile in 1983 for compact-size family sedans, compares very favorably with public transport alternatives if one is carrying a full load of passengers and contemplating regional travel. Furthermore, the move to smaller, more fuel-efficient automobiles has permitted considerable savings. Bryan (1981) calculated that an improvement from 10 to 15 mpg could result in gasoline savings of $333 to $833 per annum, depending on the mileage driven.

A 1980 travel survey by Transport Canada revealed that 90 percent of all journeys over 50 miles were made by automobile. Air travel was a distant second with 5 percent of the trips, and buses and trains were insignificant contributors. In the United States it has been estimated that automobiles account for 75 percent of all tourism-related travel (Pizam and Pokela 1983). Thus, the automobile still remains a viable option for many regional or domestic trips, and the move to smaller, more efficient vehicles does not necessarily mean less comfort since the average household size is also shrinking.

Although the three factors of motivation, ability, and mobility have been isolated in the table and examined separately, it should be evident that they are often interrelated and their total impact greater than the sum of individual parts. The fact that all three have grown and interwoven has changed the role of travel and vacations in our lifestyles. Instead of being viewed as a luxury item, with a highly elastic demand curve in relation to price, there is evidence to suggest that travel has become more of a necessity and hence less sensitive to price increases, rather like the effect of higher cigarette prices on a chain smoker. When the first energy crisis resulted in a worldwide recession one newspaper reported that a surprising number of newly unemployed people were booking overseas vacations and cruises. A survey of these people revealed that they were responding to the forces outlined in Table 3. For the first time they had the cash in the form of severance pay and time (ability) to fulfill their dreams (motive), and they were not going to let a temporary setback deny them this opportunity. Furthermore, during the early 1970s transportation companies were able to absorb much of the fuel price increase, so international travel expenses (mobility) were still within many people's budget. What gave many the courage to do this, instead of saving and pounding the pavement, was their belief that government would assist them directly with unemployment benefits and intervene in the economy to improve the general situation.

Future

Tourism is a dynamic and varied activity, where both the industry and public have proven extremely adaptable to new situations. In terms of personal mobility the crises and price hikes of the 1970s have not been catastrophic and have in fact given the transport sector time to adjust. Nowhere is this more apparent than in the aircraft industry where a new generation of fuel-efficient planes is beginning to emerge. In August 1981, the first Boeing 767 came off the assembly line, the first new model in 12 years. Likewise, there have been improvements in automobile efficiency and the move to new fuels like gasohol, propane, and hydrogen show the automobile is not going to disappear.

The ability to travel has received setbacks from inflation and rising cost of fuel, but other factors will enable people to adjust to the new situation. Foremost among these is the demographic trend in industrial nations, where the post-war baby boom has now become a major consumer group of young adults (*Newsweek* 1981). These adults differ from previous generations in that they are either deferring or canceling plans for settling down with a home and family. These people have significant discretionary incomes because they earn high incomes, yet have modest expenses for apartments or condominiums; plus they have more leisure time than most because of limited family or housing ties. They form a major portion of the travel market, as young people traditionally travel in search of new experiences and socializing. Frechtling, Director of the US Travel Data Center, has estimated that the 35 to 40 age group, which "shows one of the highest rates of travel generation," will increase by 36 percent between 1976 and 1985, and by 1990 will constitute 15 percent of the nation's population (Frechtling 1977).

Another feature of the west's demographic future that will have an important bearing on tourism is the general aging of our population. Retired people have more time for travel and many, having completed the major expenditures of purchasing a home and raising a family, now have more discretionary funds available for travel. The retired sector of society through the careful management of its time and financial assets, can become an important element of the tourism market; but as Doxey (1983) warns, a lot depends on how society treats its elderly and prepares them for their increased leisure opportunities. He notes we know relatively little about the preferences and consumer demands of this growing group. At present, many retired people have chosen to travel in the off-season to avoid the crowds and stretch their vacation dollar; some have invested in a motorhome and become the new nomads following the sun; and others have retired to popular tourist destinations in the sun-belt regions. While the latter are not strictly tourists, they have settled in touristic areas and have become an influential force in the development of these communities, as is discussed on page 112.

Finally, one must appreciate that while these demand characteristics look encouraging for the industry, the industry itself has not stood still and has continually revised its facilities and attractions. Never have there been so many choices for the tourist. The adventurous traveler can be left on a deserted island, with or without supplies, and the cautious neophyte can be chaperoned through that first major trip. Innovations such as time-sharing and activity vacations are designed to provide better value through lower-priced accommodation and multi-purpose travel. Learning a foreign language or new skill while relaxing in pleasant surroundings provides added justification and value to a vacation.

In light of continued inflation and a growing demand for public accountability, new elements are entering into the tourism picture in order to achieve more efficient use of their resources and facilities. Farmers, particularly those in the wilder scenic areas where agricultural productivity is low, are being encouraged to supplement their incomes by accommodating tourists. Regular householders in popular destination areas view summer season accommodation revenue as one way of combating ever-rising property taxes. Both of these movements will appeal to those travelers who are tired of the more impersonal hotel atmosphere, or who can no longer afford their prices. In addition, public institutions such as universities are being forced into the tourism market to supplement their educational revenues and maximize plant use. Thus, more of them are opening their dormitories to the traveling public during the summer months and offering conference facilities during school breaks.

With these and other trends futurists see an optimistic future for the travel industry. Foremost among these is Herbert Kahn (1979) who, writing in the fiftieth anniversary issue of *Travel Trade News*, extrapolates some of the past travel trends into the next half century. His examination of the dramatic changes in air transportation systems, technology and marketing provide a positive outlook for tourism (Table 2). He foresees increased mobility thanks to increased speed and reduced travel costs. There will probably be a wider range of commercial aircraft to suit various passenger priorities regarding cost, speed, and service. When one examines his predictions for 2029, however, it is apparent these dramatic changes have already entered the experimental stage or are on the drawing board. In other words, the seeds of change have already been

Tourism and its significance

Table 4 Travel industry growth trend factors, 1929–2029

		1929	1949	1969	Present 1979	*Approx. Growth	1989	2009	2029
Population	W	2.0	2.5	3.6	4.3	(2.0)	5.3	7.0	8.2
(Billions)	US	.12	.15	.20	.22	(0.9)	.24	.28	.32
Gross product	W	1.6	2.5	6.2	9.5	(5.0)	15	30	50
(Trillions of 1979 dollars)	US	.5	.8	1.7	2.3	(3.2)	3.2	6	10
Discretionary purchasing power	W	.2	.4	.9	1.4	(4.6)	2.2	5.5	20
(Trillions of 1979 dollars	US	.10	.24	.51	.70	(3.4)	1.0	2.1	4
Hotel rooms	W	4.2	3.5	5.4	8.0	(2.8)	9.2	16	27.5
(Millions)	US	1.43	1.13	1.79	2.03	(1.3)	2.29	3	3.9
Autos	W	30	50	130	230	(5.8)	400	700	1000
(Millions)	US	21	36	87	115	(2.4)	140	180	230
Auto miles	W	210	560	1300	2300	(4.3)	3000	4000	5000
(Billions)	US	150	400	980	1200	(4.3)	1500	2000	2300
Air passenger miles	W	.13	15	220	400	(6.0)	700	2000	7000
(Trillions)	US	.08	6.8	110	180	(5.1)	300	800	2000
Air travel revenues	W	.2	3	24	47	(6.8)	90	260	800
($ Billions of 1979 dollars)	US	.1	1.5	12	23	(6.8)	45	120	240
Total intercity passenger miles	W	.7	1.5	4.0	7.0	(4.7)	10	22	40
(Trillions)	US	.26	.5	1.1	1.7	(3.8)	2.3	4.5	8
Total travel revenues	W	30	70	240	450	(6.2)	800	2000	7000
(Billions of 1979 dollars)	US	10	20	80	170	(6.8)	300	800	1400

Source: Kahn (1979, 6)
Notes: W = World; US = United States. * Approximate annual average growth rate in percent for the period 1969–79.

sown, and as different as the world of 2029 appears, Kahn has in fact presented a conservative estimate of change. Like all futurology, it is the direction of trends rather than the specific predictions and details which is important and more reliable.

Development and growth are not foreseen as major problems for the industry, but problems are expected to arise because of this growth. Table 4 represents Kahn's predictions of increased wealth (discretionary purchasing power), increased mobility (auto miles and air passenger miles), and resulting opportunity for the travel industry. The pace of growth and congestion in popular destinations is expected to bring about stressful conditions. Kahn predicts:

the tourist market will continue to grow at a faster rate than will destinations. The result will be a shortage of space at desirable locations, producing a problem of how to ration what is available. (Kahn 1979, 7)

Once again the prediction is based on the present, for cases of destination congestion with associated environmental and social stress have already occurred. Kahn

takes the trends to their logical conclusion and suggests:

In general, every possible method of destination rationing may well be used in an effort to control the situation and to avoid excessive tourist pollution, which will be an increasing problem in many parts of the world. This factor may indeed become the prime deterrent to tourism expansion in the next 50 years. (Kahn 1979, 7)

It becomes apparent therefore that if tourism is to expand, and the travel industry is to take advantage of the opportunities that have been forecast, more planning and management will be needed in this area.

Papson (1979) is another seer who prophesies a bright but challenging future for tourism. He estimates that tourism may be the world's largest industry by the year 2000, handling some two billion travelers, and he too is more awestruck by its potential destructiveness to society and our environment than by its magnitude. Papson feels that:

at the levels of tourism predicted for the future, unfavorable social and environmental impacts could offset the economic benefits. Many countries may be forced to rethink their tourist policies. (Papson 1979, 249)

Such oracular warnings should not be ignored, nor should they be taken for granted. Governments and individuals should assess the issues involved with tourism's continued development and decide what form and scale of tourism they desire. It is up to them to control and direct future growth and not let the future dictate to them.

Tourism's evolution has not been without its problems, and futurists consider such problems may multiply if they are not resolved soon, possibly to the detriment of the industry's survival. It is appropriate, therefore, to review some of the major issues associated with the industry's growth before becoming involved with details concerning its management and planning. In this regard the following chapter will identify certain problem areas that have arisen, and examine governmental response to the industry's growing presence and significance.

3

Issues in tourism

Ideals and realities

The growth and development of tourism has been associated with several idealistic notions concerning its contribution to society, but subsequent experience has shown tourism, like many other human activities, can have both positive and negative impacts. The industry has frequently been promoted as a force for positive contributions to the social, economic, and natural environments of destination communities. Striving for such benefits through the vehicle of tourism development, however, has made tourism a major agent for change in every society and destination it has touched. Change involves a price, and some communities have been unaware of the costs and difficulties associated with extracting the benefits of tourism.

Many people have hoped tourism would help to foster a climate of peace and prosperity by bringing together people of different cultures and nationalities. Two examples of this sentiment are found below:

There is no better bridge between people, ideas, ideologies, cultures than travel. It can nurture understanding within a country and between countries. (Powell 1978, 3)

Tourism, in its broadest, generic sense, can do more to develop understanding among people, provide jobs, create foreign exchange, and raise living standards than any other economic force known. (Kaiser and Helber 1978, ix)

However, when the interaction of mankind and development of tourism has been examined in greater detail such worthy aspirations often face a stiff challenge and require some assistance to materialize.

A common theme in much of the tourism literature of the 1970s has concerned latent or actual hostility in destination areas where the indigenous people, "the hosts," are confronted with comparatively wealthy, and culturally different, visitors. Texts such as Turner and Ash (1975), Smith (1977), and de Kadt (1979) paint a generally depressing picture of tourism's impact, citing changed cultural values and the decay of native languages and customs. Turner and Ash equate mass tourism with past barbarian invasions,

an invasion outwards from the highly developed metropolitan centres into the "uncivilized" peripheries. It destroys uncomprehendingly and unintentionally, since one cannot impute malice to millions of people or even to thousands of businessmen and entrepreneurs. (Turner and Ash 1975, 129)

Van den Berghe and Keyes (1984) maintain the problem is particularly serious for the ethnic tourist who is in search of unspoiled natives in their natural surroundings. His very presence, and that of fellow tourists, will destroy the authenticity of the moment and setting because they are intruders. Similarly, Graburn (1976, 1984) is concerned that the inevitable commercialization of ethnic arts and crafts will lead to the development of shoddy replicas and fakes, as host communities attempt to meet the insatiable tourist demand for souvenirs.

While the majority of these negative social and cultural experiences have occurred in Third World nations, where the contrasts between native hosts and invading tourist hordes have been extreme, growing evidence of similar stress can be found within industrialized nations themselves. Role conflicts and social problems have arisen in areas of Hawaii, Scotland, and the French Alps. Women and teenagers, employed by the tourist industry, start to earn greater incomes than the men employed in traditional agriculture; the men lose pride in their new roles as waiters, bellhops, and dishwashers (Brownrigg and Greig 1976; Kent 1977; Reiter 1977).

Evidence of growing hostility towards visitors is beginning to emerge in the more popular tourist destinations which are becoming overwhelmed by the volume of business. In some areas it is evident in a growing antipathy toward tourists, as in Cornwall where they are referred to as "emmets" (ants), in southern England where they are called "grockles" (a commercially worthless shellfish). In Hawaii those tourists

Figure 4 T-shirt recording unfortunate result of territorial disputes between man and wildlife in Banff National Park

dressed in outrageous Hawaiian shirts or mu-mu's, complete with sunburn and the ever-present camera, are referred to as "howlies." In Banff, Alberta, the term "gorbies" is used to distinguish the awkward and gawking visitors. A sign of the times in Banff is production of a T-shirt which facetiously records the loss of three tourists to bear attacks one year (Figure 4). In a few regions the hostility is no longer latent with the appearance of anti-tourism graffiti, property destruction, and personal violence. Examples of this include the "Yankee go home" posters in the Europe of the 1960s, the firebombing of second homes in North Wales, and reported assaults on Canadian visitors in Hawaii.

The World Council of Churches has examined the issue of tourism-induced social stress and concluded that promotion of human understanding requires more than a simple transfer of people from one region or culture to another. It recommended in its report *Leisure–Tourism: Threat and Promise* (1970) that the industry acknowledge its social responsibilities, by providing more accurate information on the countries to be visited and by arranging informal meetings with local people. It calls for short, pre-trip courses stressing the political, social, and economic issues of destination areas and an extension of "meet the people" programs which have been successful in Sweden and Germany.

The flow of tourists and their revenue to peripheral regions has been viewed by some as a counterbalance to the economic pull of our urban–industrial centers. Christaller, the pioneer of central place theory, states:

There is also a branch of the economy that avoids central places and the agglomerations of industry. This is tourism. Tourism is drawn to the periphery of settlement districts as it searches for a position on the highest mountains, in the most lonely woods, along the remotest beaches. (Christaller 1964, 95)

Studies of national economies in underdeveloped countries have shown a considerable amount of generated tourism revenue has returned directly to the tourist-generating countries (Bryden 1973; Hills and Lundgren 1977). In one study it has been estimated as much as 77 percent of the tourism money returned to these urban–industrial economies (Perez 1974). This return flow is created by payment of loans and dividends on foreign investment, the importation of goods and services to supply the tourists, and the salaries of senior personnel who are often temporary residents. It has been given the apt name of "leakage," for a community may feel it is building a prosperous industry but when the final bills and bank charges are paid there is often much less left in the community account than expected.

Such a situation is not confined to underdeveloped countries; it can and does occur within advanced economies where small and peripheral communities attempt to transform some local resource into a tourist attraction. The development of mountain resorts or the renovation of heritage usually requires capital and manpower in excess of local supplies, consequently these tourism developments rely on investment and labor from distant urban–industrial centers and face the same leakage situation.

As an agent of transformation, tourism has been friendlier, in general, to the environment than many other activities and past industries. The conservation of beauty and heritage are key factors to the industry's development and survival and there are many examples of its support for the protection of natural and

Tourism and its significance

cultural resources. National parks around the world owe a great deal to the encouragement and political pressure of the tourism industry. The development of Yellowstone National Park in 1872, which was the forerunner of the concept, was intimately connected with the construction of access routes and tourist accommodation:

When parks such as Yellowstone and Glacier began to emerge in the 1870s, 1880s and 1890s the railroads built lines to them and constructed hotels and other facilities in and near them. They attempted to attract tourists from all over the world. (Nelson 1973, 71)

In central Africa the opening of the Saint-Floris National Park permitted a more effective protection of wildlife, for tourism revenues allowed the proper maintenance of trails and ranger camps, and the presence of tourists helped to keep poachers at bay (UNEP 1979).

The preservation of historic buildings is often supported or financed by tourism-related interests. The renovation of "old town" districts in the older North American cities is frequently founded on a business sector expectation that it will add to the touristic appeal of these cities. Churches which have lost their congregations have at times been saved by changing to a tourist function, such as a museum or "brass-rubbing" center.

The benefits of tourism extend to our cultural environment and daily life because of the diverse nature of its resource base and the intricate way in which it is woven into a community's regular activities. The presence of tourists often adds to the amenities of local areas. Perhaps the most famous example is the live theater of New York and London's West End, which depends on tourist ticket sales to sustain its existence. Of no less importance to other towns and cities are the tourist revenues which support their pageants, sports events, and tradefairs. "Institutions" such as Paris' Eiffel Tower, Seattle's Space Needle and Science Center, Munich's Olympic Stadium, and Montreal's "Man and His World Exhibit" on the Ile Saint-Hélène were created for special events and have remained as prime tourist–resident amenities.

A paradox of tourism, however, is that the industry carries within it the seeds of its own destruction. Successful development of a resource or amenity can lead to the destruction of those very qualities which attracted visitors in the first place.

The development of tourism is occasionally under- taken in such haste and without proper planning that it simply outstrips the local infrastructure and resource base, resulting in unexpected costs which further reduce its overall economic benefit to the community. The problem here is tourism's diverse and unco-ordinated structure, with numerous individual entre-preneurs striving to make a profit within their own short-term horizons:

Examples include the construction of hotels on Majorca without proper transport and sewage linkages, the continued construction on both Ibiza and Majorca despite clear warnings of insufficient water, and the rapid and heedless construction of hotels on the coast of Kenya, which now struggle to reach 50 percent occupancy owing to the unforeseen coincidence of the European tourist season and monsoon rains in Kenya. (Dilsaver 1979, 113)

Elsewhere the tourists themselves are the prime cause of environmental damage, although the destruction is usually unintended because most visitors come to admire a scene or event and the businessman's prosperity depends on an amenity's survival. Sochor (1976) reports more than 300 mountaineering expedi-tions since 1949 have caused widespread deforestation, pasture destruction, and serious accumulation of litter on the slopes of Mt Everest and other peaks in the Himalayas. Stonehenge has been placed behind a perimeter fence to protect it from the pressure of countless feet which were compacting the soil around the stones and threatening to tilt and topple the remaining lintels.

It becomes evident from this short review that tourism, as an agent of transformation, can change the social, economic, and physical relationships of com-munities where it has been adopted. These changes are often slow to emerge or to be appreciated because they can be both desirable and detrimental, so when the net balance is finally determined it is often too late to reverse or redirect the development process. In fact a good simile for the modern tourism industry would be that of a household fire. When the fire is contained and managed within the hearth it offers beauty and comfort to the household. When it runs out of control it can destroy the very household it was designed to support.

To maximize the benefits and minimize the dis-advantages of tourism's power to transform resources and host communities, it is necessary to formulate clear planning and management policies. A logical source for such planning would be the government, because "the reasoning prevails that the environment and its resources belong to the people who inhabit an area. Given this outlook, responsibility and accountability for tourism management lie with the government empowered to represent the people" (Kaiser and Helber 1978, 12). Government involvement, however, has been slow to emerge in the *laissez-faire* economies of the west, and has only come to the fore with the development of mass tourism and its consequences on national trade accounts.

Government involvement

Government interest in tourism stemmed from concern over its economic significance, particularly its sources of revenue. According to Lickorish and Kershaw, as quoted by Middleton, this alone was sufficient reason for government intervention in the development of tourism:

Justification of such intervention is the tremendous financial stake, taxes paid by various enterprises, indirect taxes paid by visitors and the employment provided in areas where alternative ways of earning a living are not usually available. (Middleton 1974, 11)

Thus, it comes as no surprise that the governments at national and regional levels have been actively promoting tourism and aiding facility development through the provision of grants and subsidies. Britain's Development of Tourism Act (1969) inaugurated that government's formal involvement with tourism planning in response to a growing travel deficit. Its goals were to provide more effective promotion abroad (British Tourist Authority) and at home (Tourist Boards on a regional basis), to encourage hotel construction and to direct development to economically depressed areas. Likewise, the more recent Travel Industry Development Subsidiary Agreements (TIDSA), signed between the Canadian federal government and various provinces, were conceived as a partial response to Canada's growing travel deficit—a deficit which had reached $1.8 billion by 1978. In all these federal–provincial development plans the prime goal was to develop the attractiveness of a province and make it more appealing to foreigners, especially United States visitors, and Canadians alike. The United States government formally joined in the promotion and stimulation of tourism with its 1981 National Tourism Policy Act,

although there had been considerable local and state promotion beforehand. The newly created United States Travel and Tourism Administration's basic mission is "to promote U.S. inbound tourism as an export" (Edgell 1983, 429), in an attempt to reduce its traditional travel budget deficit that has become an increasing burden as traditional visible exports have declined.

The most remarkable case of government involvement in tourism for economic development purposes occurred in Spain. Tourism development and promotion was used as the main financing force for the 1964 Spanish Economic and Social Development Plan. By that time tourism was the largest export sector in the country:

earnings covered 82 percent of the commercial balance deficit, financed about 40 percent of all imports and equalled 93 percent of the total value of Spanish exports. Little wonder that a prominent banking concern has likened tourism to "manna falling from heaven, impelled by the favorable winds of stabilization". (Naylon 1967, 33)

Using the momentum of mass tourism during the 1960s, Spain invested large amounts of public and private capital in tourism infrastructure and facilities to provide employment and raise living standards in various regions. These included established tourist destinations in the Balearic Islands and Costa Brava and new developments in underutilized areas such as the Costa de la Luz and Canary Islands. The timing of this investment program was perfect. The 1960s and early 1970s were the prime growth period of international tourism, when many northern European holidaymakers ventured from the fickle weather of their traditional home resorts to seek the sun and novelty of package tours in the south. By 1971, 26 million visitors were leaving $2.2 billion in foreign currency in Spain, and the industry was employing 1.4 million people or 11 percent of the labor force (Parsons 1973).

Spain's example of tourism-induced economic development has been emulated by Yugoslavia on its Adriatic coast. Three five-year economic and social development plans between 1955 and 1970 specified that tourism be treated as "an activity of special importance for the development of the country in general" (Mihovilovic 1980, 111). Accordingly, facilities were developed for tourists along the Adriatic coast at sites with tourism potential and charter links with western Europe encouraged. According to Mihovilovic, by 1980 it was expected that foreign currency earnings from tourism would amount to $1.2 billion (at 1975 prices).

Over time, government involvement with the industry has extended beyond economic concerns and revenue generation because with its growth came increasing evidence of its physical and social ramifications. First among these is the fact that tourism, like any other economic activity, competes for resources. Government agencies needed to accommodate tourism's growing needs with the demands of more traditional resource sectors like fishing, forestry, and agriculture. Furthermore, such concerns over resource allocation had to be accommodated in an era of environmental preservation, brought about by a growing awareness of the world's resource limitations and interrelated ecosystem. In North America's western states and provinces conflicting demands for resource exploitation and recreation have become a major issue for government (Hammond and Andrus 1979; Ingram 1981; *Newsweek* 1983). Federal and state/provincial governments own considerable tracts of land within the Rocky Mountain chain where increasing user pressures have forced them to consider multiple-use and self-sustaining management strategies. Such government policies are needed if the recreation and tourist demands of a growing urban population for lake and ski resorts can be balanced with increased demands for power (hydro-electric, coal, oil sands), the needs of traditional users (forestry, fisheries), and their responsibilities to future generations (land reserves, including national and state/provincial parks).

In Europe, the scale of tourism movement and more intensively developed landscape has forced governments to integrate tourism into local land-use patterns and lifestyles, or even become directly involved in its development. The British national parks encompass productive farmland and urban areas of considerable size, so their growing popularity as tourist destinations requires careful integration of the leisure industry into an existing economic and social system. In 1974 the Sandford Report of the National Parks Policies Review Committee recommended, and the government accepted, that landscape conservation should take precedence over recreation use. This included a duty to pay heed to the needs of agriculture and forestry, and the socio-economic well-being of local communities. Subsequent management plans of the ten National Park Authorities attempted to meet these requirements. However, not all successive governments have been

wholehearted in their support for a conservation priority, and retention of traditional landscapes has come under intense pressure from the growing agri-business farming methods.

In France the desire to develop a new area of the Mediterranean coast for tourism, to reduce the pressures on the Côte d'Azure and utilize the tourism potential of nearby coastal areas, has led the government to initiate the Languedoc–Roussillon project. Among the multiple purposes of this massive regional development plan (US$18.5 billion invested by 1979) was the creation of five tourist units (Figure 5). The purpose was to raise the income and employment levels of this depressed area, to provide new recreation and amenity facilities for local residents as well as visitors, and to provide an increased opportunity for social tourism projects (Willis 1977; Clarke 1981). The early experiences of the Languedoc–Roussillon project have not been as positive as first hoped, especially in terms of stimulating regional employment and economic growth, and now the French government seems to be adopting the view that it takes time for an underdeveloped region to become an established tourist Mecca.

One problem which the French and other governments have come to appreciate is that a major obstacle to development and planning in tourism is the fragmentation of the industry. For many small businessmen tourism is the last bastion of free enterprise, where with relatively little capital but with good timing and good ideas fortunes can still be made. In this sort of atmosphere, to decide on a public policy is one thing, to communicate this goal to all the companies, businessmen, and communities affected, and coordinate their actions is another. The overall fragmentation of the industry makes it easier for development conflicts to arise and facilitates a situation where the final outcome of individual decisions can place a great strain on the natural and human resources of destination areas. As Gunn sums it up:

the evidence of fragmentation of tourism development is mounting. As the volume of tourism expands and as development increases, many segments of tourism are running on collision courses with growing frequency. These conflicts appear to be expressed in reduced satisfactions to visitors, reduced rewards to owner–managers and erosion of basic resource assets. (Gunn 1977, 92)

Acceptance of this fact has compounded government

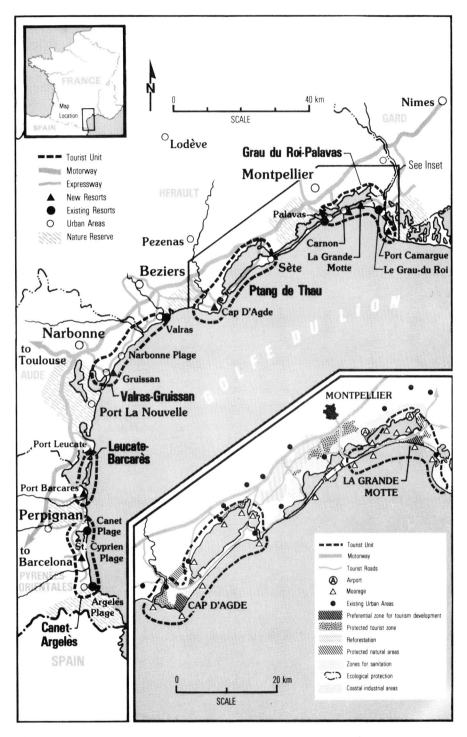

Figure 5 Languedoc–Roussillon regional development incorporating Tourist Units
Sources: Clarke (1981) and Pearce (1981)

involvement with tourism, for it alone possesses the necessary financial resources and legislative power to redirect and coordinate the industry along more desirable courses of action.

Government response to this fragmented growth industry, its numerous resource demands and various impacts, has been the gradual creation of tourism departments and ministries and an evolution of policy. In most western governments tourism agencies have been linked with trade and commerce ministries, reflecting its business orientation in legislative minds. In a few national and state/provincial governments where tourism has grown into a major economic activity, often within the top three activities in terms of employment or revenue, it has been accorded its own ministry. The initial goal of many agencies was to assist in the creation of an attractive and competitive tourist product. This involved cooperation with the industry and related government departments to stimulate business and supplement facilities through promotion and physical planning. Millions of dollars were spent on the promotion of traditional and new destinations in the belief that the economic return on such "investment" would be justified. New facilities were encouraged through subsidies, tax incentives, or outright grants, especially in areas of high unemployment. This economic and plant inventory emphasis, however, has gradually been replaced by a more comprehensive planning approach as the complexity and impacts of the industry have become apparent.

Fragmentation of the industry, which has been viewed as a barrier to comprehensive development and maximization of revenue, still retains some merit if it forms the basis for local diversity and character. The joy of travel includes noting regional variations in landscape and culture, as reflected in local architecture, customs, and food. Memorable visits can be made by the personal touch of individual owners and operators. Therefore, the problems of fragmentation must not be confused with, or transposed into, the boredom of conformity and mass production.

Mings considers the tourist industry's development prospects are at a crossroads and government involvement will play a major role in its future. As he sees it:

Rapid growth of any industry requires considerable study and planning in order to maximize its potential assets and minimize its potential liabilities. Commonly, tourism has not received the benefits of sufficient research to enable proper planning. Consequently, development in most places falls short of

achieving optimum impacts. Simply, too many countries have plunged headlong into an activity with inadequate and, occasionally, naive understandings. (Mings 1978, 2)

Governments, according to Mings, have three options in the face of this situation. First, there is the "no change" option, which consists of ignoring those problems and protests associated with the industry. Such a "hands off" approach is likely to be hazardous for both tourism and the government because the industry depends on local support and no elected government can disregard unpopular and unsuccessful activities for long. Second is the alternative course of action of withdrawing public support for tourism and even attempting to curb private promotion of tourism. In this case a danger exists that government officials under attack may react prematurely, without the benefit of adequate investigations. It may be the case that "whereas at one stage a few years ago officials jumped on to the tourism bandwagon with unwarranted haste, many are now in danger of jumping off in much the same unreasoned fashion" (Mings 1978, 3). The third option is to pursue rationalization of the industry so as to render it more beneficial. This involves an assessment of the industry's problems and prospects, followed by a plan of action to remedy weaknesses and direct the industry toward long-term goals. Underlying this third option Mings outlines two major issues:

1) Can the various objectives to tourism be remedied satisfactorily? And if the answer appears to be yes:
2) Will the contributions (economic, social and environmental) of the surviving industry be of a sufficient magnitude to warrant public support? (Mings 1978, 3)

As Mings notes, none of these three options exist in their pure form, but "most countries have borrowed some characteristics from all three options." The rapid and inadequately planned growth has created a myriad of unexpected and undesirable problems, placing tourism development at a crossroads. Either the industry's shortcomings will be attacked and its potential benefits realized, or the necessary public support will be redirected to other areas of social and economic investment.

Community approach

The purpose of this book is to examine the two issues raised by Mings and offer a method by which the

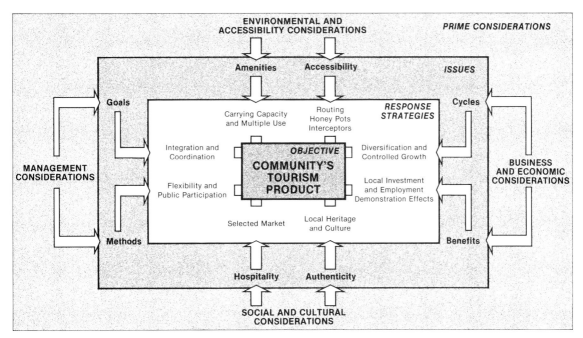

Figure 6 Major components for a community-oriented tourism strategy

industry's contribution can be directed toward community goals, and thereby warrant public support. The industry possesses great potential for social and economic benefits if planning can be redirected from a pure business and development approach to a more open and community-oriented approach which views tourism as a local resource. The management of this resource for the common good and future generations should become the goal and criterion by which the industry is judged. This will involve focusing on the ecological and human qualities of a destination area in addition to business considerations.

A community approach to tourism management requires a complex combination of interlocking parts, leading to a general goal that can be identified and measured. Figure 6 is an attempt to outline the major components of a community-oriented tourism management strategy and forms the basis of this book's structure. The objective of this strategy is to produce a "Community Tourism Product" which like the traditional tourist product will be an amalgam of the destination's resources and facilities; but in this case it is one which the community, as a whole, wishes to present to the

tourism market. To research this goal three separate stages are identified and discussed.

The prime consideration in any planning or management scheme is what components to consider. In this case environmental and accessibility considerations have been selected first because of the industry's dependence on its resource base and connectivity with tourist-generating areas. The presence of resources and a potential market, however, do not necessarily make a viable industry, so business and economic considerations need to be considered next. In addition, the fact that tourism is so dependent on local hospitality makes it mandatory that development proceeds in accord with the desires and customs of local people, thus social and cultural considerations need to be included. Finally, management of a community product provides a range of options. By placing tourism in a community perspective it becomes only one of several functions and opportunities for an area, and must be planned in accordance with its relative importance and contribution.

Within each of the four consideration areas identified in Figure 6, certain major issues have been selected to

37

illustrate the relevance of a community approach to this activity. They are not intended to represent all the issues within each area, but from past experience they are general problems and ones which have persisted under the old *laissez-faire* or elementary planning strategies. These represent the objections to tourism, which Mings referred to, and need to be remedied if tourism is to have a future.

To ascertain if the problem areas can be rectified, various response strategies have been examined. They have been selected in terms of a community relevance, to demonstrate the feasibility of using this approach. Again the list is not meant to be all-inclusive but has been based on community-oriented response strategies used around the world.

Succeeding chapters will investigate the inter-relationships between the local issues and response strategies in more detail. They will examine how a more humanistic and community-oriented approach can lead to a tourism product that is more in harmony with the environmental and social capacities of destination areas, while still providing an attractive long-term tourism business. The emphasis will be on destination area concerns and strategies, which is intended to complement and balance the existing literature on international and large-scale aspects of tourism development and planning.

Section 2

The environment and accessibility

To enter the tourism business a community needs to create a tourist product that will attract visitors and to provide the access so they can visit and experience the product. Competition for tourists is intense, and growing more so, as communities look on this activity as a relatively non-polluting growth industry which is labor intensive and supportive of local amenities. One theme which is emerging from this competition is the need to offer a quality product combined with a pleasant travel experience. This requires destinations to look internally to ensure their basic tourism resources are protected, and to look externally to examine ways of improving the route and travel experience involved in reaching them.

It has been noted that tourism development carries within it the seeds of its own destruction, and this factor should be considered in all development and planning proposals. If the number or concentration of visitors, both in spatial and seasonal terms, exceeds a community's physical carrying capacity, deterioration of such basic resources as landscape and water supplies can occur. It will transform what was intended to be a non-consumptive, renewable resource industry into yet another short-term boom and bust enterprise.

Since tourism sells personal experiences, deterioration of the environment need not be the first sign of trouble for a destination. Negative vacation experiences can occur much earlier, when visitors with different expectations find themselves in conflict with each other over the use of community facilities and amenities. Some types of tourist are more tolerant than others in terms of what they expect, but if a destination is to maintain a good image it must do its best to match the expectations of those groups it wishes to attract.

Since few destinations can offer a unique attraction guaranteed to draw visitors, most have to consider their relative competitive position. An important feature will be their access to major tourist-generating regions and possible competitors that can intercept potential visitors, especially in the case of automobile travelers. Therefore, a destination must consider the route and travel needs of its visitors as well as their stay. It may be necessary for several destinations to cooperate and combine their various attractions into a regional package in order to offer a meaningful and tempting package to the tourist.

In response to these challenges tourism agencies and local planning authorities have inaugurated various strategies. These include increasing the supply of destination areas in order to spread the demand more evenly and reduce the physical crowding; the classification of destinations to indicate the primary tourist activity offered in the area; and the zoning of land within destination areas to separate and guide the various visitor expectations to specific zones, in order to minimize user conflicts and environmental stress. Behind much of this planning lie the twin concepts of carrying capacity and multiple use, which are proving to be useful tools in the management of our natural resources.

Management is the key to accessibility problems as well, especially where engineering solutions, such as new and bigger highways, appear to be inappropriate or too expensive. Perception and stereotype images play a major role in travel decisions and these mental attributes are being used, increasingly, to lure or deter the visitor. To attract visitors, scenic and heritage routes have been developed, and "honeypot" attractions have been created, which combined with information and promotion programs can lure tourists into previously underutilized areas. Where visitor presence has

The environment and accessibility

become overwhelming, particularly in terms of the "windshield tourist," visitors are being induced out of their automobiles to walk or use public transit. Access is the key to resource use in tourism, so these two features have been placed together in tourism management and this text.

Although the bulk of this section deals with the natural environment and regional travel patterns, there are numerous parallels to the problems and strategies within urban-based tourism. For example, the problem of resource and image integrity faces the city of Athens, where pollution is eroding the Acropolis and authorities have begun to replace parts of the original with replicas. Perceptual awareness and mental maps are important concepts in the city, where the works of Lynch (1960) and Porteous (1971) indicate respectively their relevance to finding one's way around the city and to particular destinations. Finally, access and information sources are perhaps even more relevant to tourism management in the city, when visitors are so close to their objectives yet often frustrated due to a lack of access or precise directions. What can be more frustrating than to see beach access denied by private property rights, or to be unable to locate a publicized attraction because of poor signposting and inadequate directions? Both of these problems are now being addressed by more cities, in the form of guaranteed access to amenity attractions and more information centers on the outskirts of town, to advise tourists before they enter the urban maze.

4

Environmental–accessibility issues

The biggest concern for destination communities should be conservation of their natural tourism resources, for this is their *raison d'être*. Successful tourism development leads to increased numbers and the possibility of visitor-induced stress on a community's physical environment. The problem is most acute in those areas with outstanding scenic beauty or recreation opportunities possessing good access to tourist-generating regions. They are becoming overwhelmed with tourists and need to conserve their attractions by controlling growth.

Resource integrity

A prime example of this situation are those national parks offering urban tourists the opportunity to view scenic grandeur, wildlife, and participate in outdoor recreation. In the USA their appeal has ballooned, with visits to national parks increasing from 80 million in 1960 to over 300 million by 1980 (*Newsweek* 1981). By 1982 the number had reached 334 million, of which 245 million were "recreation visits" (National Park Service 1983). Despite this impressive growth, the supply of national park space has failed to keep pace with demand, especially in the eastern states.

The busiest national park, by far, is the Great Smoky Mountains National Park in North Carolina, which is the closest wilderness park to the industrial northeast. This park regularly receives over 8 million recreation visits a year, which, when coupled with the 14 million recreation visits to its companion Blue Ridge Parkway, makes it a major tourism magnet in the eastern United States. Many of the visitors to this area stay overnight in the gateway service town of Gatlinburg, because of the restriction on overnight accommodation in the park. As a result Gatlinburg is "now more akin to Las Vegas—a tourist's dream perhaps, but a planner's nightmare barely 800 meters from the park boundary" (Coppock and Rogers 1975, 510).

Yosemite National Park receives an average of 2.4 million visitors a year, because of its appeal to the day-trip market out of San Francisco and Los Angeles (van Wagtendonk 1980). In addition to serving the drive-through visitor, Yosemite accommodates those who wish to stop-over, providing campsites, cabins, and a hotel in Yosemite Village. At times the valley which contains this village and attracts most of the visitors becomes an off-shoot of Los Angeles, complete with traffic jams and smog conditions—the very conditions tourists are trying to escape. Indeed, some find the existence of a tourist center offering creature comforts and convenience incongruous in a national park setting. One of these is Sax, who maintains:

Tourism in parks today . . . is often little more than an extension of the city and its lifestyle transposed onto a scenic background. At its extreme, in Yosemite Valley or at the South Rim of Grand Canyon, for example, one finds all the artifacts of urban life: traffic jams, long lines waiting in restaurants, supermarkets, taverns, fashionable shops, night life, prepared entertainments, and the unending drone of motors. (Sax 1980, 12)

In response the National Park Service has attempted to reduce the scale of Yosemite Village and its facilities, plus reduce the number of automobiles entering the valley.

In Canada the situation is much the same. There has been more than a tenfold increase in visits to national parks since 1950, with 20.7 million visits recorded in 1980. Within the Canadian system, Banff National Park

Figure 7   Banff Township in mid-summer, complete with hotels, restaurants, stores, and crowds

has the highest visitation record at 3.6 million, despite the fact that it is well removed from the population centers of southern Ontario and Quebec. In fact, Canada has the same spatial imbalance as the United States with most of its national parks in the north and west, far away from the densely populated areas of central Canada.

Banff's popularity owes a great deal to its location astride the Trans-Canada Highway, which is Canada's principal east-west highway, and its proximity to Calgary. The park is only an hour's drive from Calgary, via the four-lane Trans-Canada Highway, which makes it a veritable backyard playground for this metropolis. Unlike many other national parks, Banff receives no winter reprieve from tourism because of the ski facilities which have been developed in the park. It now has a twin-season peak, and although summer is busier than winter, it is not unusual to see line-ups for the ski-hill gondolas (*Globe and Mail* 1982). This situation

could become worse as the area becomes better known through its 1988 Winter Olympics exposure.

The pressure on Banff's facilities has become intense and has had to be met by controls and diversion. The service center of Banff township has developed into a small town of 4000 permanent residents, complete with hospital, cinema, and nightclubs (Figure 7). "The continuing urbanization of Banff [township] became incompatible with the emerging preservationist policies of national parks" (Todhunter 1981, 39), and strict limits have been placed on future expansion. Such limits, however, do not diminish the demand for access and accommodation, so this has been met by diverting development to the park's gateway community of Canmore. The result could be the rise of another Gatlinburg, with all its attendant social problems (Cheng 1980), and no respite for the park's landscape and recreation facilities.

The popularity of North America's national parks is

Figure 8   Climbers on Stanage Edge, Peak District National Park

not only reflected in the growth of services and accommodation, but more significantly in terms of increasing degradation of their environmental attraction (Jordan 1979; Marsh 1983). Tourist activities and tourist facilities often involve landscape and habitat change, the elimination of wildlife, soil compaction, and erosion. Trees have been cleared for ski slopes and campsites; "nuisance" animals, especially bears, have been removed or shot; and the human use of campgrounds and trails has compacted soil and altered vegetation cover. Most conflict occurs in valley bottoms, where tourist facilities and routes are located, because these areas often form the crucial habitat zones for wildlife species. But as the more adventurous tourists penetrate the upland and less accessible areas even these sanctuaries are disappearing.

In Britain two of the busiest national parks are the Peak District and Snowdonia Parks. The Peak District is located between two urban–industrial fingers and is within a comfortable driving range for afternoon trips or day outings. Most visitors are "windshield tourists," gazing at the landscape as they drive leisurely through the park. Consequently, a major concern in this park has been traffic management, but congestion can spill beyond the highway into the natural environment itself when there is a particular attraction or reason. One example is Stanage Edge (Figure 8) where the escarpment face has become such a popular practice spot for rock climbers it is difficult to find uneroded handholds or a clear route to the top (Patmore 1972, 121).

Snowdonia has long been a popular destination. On a

43

The environment and accessibility

busy day there can be over 100,000 visitors within the park, contributing to an annual figure of over 9 million visitor-days spent in the park. Such numbers have led to general road congestion and delays for visitor and resident alike in this rural area. They have led also to over-use and vegetation erosion in popular recreation sites, such as northern Snowdonia, the Merionnydd coast, and around Cader Idris.

Congestion and environmental stress from tourism are not confined to mountainous or upland areas, for similar problems have arisen along coasts and water-ways which have long been magnets for tourism. McHarg (1969) was one of the first to stress the fragile and interrelated nature of dune coastlines. He pointed out the danger of constructing homes and recreation resorts adjacent to beaches on unstable dunes, and the disastrous outcomes of attempting to stabilize the natural processes of coastal erosion and accretion. A common problem is that the major tourist attraction—the beach—is extremely tolerant and resilient, which can lull unsuspecting developers into a false sense of security regarding the surrounding area.

While the beach is resilient because of tidal cleansing and the protection it affords to burrowing animal life, the back area dunes which people need to cross are fragile (Figure 9). The primary dune is secured and held in place by dune grasses that are vulnerable to trampling. If the grasses are destroyed, wind erosion will remove the loose sand and breach the dune, exposing inland areas to flooding. The trough behind the primary dune is more tolerant because the presence of groundwater helps maintain the vegetation and its binding roots. The secondary or inland dune is nearly as vulnerable as the primary dune, and if it is to be used as a secondary defense against flooding the

vegetation cover and profile must be retained. The backdune is the most tolerant in terms of development because it is the most stable and mature, with more extensive vegetation and fresh water supplies.

Where there are dunes there are good sandy beaches, which attract large numbers of people and generate considerable revenues. It has been calcu-lated, for example, that the dune-backed beaches of Norfolk can yield revenues of up to £68,000 ($US123,000) per kilometer per year in Lowestoft, £23,000 ($US42,000) in Great Yarmouth, and £14,000 ($US25,000) in Cromer (Simmonds 1977, 4). To reach beaches such as these often requires crossing vulnerable primary dunes, with most traverses occurring close to parking lots serving the beach area. This places excessive stress on the dune because the trampling and mechanical pressure of large numbers of people is concentrated in one area, hastening the destruction of dune grasses.

In Northern Ireland's Portrush and Portstewart area it was thought that the "slow but creeping rates of coastal deterioration do not arouse the public's interest in nor its appreciation of the environmental dangers involved" (Eastwood and Carter 1981, 281), but in the Studland Heath Nature Reserve, Dorset, a more positive approach has been applied to the problem of dune damage. Taking advantage of the concentrated dune-crossing route the Studland Heath authorities have "hardened" the environment by providing duckboard paths, to limit the negative impacts. The feeling is that "given a choice, people prefer to walk along a fairly firm path rather than through soft sand, so the provision of defined routes from car park to beach will often alleviate erosion problems" (Cox 1980, 60). Further-more, in addition to explaining the bureaucratic interference with freedom of movement in the dune

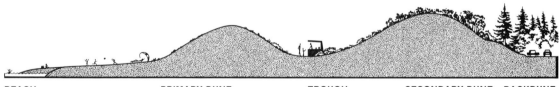

BEACH	PRIMARY DUNE	TROUGH	SECONDARY DUNE	BACKDUNE
TOLERANT	*INTOLERANT*	*RELATIVELY TOLERANT*	*INTOLERANT*	*TOLERANT*
Intensive recreation	Few paths to	Limited recreation	Limited pathways	Most suitable
No building	minimize breaching	Limited structures	No buildings	for development
	No buildings because			
	of instability			

Figure 9   Cross-section of coastal dunes
Source: McHarg (1969, 14–15)

area, Cox suggests that:

Telling people why you have fenced and planted an area of dunes can help reduce the amount of thoughtless damage that occurs. . . . The trails and [information] centre are perhaps the most useful [methods of imparting this information] as they can be laid out to deliberately lead visitors away from certain sensitive parts of the dunes. (Cox 1980, 61)

The concentration of visitor activity in dune areas is not limited to beach access, for the very nature of dunescapes, steep slopes and poor footing, tends to focus users along a few favorable routes. This has been noted and taken advantage of in the Spirit Sands area of the Spruce Woods Provincial Park, Manitoba, where up to 30,000 visitors a year come to view this unusual inland feature. To accommodate this intrusion into a fragile landscape, while protecting the environment, the park management has developed an interpretive trail and made efforts to stabilize its neighboring slopes.

Interwoven within the dune landscape can be salt marshes which, despite their unimposing appearance, play a vital role in providing a wildfowl refuge and nursery for many fish and crustaceans. The drainage or filling of these areas can provide beach-access land for tourist facilities, but at the cost of declining fish stocks and lost nature study opportunities. Furthermore, the pollution of such areas with untreated sewage and other waste products is likely to have a later effect, as its influence is absorbed into the food chain, culminating in man himself.

One coastal waterway and marsh area which is facing increasing tourism and other development pressures is the Norfolk Broads. This man-made system of 48 broads (lakes) and 200 kilometers of partly tidal, navigable waterways stretches inland from the resorts of Cromer, Great Yarmouth, and Lowestoft:

The two areas of concern to environmental managers are the persistent loss of natural habitat with consequent effects on associated plant, animal and insect species, and the alteration of the characteristic landscape. Both of these are not only morally and aesthetically unfortunate but could result in very costly dredging and bank maintenance operations if the local tourist industry and agriculture are to be maintained. (O'Riordan 1979, 51)

In terms of tourism, the major concerns are to preserve waterways and broads for the large boat rental business, which earns an estimated £12 million ($US21 million) a year; plus conserve the natural habitat of surrounding marshlands, which add to the tourism

experience by sheltering large numbers of birds and other wildlife. To conserve this area will require management measures that link the land with the water in a zonal approach, rather than the conventional separation of land management from water management, according to O'Riordan. As an example he cites the need to protect 20,000 hectares of low-lying marshland from flooding by building up the protective river dykes and reducing the speed limit and resultant wash of passing cruisers.

Although water recreation has great appeal for tourists, the industry has been lax at times in protecting the integrity of this resource. A flagrant example would be certain rapidly developing areas of the Mediterranean, where:

Local and national governments, in their eagerness to attract more tourists in order to develop the local economy, as well as to improve the balance of payments, are often ready to disregard zoning regulations and other qualitative standards. The results of such indiscriminate development are often ruined beaches, polluted coastal waters and overloaded public services. (Gonen 1981, 381)

But this problem can arise also in established tourist destinations, where maturity and self-interest would be expected to guide the conservation of principal tourism assets. The principal attraction of the Okanagan Valley in British Columbia is its lakes, but as settlement and agriculture have developed, sewage and fertilizer residuals have entered the lakes raising the coliform count and encouraging weed growth. By 1969 the issue of water quality was being raised in the local media, but the industry response was "a vehement reaction from the resort owners in the area who insisted that the lake was 'pure and pristine,' with the debate merely 'hindering our tourist season and whole economy'" (Dearden 1983, 83). By 1980 the milfoil weed problem had become acute in Okanagan:

Initially, the weed demonstrated a preference for areas with high nutrient loadings, such as at sewage discharge points, and the mouths of creeks with agricultural run-off, or high sediment loads resulting from headwater logging practices. . . . By 1980 some 700 hectares of the littoral zone (near the shore) in the Okanagan Lakes System were colonized. (Dearden 1983, 84)

At this stage the industry finally cried "foul." Resort owners and the Chamber of Commerce which had earlier defended the lake's pristine condition now started to call "for 'no expense to be spared to rid the

The environment and accessibility

weeds from the lake,' claiming that it was a 'disgrace to let tourists see the beaches'" (Dearden 1983, 85). By this point the Okanagan Lake's recreation image had been tarnished and business started to falter; a situation that was not helped by further adverse publicity associated with the harsh remedies proposed to rectify the situation—namely, the application of the chemical weedkiller, 2,4-D.

Image conflicts

Tourism is a very personal use of discretionary time and income. As such, tourists' perceptions of the natural environment are, in many ways, as relevant to a quality travel experience as its physical characteristics. If beauty is in the eyes of a beholder then we can expect that what is acceptable to one group of tourists may be intolerable to another. Stress has been documented between various vacationing groups, when the activity preferences and perceptions of one group have been upset or constrained by the activities of another. It can occur also between visitors and residents, either in the form of different priorities or as a conflict of interest and perception between local decision makers and the visitor.

Perceptual differences between various visitors and their potential for conflict was noted in Lucas' (1964) study of wilderness perception in the Boundary Waters Canoe Area of the Superior National Forest. Lucas contended:

All resources are defined by human perception. . . . The importance of resource perception is particularly obvious for recreational, scenic, and amenity resources because of the internal, personal, and subjective way such resources are used. (Lucas 1964, 409)

The wilderness was a major attraction for canoeists and auto-campers, but both had different perceptions and uses for this feature. Canoeists generally sought isolation and a "natural" setting for their wilderness, whereas auto-campers viewed any area inaccessible from the highway as wilderness—a backdrop to be admired but not entered. Accordingly, the auto-campers' perception of wilderness was not disturbed by the presence of canoeists in their panoramic backdrop, but for the canoeists the presence of others and the appearance of vehicles destroyed the illusion of wilderness and their recreation experience.

Lucas' seminal work has been followed by a series of case studies which reveal several factors relating to the perceived recreational conflict of various groups. Murphy (1975) noted that the conflicting demands water-skiers and fishermen placed on a body of water led to two outwardly similar lakes being divided up between these two groups—a process of natural selection and territoriality. Jackson and Wong's study (1982) of cross-country skiers and snowmobilers found their perceptual conflict to be asymmetrical, with the skiers viewing snowmobiles as a negative interference whereas snowmobilers enjoyed or were indifferent to meeting skiers. Consequently, Jackson and Wong felt that perceived recreational conflicts could be better understood by examining recreational orientations and motivations in addition to the actual choice of activity. They found that:

cross-country skiers show an aversion to mechanization in recreation and are motivated to recreate in order to fulfill needs of solitude, tranquility, physical exercise, and to develop an awareness of the natural environment. Snowmobilers are machine-oriented, with a leaning towards socialization, adventurousness, and escapism. Cross-country skiers choose their activity precisely for the reasons which make it susceptible to impact, whereas snowmobilers choose theirs precisely for the reasons which may generate those impacts. (Jackson and Wong 1982, 59)

Such revelations are of major concern to destination development and management, for whenever a gap exists between the predetermined market objectives and the actual status of a tourist product or resource an image and marketing problem exists.

Management and changed behavior are obviously called for in situations where environmental stress has led to violence and degradation. Group differences have led to vandalism and rowdyism in Ontario's provincial parks. White, Wall, and Priddle (1978) report a rise in antisocial behavior in the parks, as teenagers and young adults, in search of parties and carousing, conflict with family campers seeking peace and quiet in the evenings:

In 1975, 41,246 people were involved in [incidents of rowdyism] generating 2,994 complaints from campers. In consequence, 6,640 campers were evicted from 1,162 camp-sites. . . . Damage to park property was estimated at $30,663 and to private property a further loss valued at $17,493. These events took place even though 14,678.5 man-days were spent by Ministry of Natural Resources staff, and 2,371.5 man-days by police, in enforcement of laws and regulations. (White, Wall, and Priddle 1978, 14)

In the United States, park rangers are now required for policing as much as for nature interpretation. "With major crimes on the rise in the parks, more and more rangers receive law-enforcement training" (Jordan 1979, 45)—including small arms training.

Stress can be seen in terms of the natural environment when the commercial aspects of tourism overrule conservation or aesthetic considerations. The trampling of thousands of visitors to Land's End in Britain had resulted in serious soil erosion of this privately owned and operated property by 1976 (Figure 10). In Gettysburg, Pennsylvania, the site of the National Military Park has been overshadowed and besmirched by a 307-foot viewing tower erected by a neighbouring entrepreneur.

Questions involving destination image and different perceptions extend to the relations between the hosts and guests in a tourism environment. Residents of destination areas have been found to possess different recreation priorities compared to their visitors. McCool (1976, 1978) has hypothesized and confirmed that residents would participate more frequently than tourists in certain activities, which can lead to local demands for one type of recreation facility while the visitors are looking for another. Using McCool's five-fold typology of recreation activities Jackson and Schinkel (1981) have identified similar distinct recreation preferences among the residents and tourists of a destination area (Table 5). They found the residents and tourists were similar in only one activity class, whereas

local residents expressed a stronger preference than tourists for activities such as resting and relaxing, swimming, boating and canoeing, while tourists more frequently preferred activities such as sightseeing, hiking, photography, visiting and meeting people. (Jackson and Schinkel 1981, 361)

They note that while no inter-group or inter-activity

Figure 10 Erosion at Land's End, England

The environment and accessibility

Table 5 Planned participation of residents and tourists in the Yellowknife region of the Northwest Territories

Activity classes	Activity components	Residents (n = 138) percentage	Tourists (n = 159) percentage	Total (n = 297) percentage	Chi-square
Appreciative–symbolic	Sightseeing, hiking, photography, enjoying the outdoors	16	62	40	62.18*
Extractive–symbolic	Fishing, picking berries, collecting rocks, bird hunting	50	53	52	0.14
Passive–free play	Resting and relaxing, getting away from the city, camping, cooking, reading, enjoying camp-fire, cards	59	15	35	61.59*
Sociable–learning	Visiting friends and relatives, shopping, meeting people, drinking and partying, nature study	4	23	14	21.90*
Active–expressive	Swimming, boating, canoeing, beach activities, children's play, horseshoes, frisbee, volleyball	46	16	30	30.32*

Source: Jackson and Schinkel (1981, 357)
Note: * Significant at 0.001 level.

conflict was evident at the time of their study such "differences in activity orientation suggest that in a situation of greater competition for recreation resources ... such conflicts are likely to occur" (Jackson and Schinkel 1981, 362).

If conflict is to be avoided or reduced some form of management will be needed to develop the widest range of tourist experiences, to segregate conflicting activities and maximize community benefits. In the past this has required input from the experts (regional and local planners, park managers, tourist boards, and businessmen) to judge the perceptions, motivations and preferences of visitors and residents alike. If such experts had a clear understanding of visitors' percep- tions and preferences and the local community's priorities and capacities such a system would be acceptable and functional, but unfortunately numerous studies have revealed consistent divergence between the views of experts, visitors, and local residents (Lucas 1964; Hendee and Harris 1970; Clark *et al.* 1971; Peterson 1974; Wellman *et al.* 1982).

In a review of evidence presented to the Select Committee on Scottish Affairs concerning "appropriate uses" of the Scottish countryside, Sewell identified several distinctive perceptual differences among groups making presentations to the Committee. These included the conservationists and naturalists who "appeared to see the countryside as a last bastion in the maintenance of diversity in ecological systems, and in a broad sense, a means of prolonging the survival of the human species" (Sewell 1974, 244). The outdoor recreationists who "viewed with alarm the continual expansion of forest development in the countryside" contradicted the forestry interests which "believe that the modification of the environment is inevitable, and suggest that such modification brings many more social benefits than a policy of non-development" (Sewell 1974, 245). In contrast to the urgency of various pressure group briefs, which tended to emphasize present or potential conflicts and call for shifts in policies or modifications of existing institutions, the general picture presented by the officials was "that there were no major problems, and that should they arise, the existing framework was adequate to handle them" (Sewell 1974, 246).

Such diversities of perception and interest can lead to underutilization of prepared recreation facilities or conflict between various user groups. Hendee and Harris (1970), for example, found four distinctive differences of opinion between the managers of wilderness areas and their users in the Pacific North- west, which led to over-capacity development and an underrated willingness of visitors to cooperate with meaningful management controls:

First, managers did not credit users with as responsive an attitude as they actually exhibited toward suggested measures of behavior control. For example, most managers did not recognize that typical users support most camp clean-up practices, favor charges for use and mandatory fire permits; oppose short-cutting trails, camping wherever one pleases . . . in general wilderness users seemed responsible and responsive to reasonable measures of control but were not always credited with such an attitude by managers.

Secondly, managers attributed to users more support for recreational development in wilderness than most users actually expressed.

Third, despite the fact that managers over-estimated demand for campsite development in wilderness, they also over-estimated the prevalence of purist philosophies among typical users. . . . For example, managers did not anticipate that most users were willing to accept the use of helicopters (for bringing patrolmen to and from wilderness) . . . that portable radios are unacceptable in wilderness to only a minority of users or that most users favor control of heavy infestations of forest disease.

Fourth, managers tended to perceive users as clearly opinionated and did not anticipate the high proportion of users who were neutral in their response. (Hendee and Harris 1970, 760–1)

An example of conflict is provided in Overton's analysis of game laws designed to protect Newfoundland's caribou herds. A series of legislative acts, starting in 1879, restricted hunting and attempted to raise it from a subsistence activity to one which took its place in a commercial economy:

With the introduction, extension and enforcement of the game laws, conflicts become increasingly common, because there was now a formal code which could be violated. Moreover, much of the impetus for the development of game laws came from the advocates of the tourism industry who viewed the caribou as a tourism resource rather than a food staple for those engaged in fishing. . . . The main locus of conflict was between the poor settlers and the state. As game laws made it more and more difficult for people to kill deer for their personal consumption and for sale, the crime of poaching increased. (Overton 1980, 46)

The intent of Newfoundland's game laws has not been achieved in the main since the size of the herd is greatly diminished and local residents, particularly native Indians, continue to protest about environmental laws designed to protect business interests.

Resource allocation

The incidents of physical deterioration and user conflict reflect an overall competition for scarce resources in our modern world. Nowhere is this more apparent than in the current debate concerning the future of North America's wilderness parks. These parks face the dilemma of preserving the integrity of a natural environment while making it accessible to millions of visitors. They must reconcile the numerous and conflicting demands placed on their resources by various tourist types and extractive industries. But above all, the true meaning and purpose of these parks has to be determined.

National parks are being asked to fulfill a multitude of functions, some of which are incompatible. Bryan outlines four major objectives in the Canadian system:

The park system attempts to satisfy a demand for outdoor recreation in areas of magnificent scenery, to provide sanctuaries for the protection of wildlife, to preserve areas of wilderness, and to preserve parts of the Canadian national heritage. (Bryan 1973, 276)

To achieve such ends would require parks to (1) cater to all types and quantities of recreation demand; (2) become extensive, unenclosed open-air zoos; (3) establish areas of sufficient size and variety to meet the diverse perceptions of wilderness; and (4) establish areas that are large enough to be ecologically independent, so that the natural heritage can be perpetuated. This last function may require reserves of land large enough to accommodate natural events like forest fires, without intervention by man.

There is no doubt that such multiple goals have already led to conflict and compromise. The development and commercialization of river rafting on the Colorado River through the Grand Canyon National Park generated a lot of criticism. The number and noise of these large inflatable craft was beginning to destroy the solitude and wilderness of the canyon floor, so in response to conservationist protests the United States Park Service proposed a ban on all motor-assisted craft in 1985. The proposal to expand skiing facilities at Lake Louise, complete with a new resort village, generated considerable opposition in the early 1970s (Sadler 1983); but the conservationists' success in halting the development may be short-lived if current proposals to use Lake Louise for part of the 1988 Winter Olympics go ahead.

Much of the recreation–conservation dilemma has

The environment and accessibility

Table 6 Visitation levels of selected North American National Parks

Nation and date of visits	National Park	Location	Number of visits
Canada[1] 1979–80	Banff	Alberta	3,642,928
	Forillan	Quebec	708,440
	Fundy	New Brunswick	840,931
	Glacier	British Columbia	1,359,782
	Gros Morne	Newfoundland	200,043
	Jasper	Alberta	1,849,632
	Kluane	Yukon	7,034
	Kootenay	British Columbia	2,353,678
	La Mauricie	Quebec	238,019
	Pacific Rim	British Columbia	553,632
	Point Pelee	Ontario	455,579
United States[2] 1982	Badlands	South Dakota	1,030,500
	Carlsbad Caverns	New Mexico	782,000
	Crater Lake	Oregon	435,600
	Everglades	Florida	550,200
	Grand Canyon	Arizona	2,293,100
	Great Smoky Mountains	North Carolina/Tennessee	8,177,900
	Hawaii Volcanoes	Hawaii	1,995,400
	Mammoth Cave	Kentucky	1,526,700
	Redwood	California	467,100
	Shenandoah	Virginia	1,752,000
	Yosemite	California	2,415,600

Sources: [1] Eidsvik (1983, 247)
[2] National Park Service 1983.

been caused by tourism's growth rather than by a change in tourist tastes. Sax (1980) observes that a contradiction of objectives was present in the 1916 Act of Congress, ordering the National Park Service to both promote use and conserve resources, so as to leave them unimpaired. At that time Sax believed it "was actually a workable mandate," because although the visitors

arrived in carriages, slept in hotels, and spent a good deal of their time sitting on verandas ... they came in much smaller numbers, their impact on the resources was much less, and, despite the comforts they provided themselves, the setting in which they lived in the parks was fairly primitive and marked a sharp contrast with life at home. (Sax 1980, 11)

Now with the arrival of millions of visitors at certain accessible and popular parks (Table 6), plus the provision of increased tourism infrastructure and facilities, the conceived balance has become untenable in some locations.

The competition for wilderness areas is becoming more intense as different groups and users place their claim. The large areas of land set aside as national parks or protected areas in Alaska has upset native Indians, the state government, and industry (Hammond and Andrus 1979). A major competitor for much land in the west is the forest industry. In northern California this industry claimed that a proposed 2.4 million acre wilderness would cost the local economy 1300 logging and sawmill jobs, creating a local market for a bumper sticker reading: "Sierra Club—Kiss My Axe" (*Newsweek* 1983, 26). In British Columbia it was estimated that withdrawal of a granted tree-felling license in order to save a scenic off-shore island would cost the government $US21 million in compensation. Another important competitor is the mining industry which was a factor in causing the delayed opening of Kluane National Park, in the Yukon (Eidsvik 1983).

The cost of conserving large areas of land is becoming prohibitively expensive, both in fiscal and political terms. Withdrawal of land from the free enterprise system incurs opportunity costs, the loss of potential revenues from other users, plus the cost of assembly and operation. After the United States government purchased 48,000 acres of logged watershed to add to the Redwood National Park it needed to spend an additional $33 million to rehabilitate the area (Grosvenor 1979, 29). In Canada the cost of Parks Canada's operating budget needed to increase five-fold during the expansionary period of the 1970s. In political terms such expenses are becoming harder to justify, but even more frustrating is the complexity and trade-offs involved in establishing new parks. It took 30 years for Kluane to receive national park status and negotiations have been underway since 1965 for the Grasslands National Park in Saskatchewan.

The major road block to the development of national parks, however, lies in the confusion over their appropriate purpose and the place tourism will take in this role. The twin mandate of conserving resources for the future while developing them as core attractions for the tourism industry in the short run has been based on the notion that tourism is a non-consumptive activity. The evidence presented here and elsewhere (Wilkes 1979) shows that this is a fallacy. Tourism can lead to the physical deterioration of a landscape if it exceeds the carrying capacity of a destination and is not properly managed. In light of this, Parks Canada has adopted new policy objectives to guide future development and planning. These objectives are:

To protect for all time those places which are significant examples of Canada's natural and cultural heritage and also to encourage public understanding, appreciation and enjoyment of this heritage in ways which leave it unimpaired for future generations. (Canada 1980)

But even this attempt to clarify priorities leaves sufficient vagueness that whenever new national parks have been proposed the debate over tourism's appropriate level continues to arise (Marsh 1983).

In the United States, Sax (1980, 103) contends "most conflict over National Park policy does not really turn on whether we ought to have nature reserves, but on the uses that people will make of those places." As an advocate for the conservation lobby, Sax argues that parks should perform functions that differentiate them from conventional facility-oriented tourism. Parks should offer contemplative experiences which will renew the spirit and outdoor recreation experiences that are challenging, hence the title of his treatise *Mountains without Handrails* (Sax 1980).

There is a growing feeling in North America that national parks cannot be all things to all people in every location. Consequently, conservationists like Sax would like to lure people out of their automobiles and resort bubbles into individual contact with nature, while Marsh (1983) has gone further in recommending parks and reserves for separate functions. National park agencies are trying to reduce the pressure on wilderness areas by creating more parks closer to urban areas, and working in conjunction with state and provincial governments to provide more recreation opportunities outside the national park system. The strategies used in these attempts to maintain the integrity of national parks while meeting the increasing demands of tourists will be examined in the next chapter.

Physical access

Second to possessing attractions that will lure tourists, a destination needs some form of access to the outside world. It is desirable to have more than one form of transport if a community wishes to become a major destination or wishes to guard against changes in the competitive position of various transport modes. Furthermore, the higher a community's position on the transport network hierarchy the more competitive its position in the tourism market, for a few routes and nodes dominate the system.

The major link for most tourist destinations is the highway, and with the rise of automobile travel any area with highway access is a potential destination. Within the near-ubiquitous highway networks, however, it is the higher order highways (freeways, motorways) which have had the most dramatic impact on destination accessibility. British motorways have opened up previously isolated, and therefore more exclusive, tourist areas by bringing the populous, industrial Midlands and London regions within a few hours' drive of the Lake District and the southwest. Interstate Highways No. 75 and No. 81 bring the residents of the industrial northeast to Gatlinburg and the Great Smoky Mountains National Park. The introduction of the turnpike connecting Montreal with the Laurentians has favored ski-hill resorts located close to its exits (Lundgren 1983).

Water transport links are becoming an accessibility factor again thanks to higher energy costs and the move to public forms of transport. The fastest growing segment of water transport for tourism is the cruise ship business, and many destinations are eager to join the ports-of-call list. The modern cruise ship is a highly competitive and successful combination of travel and entertainment, that in 1980 attracted 1.3 million customers to North American cruises (Davis 1981). For destinations, a visit from a cruise ship brings revenue from the ship (fuel and provisions), the visiting passengers, and crew. In 1979 British Columbia, which has a relatively small cruise ship business, operating along the "Inside Passage" to Alaska, generated an estimated $US38 million. While much of this was spent in Vancouver, the only embarkation–debarkation port in British Columbia, some was spent in the relatively isolated communities of Alert Bay and Prince Rupert (Montgomery 1981).

The potential of waterways is not restricted to coastal areas. Long stretches of the Rhine and Danube rivers are used for picturesque cruises, and old canal systems in Britain and France are being revitalized through increased pleasure traffic using converted barges and private boats. Even hostile river stretches are luring travelers who want "white water" excitement in addition to a tranquil travel experience.

Communities are beginning to re-evaluate the tourism and transportation potential of local waterways on which they had previously turned their backs. An example of this growing interest is Helleiner's (1981) analysis of recreational boating along the Trent–Severn Waterway north of Lake Ontario. Using graph theory analysis he identifies seven distinct nodal regions of local traffic within the 386 kilometers of waterway available for continuous cruising. "Within the entire waterway, 63 percent of the trips originated and terminated in the same region," indicating that despite its physical unity the Trent–Severn is not being used as a single recreational unit with cruises along its full length. To take advantage of the cruising opportunities in this area will require further adjustment by the tourist industry, specifically the construction of more overnight facilities and the chartering of self-contained boats.

A destination's level of accessibility is conditioned by the transport technology and hierarchies which have preceded it. Nowhere is this more apparent than in the case of airline networks, which have closely followed the nodal hierarchies of previous transport eras, especially the railroad system and oceanic liner routes which they largely replaced. Most intercontinental and transcontinental passenger services are linked to major cities which were also important railroad junctions and ports (Taaffe 1962). The cumulative effect of historical linkages being supplemented by modern freeways and international airports can be seen in New York's ability to attract 17.1 million visitors in 1980, making it one of the world's top tourism destinations at that time.

Travel patterns

The physical connectivity of a destination with national and international transport networks explains only part of its market accessibility, for it also needs to take into account the location of competitors and marketing considerations. Ullman (1956) has identified three basic elements in the spatial interaction process of trade and commerce which relate very closely to the tourism market and relative accessibility of individual destinations. He proposed that the bases for regional transportation and interaction were complementarity, intervening opportunity, and transferability.

For interaction or trade to develop between two regions there must be a demand in one and supply in the other, so that they possess *complementarity*. In terms of tourism this means a region offering sunshine, splendid scenery, and opportunities for recreation could attract people from colder climates where the environment was not so conducive to rest and relaxation. Such complementarity will give rise to interaction when there is no intervening source of supply available. For example, Florida attracts more tourists from the northeast United States than does more distant California. In this case Florida is more accessible to the main United States tourist market and thus becomes an intervening opportunity as far as California is concerned.

Intervening opportunities are always developing in tourism as new destinations and attractions enter the market, truncating existing travel flows and market areas. An example of this can be found within the above example. Miami Beach, one of the prime Florida attractions for New Yorkers, has itself been intercepted with the recent opening of Disney World near Orlando on Interstate No. 4. According to Zehnder

The Disney lure was immediate. Orange County and Disney World for the first time topped the usual tourist Meccas of Pinellas and South Florida last November, the first month that the attraction was fully operative. . . . Central Florida's tourist boom appeared to be hurting the Miami area most. . . . In the first nine months of the year [1972] tourists giving Miami as their destination declined from 9.8 percent to 6.9 percent. (Zehnder 1975, 282)

The presence of complementarity and absence of intervening opportunities, however, are no guarantee of interaction. The cost of making the transfer is the final arbitrator. If distance or time required to make the trip between two complementary regions is too great, or the cost too high, *transferability* will not take place. In tourism the overwhelming preponderance of domestic travel compared to international travel would appear to offer general support for this principle, but there are other explanatory factors at work as well, as Williams and Zelinsky discovered in their research.

Williams and Zelinsky examined international travel flows over a nine-year period (1958–66) in an attempt to identify and explain the spatial patterns that resulted. They concluded the travel flows were not random, but were in fact so distinct and stable that "evidently, once established, a stream of tourists has its own inertia and one can predict future flows with considerable confidence" (Williams and Zelinsky 1970, 563). In their attempts to explain these flows, however, they met with mixed success.

They expected tourist flows would be most clearly explained by the spatial distance separating a destination from its tourist source, which equates to Ullman's transfer costs. It was predicted, therefore, that there would be low levels of interaction between distant nations and high travel volumes between contiguous nations. In terms of their data, however, the results proved ambiguous. While some distant nations had relatively low interaction levels, such as Japan and Europe, some contiguous nations also recorded poor showings, as in the case of Italians to Austria and the low volumes between France and Germany.

Having found that the physical aspects of accessibility could not account for all or most of the travel flows, Williams and Zelinsky proceeded to test various cultural, social, environmental, and economic hypotheses. Ullman's complementarity concept was observed to be functioning in Europe with the annual exodus of north Europeans to the Mediterranean countries. The lure of the sun was undoubtedly a major factor for those living in the north where summers can be so fickle. Note the desperation of one British seaside attraction where:

Hotel-keepers and seaside caterers are watching the move made by Mr. George Brenner, chairman of the Grand Pier Co., Weston-super-Mare, who is investigating the possibility of legal action to restrain the BBC from broadcasting "discouraging" weather forecasts. (Muir and Brett 1978, 139)

Other flows could be explained partially by cultural ties and strong political and commercial associations, as in the case of the United States and Britain.

The "strength and nature of the mental image of potential target areas as harbored by potential visitors" was the final intriguing hypothesis offered in this study. Again data limitations restricted any definite conclusions but the authors "gingerly offer two or three instances" where such factors may operate. They cited the special significance of Greece to British and American travelers, which may be related to its image as the origin of western democracy. Likewise Americans' image of France as a long-term ally, coupled with its other attractions, may have perpetuated their tourist flow despite political tensions during the period.

This frustrating lack of predictive power at the international level is duplicated in studies of domestic travel. Deasy and Griess (1966) found accessibility, as measured by the friction of distance, did not have the expected impact on visitor patterns to two coal-mining tourist facilities in Pennsylvania. Searching for further explanation of the asymmetrical market areas of the Seldom Seen Valley Mine and Pioneer Tunnel, they felt a combination of forces were present, but that familiarity with the mining industry and the pull of advertising were the most influential at that time. Wall's study of holidays undertaken by Kingston-upon-Hull automobile owners found that while "the major concentration of Hull car owners is still the local one. . . . This relatively simple pattern is a synthesis of a large number of holidays of varying types, lengths and locations" (Wall 1973, 128). He considers that a number of social-economic factors, especially income, education, and family size can distinguish underlying subsets in the vacation patterns. Specifically, less wealthy and lower-educated travelers were more likely to frequent local resorts while the other end of the socio-economic spectrum ranged further afield and usually toured.

Accessibility is not simply a matter of distance and physical connections, for the research discussed above reveals highly personalized factors are involved in pleasure travel. Steinbeck went so far as to equate his travels with a person and marriage:

A journey is a person in itself; no two are alike. And all plans, safeguards, policing and coercion are fruitless. . . . In this a journey is like marriage. The certain way to be wrong is to think you can control it. (Steinbeck 1962, 4)

Not everyone is the observant free-spirit exhibited in

The environment and accessibility

Steinbeck's *Travels with Charley*, but Williams and Zelinsky (1970, 567) consider the critical area of investigation should be "how potential tourists perceive and evaluate various destinations, and how such mental images can actually impinge upon travel decisions."

Personal perspective

A destination must look beyond mileage charts, transport connections, and its own boundaries to determine what type of visitor will be attracted by the route which leads to them. Travel for pleasure is a voluntary act, strongly influenced by an individual's motivations, personal experience, and perceptions. For some the quality of the journey to and from a destination can be as important as intervening opportunities or other factors. As G. K. Chesterton once observed, "the traveller sees what he sees, the tripper sees what he has come to see." Under these circumstances a vacation trip can be equated to Clawson and Knetsch's five-phase model of an outdoor recreation experience (Figure 11). Each phase can be related to the tourist's view of a trip and to a destination's competitive position.

The *anticipation stage* is where a person prepares for a recreation trip by thinking about it, which in vacation terms includes planning. "Pleasurable anticipation is almost a necessity—certainly travel agents cannot be charged with underestimating the attractiveness of areas they advertise!" (Clawson and Knetsch 1966, 33). Planning a vacation can be a most enjoyable part of a trip for the tourist, sorting out the best routes, reading about the various attractions, visiting the travel agents where dreams are formed. Murphy and Rosenblood's research into the perceptions and preferences of first-time visitors to Vancouver Island, British Columbia, found:

the distinctive planning cluster and overall accuracy of predictions on the part of the tourists indicate that their search pattern is closely related to their prior mental image and motivations. (Murphy and Rosenblood 1974, 208)

The second phase of an outdoor recreation trip is *travel to the actual site* and as we have seen travel is a necessary ingredient for tourism. Although time and distance considerations were expected to have an influence on the level of travel, "less obvious, but perhaps of greater significance, the satisfactions and dissatisfactions of travel to the site vary greatly between individuals, between routes, and between end objectives or areas visited" (Clawson and Knetsch 1966, 33). A destination's accessibility becomes, therefore, more than a function of travel cost and convenience, it also involves the quality and sight-seeing opportunities of the route. A ferry link need not mean lost time and extra cost to the traveler—to some it can be an added attraction of that route.

The third phase consists of *on-site experiences* and activities. This certainly ranks as a high priority for both the tourist and the destination. For the tourist the destination experience is usually the focus of his holiday package, whether it involves one or several destinations. The quality of the beaches, the standard of service, variety of attractions, and courtesy of residents, all go toward the site experience. What happens during the on-site visit determines to a large degree the general satisfaction of the vacation.

The fourth phase is the *return travel* home. As Clawson and Knetsch (1966, 34) note, "it is unlikely to be a duplicate of the travel to the site" because even if the route is the same the recreationists are different. They are now tired, they are heading home so the journey "seems shorter," they have memories of their day out. This concept of a different experience on the return journey is even more appropriate to tourist travel, when the memories are more extensive and the options for a different route home more plentiful. Many destinations are aware of the importance of circular routes, for they eliminate the need to back-track and provide an opportunity to see something new all the time. For this reason, tourist boards and associations develop and promote circular tours within their areas, linking several nodal attractions with scenic routes.

The fifth and final phase of the total recreation experience is the *recollection* a person has of his outing or trip. Recollections are the savoring of the trip, consisting of memories supported by souvenirs and photographs:

Recollection of one outdoor experience often provides the starting point for anticipation of another, by the same person or by others. And recollection of many experiences in time builds into knowledge, or assumed knowledge, which provides a basis for choosing among different areas and different activities. (Clawson and Knetsch 1966, 35)

Such memories are important to the traveler, for they sustain him through the return to normalcy. The tourist purchases not only a recreation experience, he pur-

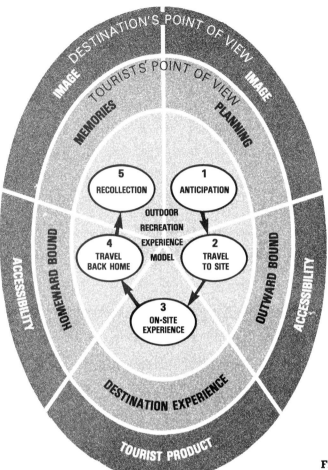

Figure 11 Destination area's perspective of a vacation experience

chases memories of those times when he broke out of the routine and tried something different.

It is the goal of tourist destinations to make a visitor's memories happy ones. A satisfactory experience is the best publicity a destination can achieve, for it promotes return visits and creates a goodwill ambassador to confirm the travel agent's publicity and convince the skeptics. The industry is deeply involved with this phase in its development of souvenir lines. These not only form convenient "gifts for the folks back home," they provide tangible reminders of the trip and increasingly they add to the dimensions of the experience. As travelers become more knowledge-able and discerning many have wished to learn more about their destinations. Books relating to local history and geography, native arts and crafts—often with small notes of explanation—tour guides and cassette tapes are evidence of a growing sophistication in the memorabilia aspect of a tourist trip.

Perceptual awareness

Since tourism involves travel, it is important to determine the ways in which people perceive different destinations and alternative routes. There are many

The environment and accessibility

definitions and interpretations of the perception process but the focus of most is on the "process of being aware" (Goodey 1971, 3). The awareness that is particularly relevant for tourism is the visitors' awareness of the environment, for the visitor seeks out the beauties of nature and' the masterpieces of man's culture and craft. The label "environment" means more than a physical setting for it includes man-made and social environments.

Any discussion of beauty and amenity raises the old saw of "beauty is in the eyes of the beholder" and that any attempt at manipulating images and attractions can only increase the appeal for some while reducing it for others. This feeling, however, has come under increasing attack from the growing evidence of environmental perception literature and the experience of mass tourism. Environmental perception studies have revealed remarkably constant group images (Hall 1959, 1966; Tuan 1974; Gould and White 1974) and common perception processes (Appleyard *et al.* 1964; Saarinen 1969; Downs and Stea 1977) despite the fact that we are dealing with an individual's personal interpretation of his surroundings. Mass tourism is built, in fact, on the

premise that certain attractions do have a broad appeal, and its marketing is designed around the concept of image.

The dominant perceptual process in tourism is the spatial framework that individuals establish in order to organize the mass of environmental stimuli and impressions which accrue over time. Such a spatial framework is evident in Goodey's model of man's perceptual map (Figure 12), which has clear implications for tourism. An individual is at the center of his own world, thus we can refer to his *personal space*. This is the area most familiar to him for it includes his home and immediate neighborhood, and can act as a term of reference by which to judge other places. As Gould and White observe, people traditionally evaluate places in terms of their home surroundings and therefore a rural–urban dichotomy in visitor perception is often evident:

Some people are definitely town-dwellers, and enjoy the sense of hustle and exchange that is always present in large towns and cities. Many who have lived and grown up in cities feel quite lost when transferred to the countryside and they long to get back to the noise and services that large urban areas provide. But there are others who dislike cities

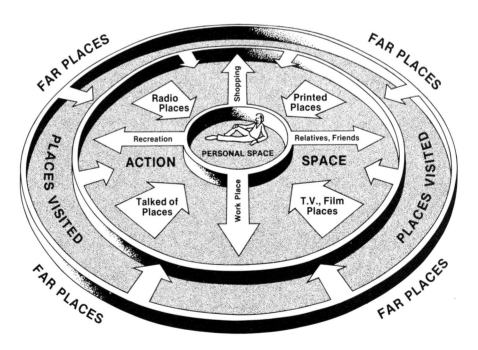

Figure 12 Man's perceptual map of his home town, surrounding regions, and far places
Source: Goodey (1971, 7)

intensely, and who would do almost anything to keep out of them. (Gould and White 1974, 19)

Such feelings have emerged when the author has taken visitors from England through British Columbia's Rocky Mountains and northern interior. Along these trips common questions have included, "Where are all the people?" and "When do we get to a big town?"

From the security of his personal space an individual takes regular work, shopping, or local recreation trips, and this extension of his awareness is referred to as his *action space*. The regularity of travel in and around his home region, plus numerous information inputs from the media and friends, helps to build up a fairly accurate image of this area, but one which is definitely restricted to his spatial behavior pattern within it. The occasional visits to surrounding areas build up a stronger and more reliable mental image than for most distant places, which helps explain the dominance of domestic tourism and growing popularity of second holidays and get-away weekends within the regional context. In terms of Goodey's model the "places visited" are areas of our city, province or country through which individuals pass occasionally, so that they develop familiarity but possess no detailed perceptions. Such imagery may play an important role in future vacation planning as rising energy costs restrict more travelers to their regional action space and own country.

Beyond the familiar lies the enticement of "far places" which are often spatially distant, but not necessarily so. *Distant lands* are no longer unknown to us, for as Marshall McLuhan coined it the world has become a "global village" since the media, particularly television, brought world news and events into our living rooms. Such coverage, however, is often fragmentary and incomplete from the point of view of future travel plans, so an individual's mental image of these distant locations often becomes distorted and colored by stereotypes. Klineberg's (1964, 95) study of international relations revealed a consistent ethnocentric perception of distant events and places, with a "tendency to see and judge external occurrences in terms of one's particular ethnic or national expectations." According to Klineberg this made it possible "for an American and Russian to look at the same phenomenon and see it so differently." But our ethnic background and cultural heritage can also influence our stereotype image of the general environment. Lowenthal (1962) suggests from his observations that Americans have a bias towards pioneer and wilderness romanticism (old towns and national parks), with a reverence for giantism both in natural and made-made scenes (Grand Canyon and skyscrapers); while in an essay with Prince (1965) he suggests that the variety and openness of the English landscape points to amenity as being the key concept to English man–environment relations.

The importance of group stereotypes cannot be overlooked in tourism for it can play an important role in travel decisions, particularly with regard to those far places where individual experience is lacking and perception limited. Tuan has expressed the power and influence of groups and culture on our perceptions very strongly in his book *Topophilia*, which is the "affective bond between people and place or setting." He states:

The group, expressing and enforcing the cultural standards of society, affects strongly the perception, attitude, and environmental value of its members. Culture can influence perception to the degree that people will see things that do not exist, it can cause group hallucination. (Tuan 1974, 246)

Such group stereotypes or hallucinations affect the way we view far places and the people who inhabit them. Some of these viewpoints are expressed in rather humorous "putdowns" but they contain elements of truth—as far as the "in group" is concerned. Gould and White note this facet of human perception in their discussion of Daniel Wallingford's map of the New Yorker's view of the United States (Figure 13):

As far as the New Yorker is concerned the boroughs of Manhattan Island and Brooklyn are perceived as the most of New York State, while the northern borough of the Bronx is so far away that to all intents and purposes it is close to Albany and Lake George in the Adirondacs. Connecticut is somewhere to the east, but it is mentally blurred with a place called Boston—obviously a mere village in the crook of Cape Cod. Westwards the map becomes more and more distorted and hopelessly inaccurate. States exchange names and wander to outlandish locations; California has been partitioned between San Francisco and Hollywood (after all what else is there?); and Florida has swollen to assume its proper proportion as the holiday place for New York just south of Staten Island. (Gould and White 1974, 37)

In this mental map of the "typical" New Yorker not only do stereotypes emerge, such as the United States' view of Canada being a combination of Rose Marie (Northwest) and René Levesque (Quebec); but the experience of vacation destinations, whether direct or indirect, enlarges the relative size of those locations (Florida, Adirondacs, and Cape Cod).

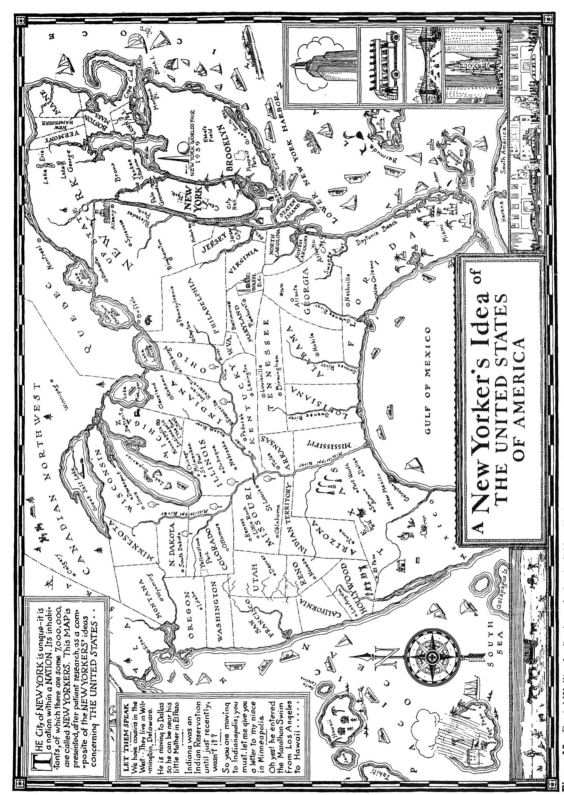

Figure 13 Daniel Wallingford's view of a "typical" New Yorker's mental map of the USA

Source: F. V. Thierfelot, Milwaukee, Wisc, USA

The reason Florida, the Adirondacs, and Cape Cod are such popular destinations for New Yorkers can be linked also to perception. Gould and White's (1974, 19–21) studies of residential preference identify six amenity factors underlying people's preference patterns, which have much in common with the considerations people make when selecting a vacation spot. The three popular New Yorker destinations offer (1) quality scenery, (2) attractive climate, (3) familiar language, (4) predictable cultural reactions, (5) political attitudes consistent with the home area, (6) accessibility. Accessibility is available either through propinquity or excellent airline connections.

5

Environmental and accessibility strategies

The physical deterioration of the environment, whether it be in a national park setting or seaside resort, is due in the main to an imbalance between tourist demand and physical carrying capacity of a destination area. Under these circumstances the expected symbiotic relationships between tourism and conservation break down and conflict develops.

A logical reaction to this situation is to increase the supply, and this was the initial response in many parts of the world. In the private sector, when a popular destination became overcrowded new destinations opened to attract the overspill and potential business. In the public sector various governments have expanded their park systems during the post-war years; but unfortunately most of this expansion took place in areas well away from the urban–industrial heartlands. This has perpetuated the market imbalance, where "less than one-fifth of the reserve of USA recreational land is accessible to the public" (Coppock and Rogers 1975, 509), and "only 6 percent of [Canada's] park area is in the eastern provinces, where 73 percent of the population live, and most of the eastern parks are remote from major population centres" (Bryan 1973, 277). In Britain the ten national parks that have been established are distant from the country's population axis, which runs from southern Lancashire to south-eastern England.

Increasing the supply of park space is a partial answer only, when park status brings with it increasing numbers of visitors and the pressure for more infrastructure and facilities. Eidsvik notes how park status raised visitation figures in certain areas of Canada,

particularly when national parks were accessible to either urban areas or major highways (Table 6). Budowski (1977, 3) feels that "for the majority of cases [in North America's national parks] the relationship between tourism and conservation is usually one of coexistence moving toward conflict, mainly because of an increase in tourism and the shrinking of natural areas." As a result the more accessible national parks continue to bear the brunt of tourism demand (Wilkes 1979; Sax 1980).

To retain the idealized symbiotic relationship between tourism and conservation necessitates management strategies in addition to more land area. The basis of most strategies has been to separate incompatible land uses, either by setting aside parks for different purposes or subdividing existing parks into specific use zones. The first process involves park classification and the second internal classification, or zoning. The two processes have been used in conjunction, with new park areas being allocated distinct purposes and classifications while the popular existing parks have attempted to separate incompatible objectives through zoning.

Functional differentiation through park classification

The separation of functions through park classification has been used widely in those countries possessing abundant government-owned land, which facilitates the assembly and designation of new parkland. In the

United States a 1964 Wilderness Act established a protected system of wilderness areas. These are large tracts of land devoted to conservation that still admit man, but as a visitor only, and with development restricted to trails and rudimentary campsites. Road access is provided to the perimeter only, and such roads are often unsurfaced logging roads, so those who do enter are few in number and empathetic naturalists by inclination. Canada introduced its Wildlife Act in 1973, but the first tangible product of this legislation did not appear until 1982, when the Polar Bear Pass Wildlife Area was established on Bathurst Island. In both countries the wilderness areas are located far from major population centers which limits their accessibility, while the lack of facilities restricts their appeal to true nature enthusiasts. This enables them to fulfill their prime function of conservation without resorting to restrictive visitor policies.

The importance of isolation for wilderness conservation becomes apparent in the few cases where such classification has been established closer to population centers. British Columbia's Ecological Reserves Act of 1971 has produced numerous small ecological reserves, many of which are close to expanding urban areas and industrial activity. Under these conditions they share the same fate as the lands around them, becoming susceptible to encroachment and resource exploitation. Ingram (1981) feels these reserves need more protection from the market forces to avoid increasing numbers of visitors and the negative externalities of man's urban–industrial society. He recommends they be protected by buffers, either of provincial parkland or unallocated public land.

In addition to supplying more conservation areas, governments have attempted to reduce the tourism pressure on national parks by expanding outdoor recreation opportunities elsewhere. The type of park and service offered has been expanded to accommodate a wider range of tastes, and these recreation parks have been located in more accessible areas. For example, Parks Canada now administers canal systems and historical parks in addition to its traditional and internationally renowned national parks. "The thrust of the late 1960s and early 1970s was to put in place an organization which could respond to growing pressure for expanded outdoor recreation opportunities and to ensure that the nation's natural and historic resources were adequately protected" (Eidsvik 1983, 242). In the United States, the Park Service has begun to "bring

parks to the people" and has established the national recreation area concept, which attempts to conserve and make accessible natural areas close to major cities. These include the Gateway National Recreation Area, composed of 26,000 acres divided into four main units scattered around New York harbor, the Cuyahoga Valley in the Cleveland–Akron area, and Golden Gate in San Francisco. "Although Gateway has only 1 percent of Yellowstone's acreage, its visitors (9 million in 1978) outnumber Yellowstone's four to one" (Levathes 1979, 89).

National government policy in this direction has received considerable assistance from provincial and state governments which have developed their own park systems. In many cases the outdoor recreation opportunities simply offer more convenient outlets for relaxation in a natural setting, but in some instances government has combined with the private sector to provide resort-type facilities. Certain state parks in Kentucky and Ohio come complete with lodges, cabins, swimming pools, golf courses, horseback riding, and convention facilities (Lundberg 1976, 171–4). In British Columbia the government is "privatizing" some of its provincial park facilities, including the Manning Park ski lodge and associated facilities.

In Britain where the pressure for recreation space is intense, areas of outstanding natural beauty and heritage coast have been given special designation and added to the country's inventory of conservation–recreation areas. Despite the addition of these protected landscapes the pressure on the more accessible national parks has continued to grow, so the idea of "honeypot" distractions has been developed. These honeypots often take the form of country parks, which are small regional facilities that can intercept or divert some of the traffic bound for the countryside. They are normally located close to urban areas so they can provide a day outing, with "a variety of attractions for family recreation . . . and meet certain standards in the provision of parking space, lavatories and supervision" (Hookway and Davidson 1970, 25).

Examples of the country park honeypot approach can be seen in the Llanberis and Clwyd country parks in North Wales, which intercept some of the traffic heading towards Snowdonia National Park. In the south of Wales the Afan Argoed country park, located north of Swansea, is designed to divert some traffic from the congested Gower Peninsula. This park, like many others, has incorporated a cultural exhibit to comple-

The environment and accessibility

ment its recreation components. It contains a mining museum that reflects conditions in the coal mining valleys of South Wales during the nineteenth century. Another country park built around an historical theme is Knebworth, north of London. This park offers Londoners the opportunity to combine a visit to a stately home, picnic in the grounds and take advantage of special events such as jousting tournaments. By 1978 almost 150 country parks had been designated, and Green (1981, 51) contends "fears that they would become 'honeypots' overrun by trippers, ice-cream vans and swings and roundabouts have not been realized. On the contrary, they have served additionally to protect wildlife and landscape."

Functional differentiation through zoning

While new parkland and strategically placed interceptors may slow visitor growth rates in the national parks, the pressure on park environments will continue as long as they remain magnets to travel. To deal with this problem, parks have adopted the urban planning strategy of land use classification and zoning. "Zoning classifies park areas for certain kinds and groupings of use or non-use and, in so doing, defines spatial limits of future use allocations" (Hoole and Downie 1978, 10). It provides a broad framework for land management, that attempts to balance the parks' twin mandate of preservation and visitor access by setting aside some areas for primarily preservation purposes and others for recreation and visitor facilities.

Parks Canada has developed a five-class zoning system that allocates land use priorities to different areas of a park (Figure 14). At the preservation end of the continuum are the *special* preservation areas. They are based on specific and sometimes small areas within the park which possess unique, rare, or endangered species. Regardless of this primary function, however, public use is still permitted, although with strict control via permits and restricted access. The second zone is classified as *wilderness* and represents areas with specific natural history themes and environments. These areas provide outdoor recreation opportunities for hiking and primitive camping, with the activities widely dispersed so as to be consistent with the primary preservation role. The third zone is classified as *natural environment* and is intended to permit those intermediate levels of outdoor recreation that are compatible with natural settings. Motorized access is allowed for the first time, but on a limited basis to the periphery of this zone. In this way visitors will have easier access to the zone, but to enter it they must use strategically located and well-maintained trails. This permits the park service to provide trails and simple campsites within the natural constraints set by the environment. The natural environment zone represents a balance between preservation and visitor access goals, and as such is the crucial buffer between the parks' two contradictory functions.

The fourth and fifth zones represent those areas where visitor activities and supporting facilities will be located. They are the smallest zones by far yet still contain elements of landscape and wildlife preservation. The fourth zone, *recreation areas*, is designed to provide general outdoor recreation opportunities and facilities. This involves the provision of campgrounds, complete with full facilities, boat ramps and permission to use power boats, ski hills with their associated facilities, and of course more extensive motorized access. Such recreation opportunities are provided in locations which can maintain the activities with minimal impairment to the environment, and interpretative services are used to explain the local ecosystem and man's place within it. In zone five, *park services* are areas that provide centralized visitor support services and park administration functions. Even in these highly developed, sometimes urbanized, areas the preservation of natural values and environmental qualities is attempted, with the location, design, and size of the infrastructure and buildings being made as compatible as possible with the national park setting. Within the debate concerning their appropriateness in a national park, there is a move to reduce or remove these urban service centers. Kootenay National Park is moving its service facilities outside of the park and Yosemite is downsizing its village (Binneweis 1984). In those wilderness areas and parks where the prime function is conservation these last two zones may be eliminated altogether.

Internal classification and zoning is now used widely throughout the world's national parks, and in most cases the zoning is based on a visitor–preservation continuum (Dasmann 1973). In Britain

The government has advocated a form of zoning as a basis for recreation management policies and this advice has been followed in all the final National Park Plans. . . . Management

ZONES

I   II   III   IV   V

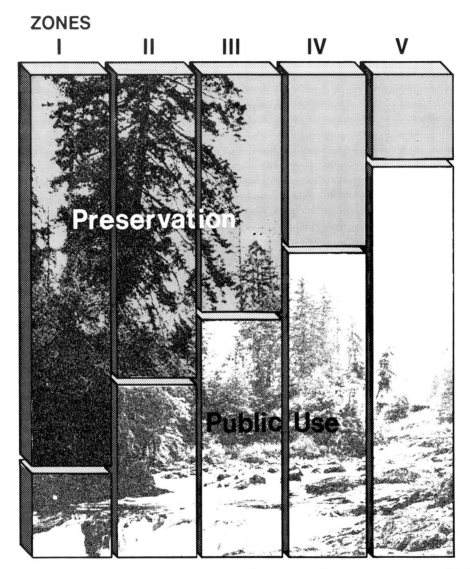

Figure 14 The relative emphasis on preservation and use in individual zones of the zoning system for National Parks
Source: Downie (1984)

policies aim to preserve remoteness by not improving access; to protect vulnerable areas and sort out the problems of overused sections ... and to promote the underused areas (invariably forests) which have some spare capacity for recreation. (Dennier 1978, 179)

In the United States' forests, different recreation experience levels have been linked to various preservation priorities. There are five levels and associated

usage zones involved. Level one is the forest environment that is kept as natural as possible, with access limited to foot trails and a recreation experience of solitude and physical exertion. Level two presents a slightly modified forest environment where solitude and escape are still the intended experience. Level three is a moderately modified environment with camping facilities including flush toilets, but the aim is still to provide exposure to nature with an emphasis on outdoor living. Level four presents highly modified sites where full camping facilities are provided, including electricity hook-ups. The emphasis is on comfort while experiencing some natural landscapes. Level five represents fully serviced sites, with all roads surfaced, complete recreation facilities, including store and laundry. The experience is resort-oriented with swimming pools, tennis courts, and golf courses set amongst magnificent scenery.

This world-wide experience has revealed some problems with the internal zoning strategy. There is a common danger that zoning will become the planning goal itself, rather than a planning tool to bring about that goal. Such a situation can lead to rigid classifications and overly simplistic methods of development control, that fail to keep up with changing environmental conditions (natural disasters or changing migration patterns) or changing visitor requirements (increase in bus tours or backpacking).

Zoning has been accused of "balkanizing" natural ecosystems into artificial units, rather than accommodating the complex interrelationships that exist within the natural systems of a national park. A major concern is that the preservation-oriented zones are not large enough to contain the migratory range of animals such as the grizzly or bighorn sheep. Although the visitor-oriented zones may occupy little land, the highways connecting the various activities run through the valleys which are vital routes for wildlife and may disturb their normal migratory patterns (Nelson *et al.* 1972).

Classification systems and zoning provide a popular method for differentiating between conflicting uses and goals, by separating them into distinctive areas within national parks. As such they provide a way to reduce conservation–tourism conflicts and operate within apparently incompatible mandates. The success of this planning technique, however, depends to a large extent on the viability of two underpinning planning concepts: carrying capacity, to determine the ecologically appropriate use of a land area; and multiple use, to determine the relative degree of compatibility between uses.

Carrying capacity

While the notion behind the carrying capacity concept is simple, its application is complex, due to the difficulty of measuring change and establishing causal relationships. The fundamental concept is that each environment has an ability to sustain activities up to a certain level, but once this level is exceeded some form of deterioration can be expected in the environment and/or the activity taking place. It is generally used in two different ways according to Hendee *et al.* (1978, 171). "First, it is used to describe the ability of the physical-biological environment to withstand recreation use. . . . Second, carrying capacity has been used to express the amount of use that is consistent with some measure of quality in the recreation experience." In Barkham's words:

Carrying capacity is a phrase delightful in its simplicity, complex in its meaning and difficult to define, as in different situations and to different people it is understood in different ways. (Barkham 1973, 218)

In terms of tourism planning, the effect of different situations and visitor expectations certainly influences the carrying capacities of destination areas.

The environmental situation can vary dramatically, often within a small space. The tolerance difference between a beach and neighboring dunes has been noted already. At Lake Louise, in Banff National Park, there is a major resort hotel that can accommodate thousands of visitors a year, but placing this hotel within a sensitive upland area has required the paving of some heavily traveled trails to prevent further soil erosion. The environmental situation can also vary over time, as different seasons affect the resilience of a landscape. For example, in the Cairngorms area of Scotland ski operations have minimal environmental impacts while there is a protective snow cover on the ground. But during the summer months when ski lifts bring visitors to bare high mountain tundra, substantial soil erosion and vegetation damage has resulted in these sensitive areas (Bayfield 1971).

How visitors assess and react to signs of environmental stress will vary with their background and interests, which can make it difficult to establish general carrying capacity standards for tourism management purposes. The motive for travel is varied, resulting in a wide range of expectations within destination areas. Cohen's "explorers" would appreciate solitude and natural landscapes, and often enter their landscapes. His "mass tourists" seek companionship and creature comforts during their visits and are often prepared to view their landscapes from a bus or hotel porch. Thus there could be a different carrying capacity for every type of experience provided. Furthermore, an over-reliance on the views of any particular group can distort assessments in favor of elitist groups or decision makers, whose experience and expectations can vary from the majority of visitors (Hendee and Harris 1970; Barkham 1973; Peterson 1974). "In brief, the problem [becomes] one of balancing the aspirations and needs of recreationists against the desire of others to minimize the disruption to sensitive areas" (Mitchell 1979, 183).

Carrying capacity assessments should be viewed as a means to an end (Wager 1961, 16–17), with their contribution to tourism management being an aid to decision makers in their assessment of development impacts and trade-offs. If tourism is to benefit the community and develop into a renewable resource industry there must be more information concerning the condition of a local environment, its ability to handle additional demands, and the likely long-term impact of development proposals.

Carrying capacity is a means to an end, with the end being a set of ecological and social conditions defined as desirable. Those desired conditions, in turn, are not defined by any inherent feature of the physical setting or deterministic notion of "highest and best use." Rather, they are a product of a complex prescriptive process that involves participation by the citizenry, resource managers, and researchers, and are specified in area management objectives. (Stankey 1981, 32)

Introduction of a carrying capacity concept, therefore, will not provide exact figures for each and every development situation, but it will create a framework for analysis and assessment that could be used to make more informed decisions.

Early carrying capacity studies in recreation areas focused on the physical and biological dimensions of the environment, and were used to warn of impending physical damage. For example, Bell and Bliss (1973) studied the effects of visitor trampling in the alpine meadows of the Olympic National Park, in Washington State. Their investigation revealed the greatest amount of damage resulted from the first trampling, when the fragile plants were destroyed. After this initial destruction the hardier plants and the soil were more resistant. Their results indicated that public use of alpine areas should be restricted and channeled along specific routes. Following their recommendations, the alpine meadows of Hurricane Ridge, in the Olympic National Park, have been protected by management techniques

including the construction of asphalt paths, warnings to keep on the provided paths, and conducted tours along these paths at regular intervals.

A similar contribution to better tourism management by a biological carrying capacity study can be seen in Merriam and Smith's (1974) study of wilderness camps in the Boundary Waters Canoe Area in northeastern Minnesota, between 1968 and 1972. They found there was relatively little change in the tree growth, soil compaction and water quality of campsite environments after the initial land-use change. The greatest impact of the campsites was the degree of soil compaction after the first season but thereafter the compaction increased very slightly. It was noted also that it took up to 6 years for the soil to return to its original condition after a site was closed. Hence, Merriam and Smith recommended the existing rotation of wilderness campsites was not practical, with a site-recovery time of 6 years needed to recover from a major impact period of 1 year.

Successful tourism development involves fulfilling visitor expectations as well as attracting them to a destination. Therefore, a carrying capacity assessment must take into account the recreation activities and needs of visitors in addition to the biological parameters of a site. Although there have been too few studies of tourist preferences and expectations, there have been some studies which add a behavioral component to carrying-capacity assessments. Lucas' study of rec-reationist images in the Boundary Water Canoe Area revealed

there are two main wildernesses—the paddling canoeists' (who wanted to enter it and feel alone), and the motor-boaters' (who prized it as a background to their lake and roadside locations). . . . The differences between these wildernesses may provide a key to increasing the capacity of the area in order to provide high quality recreation. (Lucas 1964, 409–10)

Similar conclusions were arrived at by Keogh (1980) in his study of skier motivations in the French Alps around Grenoble. He identified different goals amongst differ-ently motivated skiers, such as the "sports," "aesthetic outdoor," and "social" types, which indicated the type of experience sought was not the same and could be capitalized upon to better organize space within the resorts.

The study of visitor behavior characteristics can be extended beyond the preferences and motivations of an anticipation stage to include surveys of actual tourist experience, noting their frustrations and suggested remedies. O'Riordan (1969) followed this approach in his study of Norfolk Broads boat renters. He found those with long-term familiarity with the area noted the negative impact of increased congestion, took action to avoid their worst frustrations, and were able to propose some remedies. Using their experience and suggestions O'Riordan proposed:

a plan for Broadland based upon "activity complexes", designed to provide a hierarchy of recreational uses singly and in combination, and arranged spatially so as to maximize user satisfaction and minimize user conflict. (O'Riordan 1969, 56)

The three activity complexes were a *concentrated* type, based on towns and large villages and composed of marinas, swimming pools and playgrounds; an *intermediate* type, found in the countryside where off-river mooring basins provided a base for anglers and strollers; a *secluded* type, devoted to non-activity recreation in the countryside where people study nature and "get away from it all."

It is evident from these studies that different landscapes possess different tolerance levels for visitors, and the visitors have different expectations of that landscape. Stress will occur when tolerance levels and visitor demands are out of synchronization. The move toward sound long-term tourism development will require some degree of compatibility between a destination's natural resources and the demands placed upon it by various tourist groups. A carrying-capacity assessment could be used to help identify this compatibility by incorporating three steps.

First, to facilitate tourist satisfaction a destination must examine a visitor's needs and activity patterns. This will develop different experience zones for different visitor types. Second, to establish or maintain a high quality environment requires information relating to the physical and biological carrying capacity of the experience zones, particularly the sensitive and more popular ones. Third, combining the first two steps into environmental experience zones will indicate the degree of compatibility between visitor group desires and the natural environment. The level of compatibility will help to determine which groups a destination should pursue in the tourism market, and which would fit in with the long-term goals of a renewable resource industry.

Carrying capacity is an elastic and dynamic concept open to manipulation by management for local planning objectives. As the United Nations Environment Programme (1979) states: "The environment is not just a constraint, it is a resource; it is not just a problem, it is an opportunity." In this regard tourism management in sensitive ecological areas must use carrying capacity to guide zoning procedures, not to limit visitors but to redistribute them in space and time (Budowski 1977). Two examples of this approach are offered below, one in a coastal area, the other in a rural environment.

Pigram (1980) describes how a Japanese development company has constructed an international tourist resort on the Capricorn Coast of Queensland, Australia. The site occupies over 8000 hectares and is designed to accommodate over 10,000 visitors a year in a sensitive dune and wetland area (Figure 15). Overall, the resort plan and subsequent environmental impact statements have recognized and incorporated the interdependence of tourism and the environment through carrying capacity considerations. As a result management has attempted to:

—Maintain the stability of the coastal dune system as a protective barrier.
—Nurture the indigenous flora and fauna as a natural attraction for visitors.
—Maintain tidal and freshwater wetlands as a natural habitat to counteract the built landscape.
—Provide hazard-proof structures to withstand cyclones, floods and storm surge.
—Reafforest and preserve existing woodland to serve as a water catchment area and scenic backdrop.
—Eliminate motor vehicle traffic within site.

To Pigram such planning and attention to ecological factors is "evidence of an attempt to ensure the creation of a satisfying tourism setting in keeping with ecological constraints and with minimal environmental disturbance" (Pigram 1980, 577).

The New Forest is neither new nor a forest, but it is a large tract of land containing open heath, woodland, grazing land, streams, and villages, which adds up to a popular tourist destination in southern England. On a single public holiday Sunday in 1965 this rural area was visited by 58,005 people in 20,002 automobiles (Patmore 1972, 95). With this type of popularity and pressure the Forestry Commission and local authorities felt obliged to combine forces and devise a policy to conserve the New Forest. Inherent in their terms of reference "was the fundamental requirement that we should examine

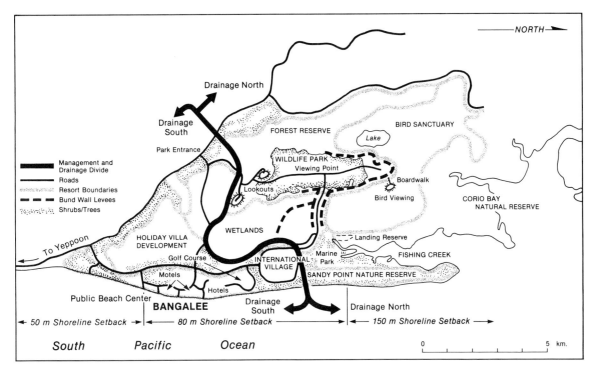

Figure 15 Plan of Farnborough resort complex, Queensland, Australia
Source: Pigram (1980)

the Forest's capacity as a place to visit. . . . The Forest's capacity would, by definition, be at a point where its inherent character would not be challenged" (Forestry Commission 1970, 7).

The main concern was to retain a balance between the three basic interests of the area, its woodland, grazing, and ecological base; and it was felt that the greatest danger to these from tourism was the lack of control over automobile access. Consequently a dispersal strategy was devised which drew motorists away from the more sensitive areas and channeled them into more tolerant zones. Certain areas were declared "car-free" to protect woodland, grazing areas, and stock, and ecologies susceptible to erosion. To channel visitors away from these areas the motorist was tempted to other locations by creating scenic drives (promoted by the New Forest Information Centre and signposting), and developing attractions such as picnic and camping sites.

Such management plans were not expected to reduce the popularity of the area nor to be without cost.

The Forestry Commission therefore recommended the continued development of country park honeypots to dilute the demands on the New Forest, and raised the possibility of instituting recreation charges:

Undoubtedly the strategy which we have proposed and the the investment and staffing associated with it will be a matter of considerable and continuing expense. Similarly, the time will come when the facilities which we propose will be congested. On both counts, it becomes valid to consider whether the visitor should be charged. (Forestry Commission 1970, 29)

Since these recommendations were made in 1970 pressure on the New Forest's recreation resources has intensified, necessitating further internal regulations and more external cooperation to maintain the environment. By 1976 it was estimated there were approximately 6 million visitors using the forest parking lots, so that its 5500 space capacity was often inadequate during peak periods (Forestry Commission 1976). Camping had grown from 618,500 to 811,700 camper-nights between 1970 and 1977, and again there were overspill problems during peak periods. The internal response to these and other pressures has been to resist expansion but to improve information and service. For example, in 1975 the Forestry Commission introduced an advance registration scheme for camping, which it now operates with the Southern Tourist Board. In addition to working with the regional tourist organization in terms of information and bookings, the New Forest has been aided by Hampshire County Council's permission, in its South West Hampshire Structure Plan, for an additional 1250 camping sites close to the New Forest. Furthermore, the same plan is advocating that new recreational facilities, such as golf courses, be provided near the forest to ease other recreational pressures (Hampshire County Council 1980).

Based on the above experiences the Forestry Commission's new Management Plan for 1982–91 envisages no new recreation facilities but continued maintenance and improvement of existing facilities, to help visitors enjoy their experience while maintaining the forest's character. Acting under the mandate that "The New Forest must be regarded as a national heritage and priority given to the conservation of its traditional character" (Forestry Commission 1981) is leading this popular destination toward multiple-use resource management. This involves conservation of the area's heathland and grassland through controlled grazing, harvesting the woodland in such a manner as to maintain its picturesque character and leave sufficient numbers of ornamental trees, and the maintenance of an acceptable balance between grazing animals and the biological stability of the open woodlands.

Multiple use

The zoning principles adopted in national forests and parks reflect an attempt to balance preservation and development, and recognize that one man's recreation is another's despoliation. But the demands on these areas of wilderness and outstanding beauty are increasing, and from directions other than tourism. Furthermore, some observers feel that "in saving natural areas from development it is difficult to foresee what will be needed to maintain them, once legally protected" (Ingram 1981, 10), because the pressure for development will increase over time. Thus, in addition to the twin mandates of recreation and conservation, national

forests and parks will need to consider other land uses, and are being forced into a multiple use situation.

Multiple use can be justified when an "incremental gain in joint resource production is equal to, or exceeds, the incremental increase in costs of achieving that level of productivity" (O'Riordan 1975, 6). There has been relatively little integrated multiple resource management in North America because the forestry and park agencies have generally interpreted multiple use as dominant use, with one function dominating land use strategies while others take on a secondary role. Reticence to adopt a true multiple use approach in the past is due, in large part, to the difficulty of assigning monetary values to intangibles such as visitor satisfaction and crowding. However, with increasing market and political pressures to use resources for more than a single purpose there has been some movement toward a more balanced approach.

In the United States an example of multiple use management can be seen in the Tennessee Valley Authority's approach to the "Land Between the Lakes" area, which was established in 1963 as a national recreation demonstration area. Approximately 170,000 acres of land is managed for timber, wildlife, recreation, and environmental education. "Multiple use was applied in a strict format. For example, timber harvests are found even within campgrounds" (Burde and Lenzini 1980, 122). In fact, the question of whether timber harvesting and tourism could coexist was examined by Burde and Lenzini.

The timber in the Land Between the Lakes is harvested selectively, taken from small areas of 50 acres or so. No attempt is made to hide the activity, but two den trees are left per acre and the slash left to decay naturally. All skid roads and log deck areas are ploughed over, limed, fertilized, and reseeded with grass. Over 2.5 million visitors come annually to the area, mainly for hunting, fishing, and hiking. A visitor survey conducted in 1977, involving various user groups (campers, hikers, picnickers, off-road vehicle enthusiasts, and sightseers), revealed that 60 percent of them did not notice the logging activities. Of those who noticed, 85 percent were not concerned. Such evidence suggested to Burde and Lenzini:

low to medium intensity cuts can coexist with both dispersed and intensive recreation activities. The results are applicable to any situation where the timber type will respond favorably to uneven-aged management, and harvest goals can be met without extremely heavy cuts. (Burde and Lenzini 1980, 130)

British Columbia's tree harvesting methods are different from those in the Land Between the Lakes area but it too is beginning to develop a more responsive multiple-use strategy, incorporating recreation and tourism needs. The principal harvesting method is clear cutting, followed by slash burn. This can leave unsightly scars along the lower mountain slopes and in the valleys of this beautiful province, as was noted by a visitor from Seattle, who later wrote:

I toured your beautiful province last month and, even as the ads say, it was Super Natural. Except for one thing: everywhere we went, those magnificent mountain slopes had been devastated by clear-cutting. A nuclear blast couldn't have wrought greater or more unsightly destruction. (Dearden 1983, 79)

To overcome this problem the provincial Ministry of Forests is encouraging logging companies to develop planned logging that takes into account land contours, its visibility from highways and aesthetic values (Province of British Columbia 1981). It suggests that belts of forest be left alongside major highways and on those slopes visible from these routes. In addition the Ministry of Forests has begun to provide recreation areas within its Crown land and forest reserves. These are usually small and primitive, but are often located next to a lake or river. They are accessible only via unsurfaced logging roads and are primarily used by local residents for swimming, picnics, and fishing trips.

The pressure for multiple use has been most pronounced in those countries and areas where many demands are placed on a limited land supply. A prime example are the national parks in England and Wales, which occupy a relatively large area of the land surface, 9 percent compared to 1.4 percent in Canada and 1 percent in the United States. Unlike the North American parks, which are vast tracts of publicly owned and little developed land with few inhabitants, these national parks are located in settled and productive countryside, where 86 percent of the land is in private ownership. Like the North American parks, however, the national parks of England and Wales have a dual mandate, to preserve and enhance the natural beauty of these areas plus promote their enjoyment by the public. To resolve this dilemma two management decisions have been suggested since 1949. Since it was not possible to consider the land-use problems of national parks in isolation from the rest of the countryside, the 1968 Countryside Act placed them under the control of a Countryside Commission, and in 1974 the Sanford

Report gave conservation precedence over recreation. It should be noted, however, that both the Commission and the Report are advisory only, with no direct control over national park planning.

National parks in England and Wales are areas within which a multitude of land uses have to be satisfied, so "in terms of national policy the national parks are not very special" (Tourism and Recreation Research Unit 1981, 90). These areas are segments of the national economy, subject to the same rules and regulations within the constraint of conserving the natural beauty of their landscape. The Local Government Act in 1972 required the national park authorities to produce a management plan, and Dennier (1978, 176) reports that "in considering management objectives and policies for landscape conservation [the authorities] agree that the fundamental problems lie with farming and forestry. . . . More afforestation and more intensive farming methods imply radical change in the traditional landscapes." In terms of recreation and tourism their major concerns were to establish further controls over noisy and crowd-generating sports such as motor rallies and scrambles, and to limit accommodation to existing settlements and farms engaged in farm tourism.

The multiple-use strategy of these plans is evident in the Snowdonia National Park Plan of 1977. It considers:

As far as Snowdonia is concerned the two aims of the National Park will continue to be conservation and provision of recreation whilst at the same time safeguarding and promoting the economic and social well-being of the people living and working in the Park. (Snowdonia National Park Authority 1977, 3.1)

Conservation is seen as "the wise use of resources" and is concerned with harmonizing these different resources with the minimum of conflict. To this end the management plans ensure all forms of development are adequately controlled and that changes in land use are in sympathy with the landscape and ecological value of the Park. Within these multi-purpose objectives recreation management is concerned with reducing conflict between visitors and the community, and between different recreationists. This involves recreational zoning of upland areas, ranging from highly managed areas where there are intense visitor pressures to diverting activities away from areas of outstanding conservation value. Other measures include more extensive information services, education and wardening services in conjunction with regional tourist boards, and promoted usage of public transport for recreational travel to and within the park, to reduce the congestion on local roads.

Accessibility

Accessibility must be maintained or improved if destinations are to attract significant numbers of visitors, but at the same time care must be taken not to overload the carrying capacity of a destination community. In this regard tourism management has taken on a two-fold emphasis. First, to develop the appeal of access routes to a destination, to ensure visitors enjoy the total travel experience. Second, to control access to popular attractions and locations so that the carrying capacity and multiple-use objectives of tourism planning can be maintained.

Increasing the quality and efficiency of access can be approached in a variety of ways. For a resort destination dependent on airline links the prime consideration is the airport. It must be capable of handling modern aircraft in a safe manner; the quality of facilities and service must ease the transfer of passengers from one mode of transport to another; it must have convenient access to major attractions and accommodation in the area. If a destination is remote from major tourist-generating regions it should attempt to increase its appeal by combining forces with its potential rivals, to provide a more attractive regional package. This process is underway in the American northwest, where Seattle, Vancouver, and Victoria have combined promotional campaigns designed to lure convention delegates and regular tourists from the distant cities of central Canada and the northeast United States.

For destinations dependent on automobile traffic similar regional strategies plus the development of circular tours can prove useful ways of increasing a limited appeal. For example, British Columbia promotes a circular tour linking Victoria and Vancouver Island with Prince Rupert, Prince George, the Fraser River Canyon, and Vancouver. In Northumbria the regional tourist board has developed cassette tape trails, for the car radio, that provide directions and information for a self-directed tour. These circular tours not only add to the appeal of existing tourist destinations, but diffuse tourism traffic and bring some economic benefits to "off the beaten path" attractions.

Most visitors do not penetrate deeply or extensively into the local environment (Plog's psychocentrics) because they confine themselves to passive sightseeing from the highway. Studies of perception from routes have revealed significant differences between tourist and commuter perceptions from the highway. Appleyard *et al.* (1964) consider that when a tourist travels through a new environment he is open and receptive to stimuli, whereas the commuter moves along familiar paths and after a while begins to follow them automatically, so the environment becomes a background and not the focus of attention. With this in mind the quality and order of the environment becomes an important factor in the tourist's perception and enjoyment. Carr and Schissler (1969) examined ways in which people observed facets of the city landscape as they moved through it and how they used memories of such features in recalling their experience. They reported that the travelers' perception and memory of a city, as seen from the highway, seemed determined by the form of the environment itself. The quality and structure of a passing landscape forms a perceptual image of the whole area for travelers and thus "the trip [becomes] a message so that highway engineers and landscapers can utilize simple perception data to improve both the transmission and reception of that message" (Goodey 1971, 37). The quality of the highway itself can also be a factor, with certain groups valuing minor roads and byways as part of the recreation experience (Brancher 1972).

A common theme in tourist routes is to base them on appealing scenic qualities—"public roads identified for their scenic value" (Dunn 1973, 1). Where there are several alternative routes in an area, tourist authorities are beginning to analyze their scenic and historic appeal, as was the case recently in southeast Alberta where Tourism Alberta selected and promoted the Drumheller–Dinosaur–Brooks tourism corridor (Sullivan 1983). In the United States there are specialized routes in certain areas, focusing on heritage, such as the Lincoln Trail in Illinois, or scenery, as in the case of various National Parkways. In Britain several experimental scenic drives have been developed by the Countryside Commission, such as those in Dovey and Gwydr Forests; and some tourist boards have been active in promoting the idea, as in the case of the Teme Valley Scenic Route (Dunn 1973).

The potential of this tour concept, to diffuse visitors, bring lesser known attractions and features into the tourism business, and increase the overall appeal of a destination has not been lost in urban areas. Whereas the European Conservation Year in 1970 stimulated considerable support for nature trails, a similar rise in urban walks and trails occurred in response to the European Architectural Heritage Year (1975) and United States Bicentennial Year in 1976 (Goodey 1979). Although the primary purpose of many such walks and trails has been to attract the tourist by capitalizing on the growing conservationist interests of the 1970s, the relevance of these informative and sometimes "eye-opening" tours for local residents has also become apparent. Goodey quotes from a letter received from the Visitor Services in Boston, Massachusetts:

It was also our desire that the Bicentennial celebration be not only for the visitors to this city, but also be to offer insights of lasting value to the citizens of Boston and the residents of these neighborhoods, therefore, it seemed most fitting to work closely with community groups to develop such neighborhood exhibits and walking trails for visitors and residents alike. (Goodey 1974, 13)

Strategies to attract more visitors through improved accessibility and better quality travel experiences are the prime concerns of new or underutilized destination areas, but in popular destination areas traffic management may require control or restriction of access. Maude (1971) feels that the natural tendency to increase highway capacities and parking facilities will have to stop, especially in rural or small town communities. Such engineering solutions will neither eliminate the problem nor satisfy the tourist, because easier access encourages more visitors and modern highways do not reflect the popular image of quiet country drives. Hence she proposes that management rather than engineering solutions be considered in attempting to balance the level of tourist traffic with the environmental capacity of the destination.

Management strategies are most apparent in the national park destinations where the conflict between large numbers of visitors and nature conservation is acute. In Britain several national parks have introduced public transit bus services to provide an alternative for the automobile user and offer increased mobility for those without automobiles. The Peak District has run a "Peak Pathfinder" service on high-season Sundays and public holidays, the Yorkshire Dales National Park has operated a similar "Dalesrider" bus service, and Dartmoor has operated a "Pony Express" minibus service. Patronage of these systems has risen slowly but

they are all dependent on a subsidy. Only the Lake District with a commercial minibus service, operating in one of the busiest national parks where there are a substantial number of long-stay visitors, has been self-supporting. Moyes (1977) notes two factors that hinder a break-even prospect for most park public transport systems. First, the general difficulty of seducing a motorist from his automobile. This is compounded when he has already used his vehicle to reach the park and may wish to traverse the park as part of a tour. Second, the demand is strongly influenced by the weather, so an erratic market makes it difficult to balance equipment and demand.

One way of ensuring better ridership for public transport systems in tourism destinations, although not necessarily a profit, is to institute a "park and ride" system. This approach has been adopted with some success in situations where private automobiles and campers were impacting the local transport system and ruining the park experience for many people. A classic example is in Yosemite National Park, where the main attraction is a narrow gorge valley with cliffs and waterfalls which can be comfortably viewed from a highway loop on the valley floor. Although it is a national park of international renown, Yosemite's proximity to San Francisco and Los Angeles means it also "serves as a local park for Californians" with considerable "drive-through" traffic (van Wagtendonk 1980, 15). The result was congestion, noise, and smog conditions which ruined the scenic solitude the park was striving to provide. The park's answer was to implement a park and ride system for the summer months. Casual day visitors are required to park at the entrance to the valley and use a shuttle bus system to view the falls and visit the Yosemite Village (Figure 16). The only visitors allowed to bring their vehicles into the valley are those campers or overnight guests who have reservations for the limited number of campsites and hotel accommodation. In Canada public transit bus service has been used in Point Pelee National Park to reduce automobile congestion, and in the Lake O'Hara area of Yoho National Park to control access to the ecologically delicate lakeshore.

In North America's newer and larger parks in the far north there is a heavy reliance on public transit. The use of buses has the appeal of reducing per capita energy costs, reducing the need for surfaced roads, and offers a unique opportunity for interpretation services. Thus some sensitive areas of Kluane National Park are

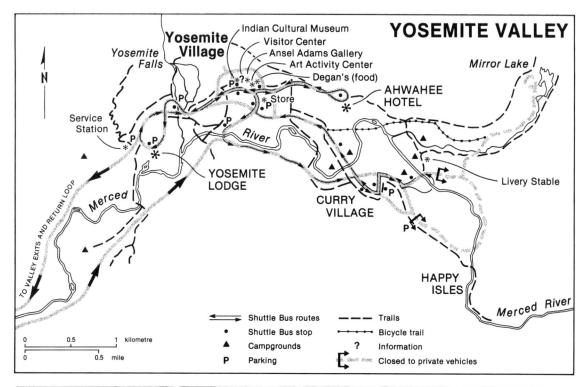

YOSEMITE VALLEY

Indian Cultural Museum
Visitor Center
Ansel Adams Gallery
Art Activity Center
Degan's (food)

Yosemite Village

Yosemite Falls

Mirror Lake

AHWAHEE HOTEL

Service Station

Store

River

Merced

YOSEMITE LODGE

CURRY VILLAGE

Livery Stable

HAPPY ISLES

TO VALLEY EXITS AND RETURN LOOP

Merced River

⟵⟶	Shuttle Bus routes	– – –	Trails
•	Shuttle Bus stop	•–•–•	Bicycle trail
▲	Campgrounds	?	Information
P	Parking		Closed to private vehicles

0   0.5   1   kilometre
0   0.5   mile

Shuttle Bus

446

Figure 16 Yosemite Valley's Shuttle Bus system
Source: Yosemite Guide, 7, 3 (1983) = US Parks Service

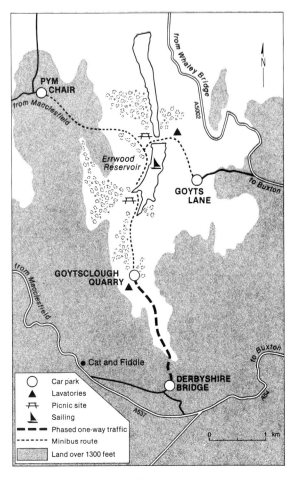

Figure 17 Goyt Valley traffic experiment
Source: Countryside Commission (1972)

footpaths, and picnic areas were provided along the valley to take pedestrians off the roadway and provide alternative ways of enjoying the scenery.

A study by the Countryside Commission (Miles 1972) found that the Goyt Valley traffic management scheme had mixed results. The number of visitors declined after the scheme was introduced, but much of that loss was in the number of drive-through tourists now the minor road through the valley was closed on weekends. Those who did visit made greater use of the valley and did much more walking. There was also a change in visitor types, with the number of blue collar and clerical worker households declining while professional and managerial increased. There were legal and practical difficulties in sealing off even a minor road to through traffic, and it was felt that the most appropriate areas for this type of solution should be self-contained cul-de-sac situations. But the initial experiment was considered successful enough to warrant continuation, because as it progressed "the attitude of visitors changed in favour of management and control" (Miles 1972, 75) and certain problems could be overcome with experience.

Pressure points occur in the countryside because of the low capacity of most rural environments to absorb growing recreation and tourist demands. Traffic line-ups can develop at narrow bridges, when visitors encounter slower agricultural vehicles or even slower livestock on narrow highways, and when they pour into small villages laid out for the pre-automobile era. But even these stressful situations can be ameliorated by traffic management, and tourism can be accommodated with minimal disruption of the local environment.

One such stressful situation where traffic management has been applied is the Gower Peninsula, South Wales. This attractive coastal area has been designated an Area of Outstanding Natural Beauty, and it is estimated that over 1.25 million people now live within one hour's drive (Glamorgan n.d., 2). To accommodate the heavy day-visitor traffic, twelve parking lots with a capacity of approximately 4000 cars have been developed around the coast. However, as Maude warned, the provision of additional facilities failed to resolve the parking problem and seven of the parking lots are regularly forced to turn away motorists. This creates problems of illegal parking, on farmland and narrow country lanes, and frustrated visitors. To deal with the problem an information system was installed in 1971, consisting of large display boards at the two main entry points to the peninsula which indicated when

accessible only by bus service, as are large areas of tundra in Mount McKinley National Park in Alaska.

A similar approach to visitor management has been adopted in the congested Peak District National Park, in England. The Goyt Valley area became a popular destination within the park after completion of a reservoir, so that "weekend recreational traffic [soon] saturated both parking space near the reservoir and the capacity of the new and existing access roads" (Moyes 1977, 209). The response to this situation was the creation of a pedestrian zone on weekends and public holidays, with a minibus service for those who could not handle the one to four kilometer walk to the reservoir from the outlying car-parks (Figure 17). Nature trails,

Figure 18   Park and ride scheme in St Ives, Cornwall

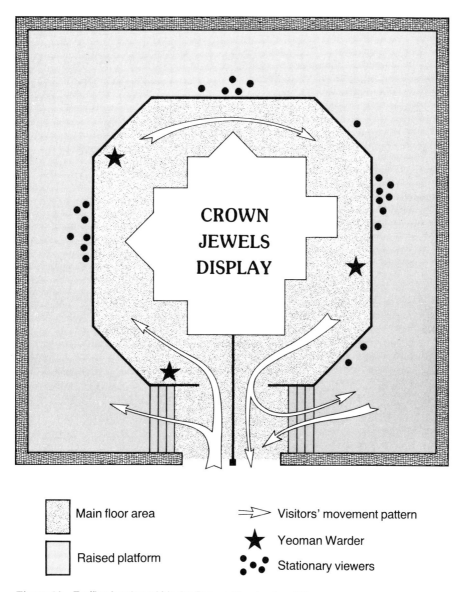

Figure 19 Traffic planning within the Tower of London Jewel House

certain parking lots were full to capacity. Although there was no direct evidence that day-trippers abandoned their visit because a target parking lot was full (Glamorgan n.d., 23), the council decided to retain the scheme. It was felt that the area had a responsibility to warn visitors of a potential problem and that some would be deterred from entering the peninsula by this simple and inexpensive operation.

The town of St Ives, in Cornwall, presents a good illustration of comprehensive traffic management that has enabled a community to retain its heritage and sanity while hosting an ever-increasing number of visitors. The narrow streets around the harbor were created for pedestrians and pack animals, yet these are now the main focus of tourist attention and have to handle up to 4300 vehicles and 40,000 pedestrians

The environment and accessibility

during a single summer day (St Ives n.d.). The town's response has been to ring its core with parking lots for visitor traffic that plans a day trip or short stop-over in St Ives. This traffic is directed by road signs and police presence to use the parking lots and the associated minibus service during its visit (Figure 18). This reduces the volume of vehicular traffic in the town center to residents and those visitors who are staying overnight, and places more pedestrians into the old streets surrounding the harbor. The system appears to work because of the good information signs on the approach roads to the town; because the parking lots are on a hillside overlooking the harbor, which enables tourists to see their eventual objectives; and because there is a regular minibus service for those who do not wish to walk. The minibus service is a commercial operation that was reputedly operating at a profit when the author visited the area in 1976.

Tourist traffic management to improve access and maintain environmental quality is not limited to countryside situations. They can be meaningful strategies in urban areas, especially where a destination faces a dual function similar to that of national parks. For example, Westminster Abbey and the Tower of London Jewel House are both concerned with accommodating large numbers of visitors while also fulfilling their respective primary roles as a house of worship and security vault.

The major concern in these two popular London attractions is to develop a circulation system that permits the original and primary function to coexist with the newer function of hosting millions of visitors each year. Westminster Abbey has created separate drop-off and collection points for coach parties, which form the bulk of its visitors. Linking the two is a one-way traffic pattern through the Abbey, which contains the tourists in certain areas and permits the retention of tranquility and services in other areas (Murphy 1982). The Jewel House is a subterranean vault designed for the apparently contradictory purposes of providing both security and access. To achieve this multiple purpose a dual-circulation system has been developed (Figure 19). Those visitors in the passageway next to the showcases must move continuously at a slow pace, while those on the more distant platform may linger and observe as long as the day's traffic volume permits. In this way security for the exhibit is maintained because of the continuous movement next to the showcase; public exposure is obtained either through a brief but close contact or a more prolonged but distant viewing (Murphy 1982).

Summary

It is evident from this review of environmental and accessibility issues and strategies that the key elements of tourism strategy must involve consideration of a destination community's carrying capacity, potential for multiple use, and ways in which to improve or control access. Although the focus has been on the physical aspects of the environment and access it is not possible, or desirable, to ignore the human elements. The term "management" is becoming more commonplace in this physical setting because tourists' perceptions of the environment and routes play a major role in their imagery and use of the tourist product. To satisfy tourist expectations within the constraints of a destination environment will require both physical and human management strategies.

Section 3

Economics and business

The one factor that should be borne in mind by any community involved with tourism is that the only constant is change. It is a highly competitive business, dependent on many external factors over which a destination area has little or no control. Success can be influenced by the weather, changing consumer tastes, economic cycles, and government policies. For example, the 1980–1 winter was a financial disaster for many ski resorts in North America due to the mild weather and low snowfall in the western states and provinces. Yet within this overall pattern of gloom there were some remarkable success stories, where local topography and weather conditions combined to provide sufficient snow and low temperatures while surrounding competitors were denied. Government policy change can cause rapid market adjustments, as when Britain imposed currency restrictions in the 1950s which essentially limited travel to the sterling areas; and when the Carter administration revoked some professional tax deductions on conference trips outside of the United States, which had an immediate negative impact on convention cities in neighboring Canada and Mexico. In these instances, as with the weather, one destination's loss was another's gain.

But if we step back from the immediacy of such events, whether they be positive or negative, it is possible to detect some predictable patterns in the tourism business. Despite the localized effects of weather and changing government policy, many successful destination areas appear to experience a series of cycles. Most are relatively short and highly visible; others are much slower in developing and require more careful observation and research to detect. They all reveal, however, that in a competitive and open system every destination area must face up to the prospect of changing circumstances.

Tourism development has a great deal of appeal for many communities because of anticipated economic benefits, such as increased income and employment. In order to achieve these rewards, communities and individual entrepreneurs are prepared to invest in the business and put up with some inconvenience. The businessman soon knows where he stands with his tourism venture, but many communities find it difficult to develop a balance sheet for this industry.

The problem is related to the dispersed nature of the tourism industry and its intertwined relationships with other industries and domestic demands. For example, a visitor purchasing at the local bakery is injecting new money into the community, making that bakery part of the tourism industry at that moment in time; but the bakery is there primarily to serve local needs and the baker is probably unaware of the tourism proportion of his trade. Under these circumstances it becomes difficult to calculate tourism's exact financial returns to the local economy, and to assess the costs of establishing such an industry. Despite these difficulties in developing an accurate account of the industry's benefits to a community there is still a large degree of faith in tourism's economic benefits, and governments continue to invest huge sums of public money in the industry.

Signs of such investment are the major development programs in peripheral and economically backward regions, based on the premise that tourism can utilize their resource base and bring prosperity in the process. Experience has shown, however, that the structural weakness of these regions is still a big obstacle to development and that tourism's role may be one of stabilizing and diversifying local economies rather than one of development.

Any assessment of tourism development should

include consideration of the costs to host communities and attempt to derive a picture of net benefits. Due to the industry's characteristics the calculation of costs is as difficult and expensive as the calculation of its economic impact. Consequently, there have been few studies that have addressed this aspect, but those few that do suggest the revenue returns outweigh the costs of developing and marketing a tourist destination— especially when there is no alternative form of development or opportunity cost involved.

With these economic issues in mind, most economic strategies in tourism have been geared to developing the greatest return from the tourism product. The major concern has been to extend the season, thereby gaining increased productivity from existing investments. A prime example of this is the growing convention– conference business. Unfortunately, to participate in this business often involves additional investment, and it throws a destination community into an extremely competitive market. Consequently, care needs to be taken over the design and use of convention facilities and the selection of a realistic market segment.

In terms of economic development, most strategies now stress tourism's potential as a supplement to the existing economic base and lifestyles of a community. Evidence of this can be seen in the promotion of farm tourism and second homes for peripheral regions. Both are designed to complement and support local community life, and both are expected to be more in scale with local economic and institutional systems. In this way it is hoped that more local resources and labor can be used, and thereby generate both increased amenities and income for destination areas.

6

Economic cycles and benefits

Short-term cycles

Short-term tourism cycles are periods of dramatic change which usually occur within a year's timespan. As a consequence they are highly visible and generally easy to predict. The most common example is the seasonality of tourism, with peaks in the summer months, troughs in the winter, and what the industry calls "shoulder seasons" between these two extremes. Linder (1970), in his book *The Harried Leisure Class*, suggests a prime cause of this peaking is the different ways of life which exist in tourist-generating and destination areas. He labels the urban–industrial generators "time-affluent cultures." In contrast, although destinations may be capable of providing year-round facilities and accommodation, they are faced with a market situation where most customers have limited vacation time and wish to utilize it during their own optimum period—the summer. This traditional orientation is further compounded by institutional factors such as factory closures, and school and public holidays.

These constrain people's summer season opportunities to a few hectic weeks. Nowhere is this more apparent than in France, where August is the traditional and institutional vacation month. The authorities estimate 11 million vacationers, approximately 20 percent of the population, are on the road during the first weekend of August. One consequence of such peaking is an annual carnage on the highway, which in 1982 included a chain reaction crash involving buses and cars that killed over 50 people.

A good example of seasonal cycles is the summer resort. It is designed to accommodate and entertain the summer surge of vacationers and as a consequence provides a stark contrast between the frenzied activity of summer and the ghost-town atmosphere of winter closures. Seasonality is not restricted to resorts, however, for summer peaking can be found in so-called year-round destinations. London, with its multitude of all-weather attractions and year-round events, still records a summer peaking and winter low (Table 7). In this case, however, much of the summer madness may

Table 7 Seasonal distribution of London's visitor arrivals

Season	1973 % Overseas	1973 % Domestic	1975 % Overseas	1975 % Domestic	1977 % Overseas	1977 % Domestic
Winter quarter	15	25	16	22	16	19
Spring quarter	26	26	24	19	25	25
Summer quarter	40	28	40	24	39	27
Fall quarter	19	21	20	35	20	29
Total no. of visits	5.8 m	10.0 m	6.0 m	10.0 m	7.8 m	11.0 m

Source: Tourism: A Paper for Discussion, Greater London Council (1978, 5)

be attributed to overseas visitors, who seem to be particularly susceptible to the time pressures outlined by Linder.

Seasonal demand creates considerable economic inefficiency and stress within the industry and local labor force. The most publicized problem is that the key revenue-generating period is squeezed into a few hectic weeks. Consequently, businesses and the community try to extract sufficient revenue from these weeks to ensure success for the full year. Price-gouging becomes the norm and even institutionalized, as governments permit the two-tier pricing system of high- and low-season rates. Service declines as plant and personnel work at over-capacity. Staff relations and skills remain minimal since labor is employed on a temporary basis and provided with little training.

An indication of peaking's inefficiency for tourism, or any system, can be found in the load-factor calculation. The load factor, which is the ratio of average load to peak load, illustrates the relative usage efficiency within a system. It has been calculated to be as low as 33 percent for urban transport systems, due to the inefficient rush-hour peaks, and as high as 75–80 percent for electric power transmission systems, where peaking occurs at meal times (Richardson 1971, 104). If this concept is applied to tourism's accommodation sector, it is possible to measure peaking's impact on usage efficiency for this important tourism component.

Table 8 provides load-factor calculations for two English destination areas to illustrate the concept. In the case of London's hotels, they experienced peak occupancy in August and a low in December, with a resulting load factor of 66.7 percent. Thus they were operating at two-thirds efficiency with their existing occupancy rates. These figures, however, do not differentiate between the many types of accommodation that are available, as do the data from Stratford-upon-Avon (Table 8). The load factors from this survey show that the overall efficiency rating can be affected by the types of local accommodation available. Here we see that the up-market accommodation has been far more successful in attaining usage efficiency than the inexpensive option.

Two explanations can be offered for the Stratford-upon-Avon situation, and within them a suggestion that seasonality is not necessarily bad for everyone. First, the up-market hotels are committed to a year-round operation in order to keep quality staff and maintain profits, so they make concessions to attract off-season trade. These include reduced "commercial rates" to the business sector, off-season rates to the public, attempts to attract convention business during the week and the public over the weekend with "get away" specials, as well as the continued activity with coach tours to the theater. In contrast, the bed and breakfast operations make little or no attempt to generate business in the off-season. Their prime function is to supplement the hotel sector and take its overspill during the summer months or offer lodging to those vacationers who could otherwise not afford to stop overnight. In this regard they play an important role during the hectic summer months, but they can only sustain such a role for a short

Table 8 Accommodation load factors

London (1975):	Jan.	Feb.	Mar.	Apr.	May	June	July	Aug.	Sept.	Oct.	Nov.	Dec.	Average
Hotel occupancy rates (%)	29	33	39	39	49	54	66	69	63	50	35	28	46

$$Load\ ratio\ factor = \frac{average\ load}{peak\ load} \times 100 = \frac{46}{69} \times 100 = 66.7\%$$

Stratford-upon-Avon (October 1974– September 1975):	Group A Expensive hotels		Group B Middle-range hotels		Group C Inexpensive hotels/bed and breakfast	
Load factor ratio	$\frac{44}{56} \times 100 = 78.6\%$		$\frac{56}{87} \times 100 = 64.4\%$		$\frac{50}{90} \times 100 = 55.5\%$	

Source: London figures calculated from British Tourist Authority, *Digest of Tourist Statistics*, 7, April 1977, 70. Stratford-upon-Avon figures calculated from Heart of England Tourist Board, *Stratford-upon-Avon Tourism Survey*, June 1976, 13.

period of time since they need to revert back to the normalcy of family life in order to survive and fulfill their primary function.

Seasonal peaking can create problems for the whole community, as well as for components of the industry. The most evident sign of a problem is the summer congestion, crowded streets, slower traffic, lack of parking, line-ups for service, to name a few. MacFarlane, in a synopsis of tourist community surveys, noted:

Residents consistently highlighted undesirable traffic conges-tion as a major effect of tourism. Traffic congestion was mentioned most frequently by 55 percent in Niagara-on-the-Lake, 47 percent in Stratford (Ontario), 20 percent in Prince Edward Island, 94 and 87 percent in Delaware, and 50 percent in Sleat (Scotland). (MacFarlane 1979b)

Beyond the visible impact of congestion are the equally serious costs of community services. Many tourist centers experience dramatic increases in population during the summer months, placing a strain on the regular infrastructure and services. To maintain levels of service requires extra facilities and the hiring of extra police, sanitary, health, and parks personnel. However, the local tax base and central government grants are usually calculated in terms of the resident population only, thus funds for extra personnel are often not available. The result is a decline in service, not only for the visitor but also for the resident, who is called upon to pay this social cost of the peaking problem.

The economic and social problems associated with the industry's seasonality again overshadow some distinct advantages to the system. Urban man, accord-ing to Milgram (1970), is like an electric circuit which if overloaded by stress and too much stimulation can burn out. Likewise, many resorts and tourist destinations could never expect to sustain the tempo and pressures of high season for many weeks without similar signs of malaise. The fact that, come Labor Day or the final Bank Holiday, the rush will be over provides a definite light at the end of the tunnel for individuals and communities alike. The lull before and after the storm helps to make the season bearable and the industry tolerable.

It is difficult to quantify such benefits of seasonal peaking but they are there to be observed and recorded. For instance, many residents only take full advantage of local amenities and facilities in the off-season. They utilize the beaches and more popular pubs when the crowds have dissipated, they return to downtown when parking is once again available and low-season rates or specials apply in the restaurants, theaters, and stores.

In addition to the human benefits of an off-season, the local environment can certainly benefit from a "between performance" reprieve. The physical pressure on flora and fauna from thousands of visitors would soon take its toll unless there was some respite, when vegetation and animals could reclaim their foothold or territory again. Many of the stately homes of Britain close for several months in order to give the family and estate time to recuperate from the season's wear and tear. Ancient fortifications arise from their ruins in the off-season as the ravages of time and clambering feet are repaired (Figure 20). Delicate foliage is given a chance to regenerate and survive during the winter months, when visitors' cameras and a favorable climate are both absent (Figure 21).

Medium-term cycles

Medium-term cycles are those which involve a change in circumstances, requiring some adjustment over several years. Tourism is a consumer industry where dynamic market forces such as demographic trends and changing consumer preferences lead to continuous cycles and adjustment on the part of destination areas. In addition, changes in the natural landscape or economic health of a country can have substantial impact on tourism patterns, requiring an adjustment to the new circumstances if a destination is to remain competitive.

Destinations cannot cater to the entire tourism market so they concentrate on particular segments of this market. In the process, however, they tie themselves to a particular demographic or interest group which is continually evolving and changing. As time passes, demographic waves mature and their demands change in accord with their life cycle. As destinations become more familiar, their attraction and novelty may wane and visitors move on, looking for new experiences. Many family seaside resorts in England and Great Lakes resorts in North America experienced a decline in their traditional market during the 1960s and 1970s, as the baby boom passed into young adulthood and families split up. Young adults and the elderly formed separate markets, cheaper air travel made distant sun-drenched destinations viable alternatives to the

Figure 20   Renovations during the off-season

WINDMILL PALMS
(CHAMAEROPS EXCELSA)

NANAIMO'S TEMPERATE CLIMATE HAS PROVIDED AN IDEAL HOME FOR THE WIND-MILL PALM. SEVERAL PALMS HAVE BEEN DONATED TO THE CITY RE-ENCOURAGING A MORE BEAUTIFUL CITY.

Figure 21   Off-season recuperation for Nanaimo's palms

traditional resort back home. Some destinations have made adjustments to these changed circumstances. Eastbourne has developed into a retirement center, focusing on a growing segment of the leisure market. Brighton has constructed a major convention center and marina to diversify its attractions and reduce its dependency on the traditional seaside market. Cedar Point in Sandusky, Ohio, has attempted to retain its position as a lakeside resort by emphasizing and developing its amusement park, which has a broader appeal than its traditional beach attractions.

Medium-term cycles can be generated by more sudden events, as well as the gradual evolution of consumer demand. Natural disasters can play an important role in a business dependent on landscape attractions. For example, the eruptions of Mount St Helens in the spring of 1980 had a devastating effect on the northwest's tourism in the following months, as people perceived the whole region to be smothered in ash. Kreck (1981) has calculated that although the immediate economic losses were substantial, with a total short-term loss of over $6.5 million, much more damaging were the news stories which emphasized the destruction and at times misrepresented the facts. The result was not only a disastrous summer season in 1980 for the adjacent counties, but continued slow business in the following year as the area was still associated with an element of danger and unpredictability.

A similar predicament arose when Hurricane Iwa crashed into the Hawaiian Island of Kauai in November 1982, just at the start of its winter high season:

There was little communication with Kauai while Iwa was blowing up a storm. TV and newspapers were going on rumor filtered through Honolulu.

Tokyo papers reported that part of the island had sunk and thousands of people had died. A bad blow, for Japanese are 15 percent of the tourist business. (Delaplane 1983)

As a result, when the physical repairs had been completed, Kauai had to start the more difficult task of repairing its "Garden Island" image and correcting the rumors concerning its demise.

Changes in national economies also bring about adjustments in tourism patterns because of the industry's dependence on discretionary income. Currency realignments, which reflect varying national economic performances, make the traveler's dollar go much further in nations experiencing a relative decline in their currency's value. Britain experienced this

phenomenon in the early and mid-1970s, when Middleton noted:

The influence of devaluation of the pound on tourist flows to the UK [tourism from the United States increased by over 400,000 visits in 1969 mainly as a result of the devaluation of the pound] has been a major factor in bringing in international tourists to the UK. The influence of the floating pound in 1973 has been a major factor in keeping British tourists in Britain. (Middleton 1974, 25)

It was the turn of North America in the late 1970s and early 1980s when its dollar fell, particularly in relation to the Japanese yen and West German mark. As a consequence, fewer Americans went on an overseas trip and more foreigners visited North America. Statistics from the US Travel Center show this trend (Table 9), which culminated in the first travel account surplus for the United States in 1981. In that year there were 23.1 million visitor arrivals and receipts of $14.6 billion (Edgell 1983, 428). But by 1983 this short-term cycle had run its course as a stronger dollar encouraged more Americans to vacation abroad (*Time* 1983).

Long-term cycles

If we change our focus to look at a longer time frame we begin to uncover new types of business cycles. In terms of an individual destination, tourism takes on the natural or ogival curve of business development, which when considered in a regional context takes on the spatial patterns of diffusion.

A common distribution pattern for both natural and man-made phenomena is the natural distribution with its familiar bell-shaped curve, or the cumulative natural distribution with its ogival-shaped curve (Figure 22). The two curves of the product cycle reflect four distinct stages in the development, one curve in absolute terms and the other in cumulative form. First, there is slow growth as the product comes on the market and seeks to establish an identity and reputation among its competitors. Second, if the product is successful it will begin to experience ever-increasing acceptance. This results in rising sales and rapid growth, which in turn tapers to the point of peak production. Third, production levels decline at ever-increasing rates as there are fewer new households who require this product and the market becomes saturated. Finally, the product enters the stage of low sales, primarily replacements, and its

Table 9 International travel to and from the United States in 1980

Origin of visitors to USA	US arrivals	% Change from 1979	Travel receipts ($ millions)	% Change from 1979
Adjacent: Canada	11,384,538	+ 6	2,428	+16
Mexico	3,200,000	+25	2,554	+37
Europe	3,400,000	+12	1,942	+16
South America	1,190,000	+25	977	+23
Asia	1,960,000	+12	n.a.	n.a.
Other overseas	1,365,000	+ 6	n.a.	n.a.
Total	22,499,538	+11	10,090	+21

Destination of US travelers	US departures	% Change from 1979	Travel payments ($ millions)	% Change from 1979
Adjacent: Canada	11,171,304	− 1	1,817	+14
Mexico	3,087,000	−10	2,564	+ 4
Europe	3,867,679	− 4	3,021	+ 6
Caribbean and Central America	2,540,935	− 1	1,134	+11
South America	489,295	+ 5	392	+36
Other overseas	1,208,739	+ 9	1,469	+21
Total	22,364,952	− 2	10,397	+11

Source: United States Travel Service, "Recap of international travel to and from the United States in 1980," *Tourism Recreation Research*, 6, 2 (1981, 19–23)

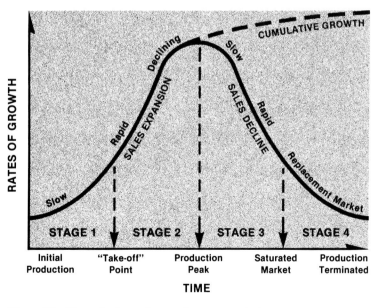

Figure 22 Theoretical growth curve for a new product

popularity wanes due to changing consumer tastes or the introduction of a new product or model. This natural curve for a product is not predestined, for an exceptional product can maintain a high position in Stage 3 for a considerable time through refinements or successful promotion. Of course many products fail to be adopted in any significant numbers so production is terminated at an early stage.

The interesting point about this natural distribution is that it can be applied to tourist destination areas, and its logic used to explain the evolution and potential decay of such areas over a long time span. Butler presents the link most clearly in his model of a tourist area's cycle of evolution:

Visitors will come to an area in small numbers initially, restricted by a lack of access, facilities, and local knowledge [Stage 1 of the product model]. As facilities are provided and awareness grows, visitor numbers will increase. With marketing, information dissemination, and further facility provision, the area's popularity will grow rapidly [Stage 2]. Eventually, however, the rate of increase in visitor numbers will decline as levels of carrying capacity are reached [Stage 3]. . . . As the attractiveness of the area declines relative to other areas, because of overuse and the impacts of visitors, the actual number of visitors may also eventually decline [Stage 4]. (Butler 1980, 6)

Butler divides this evolution cycle into six stages and his model is presented as a cumulative normal distribution, which takes on the shape of an ogival curve (Figure 22).

The first two stages reflect Stage 1 in the product cycle. First the *exploration stage* is characterized by small numbers of visitors and involves Plog's "allocentrics" and Cohen's "explorers" who make individual travel arrangements. This is followed by an *involvement stage* where the local community begins to respond by providing visitor facilities. At this stage, contact between visitors and locals can be expected to remain high as residents are becoming involved in this industry.

The third stage is described as the *development stage* and it coincides with the rapid growth in the product model. Here the community becomes a well-defined tourist market due to its advertising and success. As this stage progresses, outside companies become involved in the construction of tourist facilities, and local involvement and control declines. It is now an established tourist center and appeals to Plog's "mid-centrics" or Cohen's "institutionalized tourists." An example of this would be Hawaii in the 1950s and 1960s

when modern jet aircraft first opened up this area to the middle-class American (Kent 1977; Farrell 1982).

The next two stages represent the slowdown in growth of a product cycle. The first step is called the *consolidation stage* and represents a tapering off of growth rates. The number of visitors still increases and may outnumber the number of permanent residents. Marketing and advertising will be far-reaching, and efforts are made to extend the visitor season and market area as the local importance of this industry is appreciated. Examples of this stage would include the Hawaii of today, London, and Paris, for they all appeal to the "organized mass tourist" market identified by Cohen and the "psychocentric" described by Plog. This is followed by a *stagnation stage* where the peak number of visitors is reached, and capacity levels may have been reached or exceeded with attendant environmental, social, and economic problems. The area will no longer be fashionable and its "resort image becomes divorced from its geographic environment." Examples offered by Butler include Spain's Costa Brava and Ontario's summer cottage resorts.

The sixth and last stage reflects a range of options, which depend partly on the uniqueness of an area's tourism product and partly on the success of local management decisions. It resembles the product cycle's final stage where output can either decline and be terminated, or be maintained at a steady level because of its uniqueness or exceptional qualities. If the tourist area enters a *decline stage* the area will not be able to compete with newer attractions, and consequently faces a declining market. Tourist facilities will deteriorate and may be replaced by non-tourist-related structures and activities. In some cases accommodation is converted into condominiums, retirement, or convalescent homes, since the natural attractions still make them pleasant places to live. Examples of areas entering the decline stage are Miami Beach and old resort areas of Europe, such as Eastbourne and the Firth of Clyde. According to Butler, "ultimately, the area may become a veritable tourism slum or lose its tourist function completely" (Butler 1980, 9). In contrast to the decline scenario a tourist area could experience *rejuvenation*, either through the addition of a man-made attraction or by utilizing previously ignored natural resources. An example of the former would be Atlantic City's efforts to revive its fortunes via gambling casinos. The latter type of rejuvenation can be found in revitalized spa towns like Harrogate (conference facilities), resorts like Brighton (conference center and marina), and ski developments which have made year-round attractions of Aviemore (Scotland) and Vail, Colorado. In some cases the uniqueness of an area helps to maintain high visitor volumes, such as at Niagara Falls and Stratford-upon-Avon. However, even under these favorable circumstances careful planning and management is required to maintain the destination's image and quality of experience.

Destinations do not have to experience all the stages of Butler's model, for "instant resorts" like Cancun in Mexico and Languedoc–Roussillon generally eliminate the early stages thanks to careful site selection and planning, but the model does demonstrate that destinations can expect dramatic changes over their lifetime. Even if a resort is successful, its very success may sow the seeds of its eventual decline, thus it is important to recognize the signs of change and to plan for long-term success. As Butler cautions, it is the "growth" concept and assumption which must be questioned:

The assumption that tourist areas will always remain tourist areas and be attractive to tourists appears to be implicit in tourism planning. Public and private agencies alike, rarely, if ever, refer to the anticipated life span of a tourist area or its attractions. (Butler 1980, 10)

Two separate studies of Nice, on the Côte d'Azure, provide independent support for the notion of cyclical evolution, and at the same time illustrate how each destination is likely to develop its own variations of the Butler model. Nash (1979) concentrates on the historical evolution of Nice as an "aristocratic tourist culture," and in the process identifies three stages of development. Early growth (1763–1860) reflects Nice's development as a winter resort for wealthy invalids. Maturity (1860–1914) is linked with railroad development and larger numbers of visitors. During this stage there was considerable hotel construction and "a series of requests by the foreign communities of Nice that tourist-related projects be undertaken." Finally, a transformation (1914–36) is noted,

the crash of 1929 and the Great Depression that followed dealt a severe blow to tourism in Nice. Many of those who lived on dividends and interest were wiped out and by the time they recovered Nice had begun to entertain tourists throughout the year and cater to an influx of workers bent on enjoying a paid summer vacation. (Nash 1979, 67)

Thus Nash's narrative incorporates both short-term cycles (Nice's original seasonal appeal) and medium-

term cycles (1929 crash and its aftermath) into a longer-term cycle of development and adjustment. He concludes:

from a cultural evolutionary viewpoint one would have to say that Nice adapted extremely successfully as a tourist resort over the past two hundred years. The time of aristocratic tourism is over, but a new mass tourism has appeared to replace it. With the benefit of hindsight, one can now see that the attempts to maximize the touristic possibilities of an expanding market, begun in the aristocratic period, were an initial phase in the development of tourism today. (Nash 1979, 74)

Rudney's historical perspective of Nice's evolution focuses on another aspect of its development, linking the phenomenon of democratization with the life cycles of a resort. The democratization process came with increased access and innovative social legislation. The railroad connections and automobile enabled larger numbers and lower-income groups to visit. More visitors than ever passed through by automobile on a sightseeing tour during the lean Depression years, changing the emphasis from grand palaces to smaller hotels and rooming houses. But the major change occurred with the paid vacation (*congé payé*) legislation of 1936 which granted two weeks' paid vacation for industrial workers with one or more years of service:

Tourism on the Côte d'Azure underwent a full-scale process of democratization as thousands of workers claimed their share of the Mediterranean sun. . . . The trains filled with *congés payés* entering Nice were the Popular Front's answer to the Nazi *Kraft durch Freude* and to the Italian *Dopolavoro*. Institutionalized leisure came to be perceived as a vital piece of the labor package in a social democracy. (Rudney 1980, 222)

The above assessments of Nice's evolution and adjustment to changing conditions focus on a single location, but if we expand our horizons and definition of a destination area to include its region we note that the evolution often takes on spatial connotations. When development proceeds and mobility increases, many of the original attractions are left behind, as travelers seek out new experiences and more modern facilities. Lundgren notes these trends in the evolution of the Laurentian hills as a resort destination for Montrealers.

Major transport innovations influence cyclical developments as they alter the regional comparative advantage of destinations, thus no destination development can be seen in geographic isolation. The historical evolution of tourism development in the Laurentians

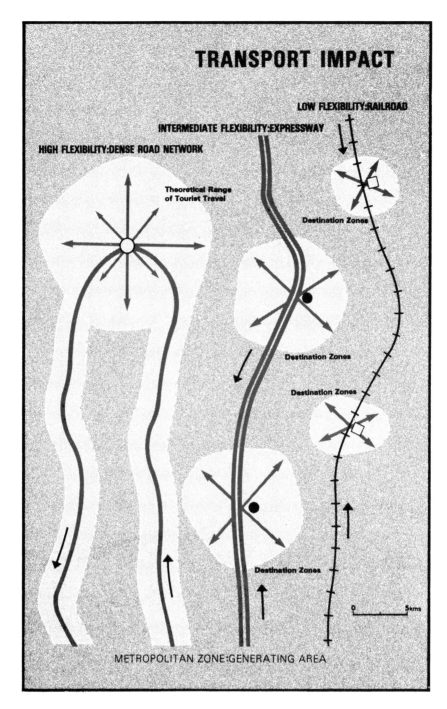

Figure 23 Spatial impact of varying degrees of transport flexibility
Source: Lundgren (1980)

shows a strong association between regional development and transport innovations. Lundgren (1983) identifies three transport eras in the Laurentians, each with its own spatial impact (Figure 23). From the 1890s to 1930s the resorts and individual cottages focused around the railroad stations and neighboring lakes, providing summer relief from the sweltering conditions of Montreal. This early pattern changed in the 1930s when the growth of a highway network between Montreal and Laurentian villages diffused tourism throughout the region. The transport situation changed again in the 1960s when a freeway link was introduced to overcome the growing highway congestion. The result was a move from the original highway network's high flexibility to the more restrictive flexibility of a limited-access highway. This has once again given comparative advantage to a few destinations, and with the growth of alpine skiing has provided an impetus to major two-season resort developments.

It is apparent from this review of cyclical forces that a destination's economic situation and prospects will be influenced by its options to extend the local season, its ability to overcome negative medium-term changes, and its position in the evolutionary process. Most planning response has been in terms of the annual seasonality, with an emphasis on creating greater economic returns through more extensive use of the tourist product. Pursuit of these economic objectives, however, could nullify the social and physical advantages of an off-season, so destinations will need to strike a balance between more revenue and more stress. Planning for unpredictable events, such as natural disasters or changing government policy, is limited to lessening their negative impacts through diversification of the tourist product. Finally, it is difficult to locate destinations on an evolutionary cycle with any precision because of the lack of hard data and the fact that various elements will be in different phases of development. However, the main contribution of this concept is that it forces planning to consider a destination's relative position within a competitive market, and to consider the long-term implications of development and marketing decisions.

Economic benefits

Tourism is a business, both for the individual entrepreneur and the community which acts as host to this activity. Both hope to benefit economically from it, but while the entrepreneur has a personal and directly accountable viewpoint the community needs to assess benefits in a broader and longer-term context, which is a more complex task. Communities cannot hope to attract all tourist types so they focus on particular market segments, which immediately affects the level of economic return they can expect. The extent of this economic return will be influenced, in turn, by the degree of self-sufficiency communities possess within national and international economies. Finally the measure of true community benefit will require assessment of the costs involved in creating and operating the tourist product.

Tourism is highly desirable to most communities because by attracting and serving visitors a community earns new or "basic" income from other parts of the country and globe. Such income is an infusion of new wealth and can be considered the equivalent of export earnings. It is "basic" because a community depends on such income in order to pay for imported goods and services, and its taxes (Tiebout 1962).

The income that tourism brings to a destination will vary according to the types of visitors attracted and their length of stay. Different expenditure rates have been associated with various types of activity and the accommodation used at a destination. The biggest spender is generally the convention delegate. Various estimates put their expenditure at $200 to $300 per convention, with an average daily expenditure of $40 to $60 (Cooper 1976; Burt and MacKinnon 1977). After taking inflation into account, such figures have probably doubled by now. Hotel guests generally spend the most per day, followed by visitors staying in bed and breakfast facilities and those using self-catering facilities, or staying with family and friends (Table 10). The high expenditure rates for hotel guests are not simply a reflection of wealthier tourists but also the growing convention–conference business, which is often undertaken on expense accounts or as a tax deduction. The lower per diem rates for campers and family visitors should be tempered by the fact that they often stay longer than the big-spending convention delegates.

Expenditure rates also vary according to the tourists' region of origin and the type of destination sought, which has an important bearing on marketing and development considerations. An expenditure survey in Hawaii, for instance, showed that in 1977 Japanese

Economics and business

Table 10 Visitor expenditures by accommodation category

Type of accommodation	Anglesey[1] (per average visitor) (£)	($US equiv.)	Greater Tayside[2] (per group per day) (£)	($US equiv.)	Galveston, Texas[3] (annual expenditures) ($US million)	Maine, US[4] (per person per day) ($US)
Hotels	29.35	70.35	17.01	40.77	39.8–49.7	36.40
Guest houses	16.78	40.21	10.66	25.55	n.a.	23.48
Bed and breakfast	15.01	35.98	8.56	20.52	n.a.	n.a.
Holiday cottages and flats	7.76	18.60	6.80	16.29	6.2–8.6	15.49
Caravans (touring)	8.73	20.92	6.66	15.96	1.8–2.4	9.09
Tents	6.29	15.08	7.07	16.94		
Friends and relatives	7.73	18.52	5.28	12.65	2.7–4.0	9.21

Sources: [1]Archer 1973, 35. [2]Scottish Tourist Board 1975, 30. [3]W. Rose, "The measurement and economic impact of tourism on Galveston, Texas: a case study," *Journal of Travel Research*, 19, 4, 1981, 3–11. [4]Maine Vacation Travel Analysis Committee, *Tourism in Maine*, 1974, 5.

visitors spent almost three times as much per person per day as visitors from the North American mainland (Richardson and Donehower 1979). Japan at this time was the more lucrative market and one which justified more intensive promotion and development. An economic impact study of Greater Tayside's tourism (Scottish Tourist Board 1975) found that major nodal towns and highland centers received the largest proportion of the region's tourist expenditures, 30 and 28 percent respectively, even though they were not normally associated with tourism. In contrast, those towns commonly associated with tourism, such as special activity centers (highland games and golf) or seaside towns, received considerably smaller proportions of the tourist expenditure, namely 12 and 9 percent respectively. The economic prominence of the inland nodes was due in part to overnight tourist stops, but also to their hierarchical dominance which drew many transients and holiday-makers from surrounding rural and coastal towns. Thus, thanks to the tourists' increased mobility, every town in a destination region has an opportunity to benefit from tourist expenditures with the appropriate marketing and development, some to a larger degree than would be expected in terms of their general image.

Multiplier concept

Visitor expenditures represent only the first stage of the economic impact on a destination community, for like other generators of basic income, tourism's contribution can multiply as the extra income passes throughout an economy. Figure 24 provides a conceptual illustration of the multiplier effect of tourist spending in a local economy, using a hotel as the specific example. The hotel's earnings from visitors represent a "direct" infusion of tourist spending into the community, usually being presented as a single unit of currency. The proportion of this dollar which the hotel passes on to its staff (represented by the household sector) and local wholesalers is called "indirect" earnings. These people, in turn, make local purchases with the revenues earned from the hotel and these become the "induced" earnings of the community. At each stage in the diffusion of tourist earnings some money leaks from the local economy to the national and international economies. The hotel, for example, can pass on only part of the initial tourist dollar to the community because it needs to account for prior purchases of outside supplies, possibly the payments for a franchise license, and taxes. Likewise, residents and wholesale and retail businesses will experience some income leakage with the arrival of their share of tourism earnings because of outside purchases and taxes. The tourist dollar spent at the hotel can penetrate the local economy extensively, but in the process it is bound to dissipate due to the leakages, and will eventually disappear.

The size of the multiplier is an important component of the economic benefit of tourism to the community, because this reflects how many times the impact of each tourist dollar goes around the local system before disappearing entirely through the various leakage channels. Its size will depend on the size and complexity of the local economy, the tourist industry's

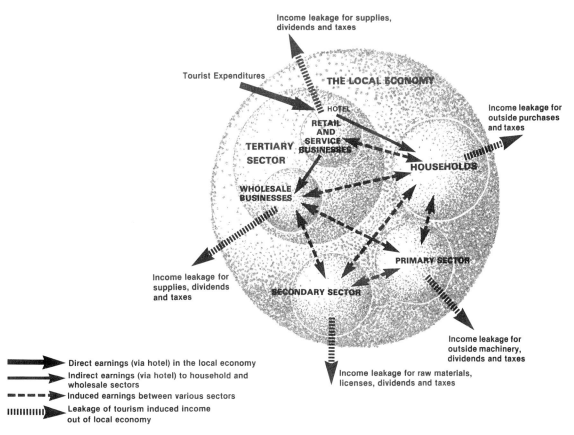

Income leakage for supplies, dividends and taxes

Tourist Expenditures

THE LOCAL ECONOMY

HOTEL
RETAIL AND SERVICE BUSINESSES

TERTIARY SECTOR

Income leakage for outside purchases and taxes

HOUSEHOLDS

WHOLESALE BUSINESSES

Income leakage for supplies, dividends and taxes

PRIMARY SECTOR

SECONDARY SECTOR

Income leakage for outside machinery, dividends and taxes

Income leakage for raw materials, licenses, dividends and taxes

Direct earnings (via hotel) in the local economy

Indirect earnings (via hotel) to household and wholesale sectors

Induced earnings between various sectors

Leakage of tourism induced income out of local economy

Figure 24 Economic impact of tourist spending on a community
Source: Kreutzwiser (1973)

and residents' need to import, and the residents' propensity to save rather than spend these earnings. Lundberg's descriptive equation of the multiplier demonstrates the relationship of these factors:

$$TIM = \frac{1 - TPI}{MPS + MPI}$$

where TIM = Tourism Income Multiplier
1 = Tourist Dollar
TPI = Tourists' Propensity to Import or Buy Imported Goods or Services
MPS = Marginal Propensity to Save by Residents
MPI = Marginal Propensity to Import by Residents

(Lundberg 1976, 157)

The impact of the tourist dollar will be reduced by the amount of goods and services imported to sustain the industry (TPI). The benefit will be eroded further by the tendency of local residents to save and thus withdraw a portion of the earnings from circulation (MPS), and by their need to buy imported goods and services for their household needs (MPI).

The more self-sufficient a community is in providing tourist facilities and services the less will be the need to import, so more revenue remains in the community to be reused by residents before disappearing to pay for those symbols of success, the Mercedes, Pentax camera, and higher taxes. Table 11 illustrates the link between the multiplier and an economy's scale and self-sufficiency. Most national multipliers are relatively large because the national economy is generally more self-sufficient than lower-order systems. However, the

Economics and business

Table 11 Tourism multiplier calculations for various economies

Economic scale	Date	Location	Income multiplier
National	1966	Ireland[1]	2.7
	1970	Canada[1]	2.43
	1974	United Kingdom[4]	1.68
	1964	Greece[1]	1.2–1.4
	1977	Mexico[8]	0.97
	1971	Commonwealth Caribbean[3]	0.88
	1974	Bahamas[2]	0.78
State/provincial	–	New Hampshire[1]	1.6–1.7
	–	Hawaii[1]	0.9–1.3
	1973	Southwest England[7]	0.35–0.45
Regional/local	1976	Ely, Montana[5]	1.67
	1977	Okanagan, BC[2]	0.73
	1977	Victoria, BC[6]	0.65
	1973	Gwynedd[2]	0.37
	1975	East Anglia[2]	0.35
	1973	Greater Tayside[2]	0.32

Source: [1] Lundberg 1976, 158. [2] J. Quayson and T. Var, *The Multiplier Impact of Tourist Expenditure in the Okanagan, BC, Canada*, Burnaby, BC, School of Business Administration and Economics, Simon Fraser University, 1981, 24. [3] J. M. Bryden, *Tourism and Development*, 1973, 155. [4] M. Hanna, 1976, 7–9, 20. [5] R. W. Lichty and D. N. Steinnes, "Measuring the impact of tourism on a small community," *Growth and Change*, 13, 2, 1982, 36–9. [6] J. Liu and T. Var, *The Economic Impact of Tourism in Metropolitan Victoria*, BC, Burnaby, BC, School of Business Administration and Economics, Simon Fraser University, 1981, 8, 12. [7] South West Economic Planning Council, *Economic Survey of the Tourist Industry in the Southwest*, 1976, 46. [8] J. Boltvinik, "The economic impacts of tourism in the Mexican economy," *TTRA Annual Conference Proceedings*, October 1979, Salt Lake City, 58.

less developed a national economy the greater the leakage and lower the multiplier effect. Below the national level come the state and provincial multipliers where economies are less self-sufficient and there is tax leakage to the national capital. At the bottom of the list are regional and local multipliers, which reflect the dependency of small communities on outside suppliers, plus tax commitments to both state and national governments.

Multiplier measurement

To operationalize the above concepts and demonstrate the economic contribution of tourism at all economic levels requires development of mathematical models that can analyze survey data. This has been achieved through the creation of a multiplier ratio which indicates the direct, indirect, and induced changes within an economic system, compared to the direct cause of the change itself (Archer 1976, 115). The commonly used multiplier in tourism research has been the income multiplier, because it reflects most clearly the eco-

nomic impact on host community residents. There are two major methods for calculating this multiplier, the "*ad hoc* model" and the "input–output model."

The *ad hoc* model has been developed by Archer to operate at regional and local levels, incorporating tourism's various component parts (Archer and Owen 1971). His tourist regional multiplier is presented as:

$$\sum_{j=1}^{N} \sum_{i=1}^{n} Q_j K_{ij} V_i \left(\frac{1}{1 - L \sum_{i=1}^{n} X_i Z_i V_i} \right)$$

where j = types of tourist accommodation
i = types of consumer outlet
Q = proportions spent on each type of accommodation
K = proportions spent on each type of consumer outlet
V = income generation in each category of expenditure
L = average propensity to consume
X = pattern of consumer spending
Z = proportion of income spent within region by the inhabitants

Table 12   Tourist income multipliers for accommodation sectors of Anglesey

Type of visitor	Income multiplier
Hotel and guest house visitors	0.25
Stationary caravan visitors	0.14
Bed and breakfast and farmhouse visitors	0.58
Camping visitors	0.35
Composite multiplier	0.25

Source: Archer (1973, 50)

Each component can be analyzed independently, and Archer calculated both the composite and individual accommodation sector multipliers for Anglesey (Table 12). Note this table indicates the highest return to Anglesey comes from visitors using bed and breakfast accommodation, even though an earlier table revealed expenditures associated with this form of accommo- dation ranked third in Anglesey (Table 10). The reason is that much of the bed and breakfast revenue stays within the local community because it goes straight into the pockets of local people, whereas a considerable proportion of the initial expenditures in hotels immedi- ately leaks out of the system to import goods and services. Hence the multiplier provides an important refinement on straightforward surveys of tourist expenditure because it reveals the overall impact of tourist spending on a local economy.

In order to apply the *ad hoc* model it is necessary to collect five basic sets of data:

(a) definition of region;
(b) the number of different types of tourists and the average length of their stay in the region;
(c) the average daily expenditure of tourists in the region and its breakdown between different types of businesses;
(d) information about the pattern in which business in the region distributes this revenue from tourism to employees and suppliers within and outside the region; and
(e) the pattern of expenditure of residential households within the region.

Such *ad hoc* models are relatively inexpensive to develop because they can operate on the basis of sample surveys and do not require a detailed break- down of the local economy and its interactions.

However, the model cannot be adapted to show how income generation via tourism affects each sector of the local economy, and for this reason it is generally considered less satisfactory than the alternative method, the input–output model.

The *input–output model* developed by Archer (1973) shows the flow of current transactions through a given economy for a particular period of time, usually a year. Various types of business activity are grouped into industrial sectors and arranged into a matrix, with the total value of all sales made by each sector to each other in the rows, and purchases made by each sector from each of the other sectors in the columns. The input– output model provides a comprehensive representation of a region's economy by showing the value of current transaction flows and following these through to include the induced effects of the initial income generation.

The origin of the regional input–output model was the basic input–output formula

$$X - AX = Y$$

where X = vector of total demand
AX = intermediate demand, as represented by the product of A (square matrix of production coefficient) and X
Y = vector of final demand

This formula has been converted into a regional model by separating endogenous (within the region) from exogenous (external to the region) final demand, producing the formula

$$X = (I - A)^{-1} \left[1 - \sum_{h = n + 1}^{p} C_h (I - A) B_h (I - A)^{-1} \right]^{-1} Y$$

Economics and business

where X = vector of total demand
Y = vector of final demand
A = square matrix of production coefficients
B_h = series of square matrices representing different household sectors
C_h = series of square matrices representing the consumption pattern in each different household sector
I = identity matrix

To operationalize the model five steps are necessary:

(a) definition of region;

(b) sectorization of the economy by placing firms into sectors and then surveying them to find their monetary flows to and from all sectors;

(c) construction of a transaction or flow matrix showing what each sector buys from and sells to each other;

(d) calculation of transactions outside of the region in terms of exports or imports; and

(e) development of a matrix for technical coefficients and a table of interdependency coefficients

Archer (1973) used the input–output method to analyze the Anglesey data, which provides a comparison with the *ad hoc* model. He found the income multipliers for

Table 13 Results of input–output model for Anglesey accommodation sectors, 1970

| Sector | Category of tourist (by type of accommodation used) | | | | |
	Hotel	Farmhouse/ Bed & breakfast	Caravan	Tent	Composite effect
	£	£	£	£	£
Agriculture	83.54	629.90	566.72	702.29	502.47
Quarrying	9.90	8.60	7.97	10.77	8.66
Textiles	0.09	0.22	0.06	0.09	0.22
Timber	3.85	2.98	3.16	4.24	3.14
Other manufacturing	7.18	15.31	13.55	23.88	13.67
Construction	120.50	63.80	104.74	37.49	107.80
Gas	11.50	6.99	2.33	3.98	4.79
Electricity	30.40	37.12	19.67	28.68	25.04
Water	20.08	16.98	8.77	12.60	12.35
Rail transport	1.38	2.78	0.15	4.47	1.13
Road transport	24.23	59.01	27.84	38.23	32.89
Postal & telecommunications	66.21	75.51	34.03	54.53	47.87
Insurance, banking & finance	16.29	49.92	27.27	41.25	30.03
Education	5.21	10.76	4.73	6.95	5.93
Garage trade	82.37	161.18	104.73	192.64	117.14
Hotels & public houses	2053.98	277.04	188.15	371.39	546.20
Caravan sites	0.65	1.45	546.73	644.37	375.28
Food shops	176.58	347.46	161.87	302.45	205.22
Non-food shops	161.72	384.93	200.20	375.15	237.15
Wholesalers	58.41	64.92	33.46	59.49	44.96
Other services	37.70	85.64	30.63	63.56	41.48
Professional & scientific	41.12	259.86	53.76	74.79	86.85
Local government	50.51	66.11	30.00	43.92	40.40
Exogenous personal spending	0	0	0	0	0
Exogenous income	0	4986.00	0	0	768.00
Total	3063.40	7614.47	2170.52	3097.22	3259.67
Multiplier	0.3063	0.7614	0.2171	0.3097	0.3260

Source: Archer (1973, 5)

the accommodation sectors (Table 13) were "of a comparable degree of magnitude, although since the input–output model probably registered more accurately the secondary induced effects of consumer spending, these multipliers are slightly higher than the ones given by the *ad hoc* model" (Archer 1973, 54).

Though the input–output model provides a satisfactory method of studying tourism's multiple effect it does have some drawbacks. First, the expense of developing a comprehensive regional input–output matrix often forces researchers to use census-derived national or macro-region coefficients for the internal linkages of smaller regions and communities. This assumes that interactions at the local scale are the same as at the higher scale, and that the technical coefficients established by the census still hold true years later. Second, the static nature of the model restricts its application to the base year of data collection, and the cost of updating the information can almost be as great as the original study. Third, the technique assumes a linear relationship between sectors, thereby ignoring possible economies of scale and other economic options open to the various sectors as business expands and contracts.

At a regional and local level, income multipliers can be used to indicate the effect on residents resulting from an injection of tourist expenditure. Provided it is possible to estimate the number of tourists visiting a destination area and their expenditure, the economic impact can be calculated by using multiplier co-efficients. If multiplier coefficients for a particular area have not been derived through a local survey, those for similar areas have been used or national coefficients have been adopted, but in these cases researchers are sacrificing accuracy for expediency.

For practical purposes it is crucial to appreciate that local multiplier studies are just case studies of local gains and no more. They leave three questions unanswered, according to Hanna (1976). First, what are the costs? Second, does the intensely narrow viewpoint of local economic analysis run counter to the development of centralized economies and national economic planning? It should not be forgotten that major infrastructure development for the industry is often initiated by central government funding and that a proportion of the tax leakage returns in the form of government payrolls and social benefits. Third, do local tourism multipliers disguise the benefits which accrue beyond the case study's boundaries? The leakages for supplies

and dividends may well benefit other parts of the national economy. The first of these concerns will be discussed later in this chapter, while the others will be addressed in the final section concerning the planning and management of tourism.

Employment opportunities

In addition to potential income benefits many communities have attempted to broaden their economic base and diversify their employment opportunities by participating in this growing service industry. Foremost amongst these are the small resource-based communities in peripheral regions, which have attempted to build upon the urban–industrial market demand for a "change of pace" and a "breath of fresh air" by promoting and developing their rural and wilderness assets. Chau identifies this potential in Canada where

a large portion of leisure and recreational travel tends to flow to economically backward areas where natural resources are generally unsuitable for agricultural or industrial purposes: snow for winter sport; the hills and mountains for climbing, hiking, etc.; forest lands for national and provincial parks. Tourism allows these areas which have been apparently disinherited to enter into stages of regional and national growth; and the resources which are unproductive for other industries, represent a source of wealth for tourism. (Chau 1973, 83)

A common response to this situation has been the creation of economic development programs designed to attract tourists and increase local employment in the process. Tourism is seen as "a particularly suitable form of economic activity for small communities where there are few alternative job opportunities" (Scottish Tourist Board 1975, 5) because it capitalizes on scenic resources, is labor intensive, and adds to local amenity facilities. As a consequence, government-sponsored tourism development has become an important regional development tool in the Scottish Highlands (Duffield and Long 1981), along France's Mediterranean coast (Clarke 1981), in British Columbia (Montgomery and Murphy 1983), and in Hawaii (Finney and Watson 1977).

A variety of economic problems have been addressed by these tourism development programs and two will be examined in detail. In the case of British Columbia, the prime concern was a dispersal of tourism volumes and revenue from the congested urban

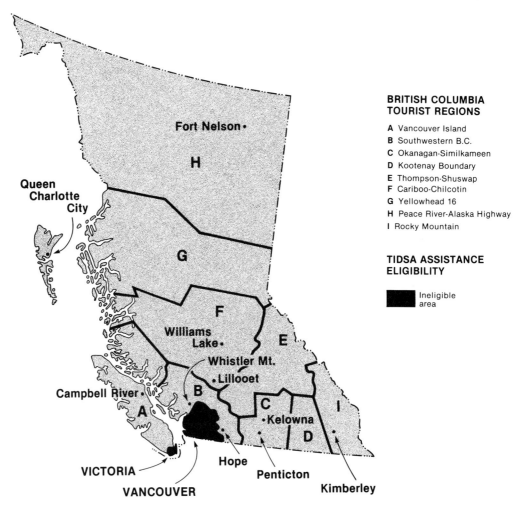

BRITISH COLUMBIA TOURIST REGIONS

A Vancouver Island
B Southwestern B.C.
C Okanagan-Similkameen
D Kootenay Boundary
E Thompson-Shuswap
F Cariboo-Chilcotin
G Yellowhead 16
H Peace River-Alaska Highway
I Rocky Mountain

TIDSA ASSISTANCE ELIGIBILITY

Ineligible area

Figure 25 Tourism regions and eligible–ineligible areas for TIDSA in British Columbia

centers of Vancouver and Victoria to the less developed regions of the province. To achieve this a $US44 million federal–provincial development program (Travel Industry Development Subsidiary Agreement — TIDSA) was initiated in 1978, and applied to all areas of the province except for the two metropolitan areas of Vancouver and Victoria (Figure 25). Among its dispersal objectives was the attempt to diversify the economies and employment opportunities in small rural towns and single enterprise communities, by improving their amenity characteristics and upgrading or building tourist facilities.

In Scotland the initial concern was "to stem the tide of depopulation through emigration that had characterized the [Highlands] area for many decades" (Duffield and Long 1981, 408). The prime objectives were to provide more rural employment and to make communities more attractive places in which to live and work, with special emphasis on the needs of the young skilled and educated workers who formed the bulk of out-migrants. Tourism was seen as a means of supplementing the traditional primary sector with tertiary employment that would provide new opportunities, especially for the female workforce. Furthermore, by making the region more attractive for visitors it was hoped that it would become a more attractive place for permanent residence.

Despite their different priorities, British Columbia and Scotland have adopted similar policies, and in the process have experienced similar frustrations. Scotland's attempts to stimulate economic development through tourism have been underway since the Highlands and Islands (Scotland) Act of 1965, and have provided evidence of several difficulties. British Columbia, on the other hand, has only just completed its five-year TIDSA program, but even here early results point to similar problems and stumbling blocks.

Brownrigg and Greig (1976) focused on three aspects of tourism's contribution to economic development in rural Scotland, its economic benefits, employment benefits, and immigration impact. In terms of economic benefits they found that most of the cash injected into countryside regions, by investors and tourists, leaked out of the local economy because of the high dependency on outside goods and services in these areas. Low multipliers were the rule for small rural communities and "the benefits from tourist expenditure are more apparent than real—it involves a lot of noise and activity but, at the end of the day, locals have surprisingly little to show for it" (Brownrigg and Greig 1976, 7). In terms of employment, most of the newly created jobs required little training or skill and consequently paid the minimum wage. Furthermore, the industry offered mainly seasonal and female employment, which provided little relief to the hard-core male unemployment. Where particular skills were required, such as in the hotel sector, the industry often turned to outside expertise rather than provide on-the-job training for local people. With these observations it is not surprising that Brownrigg and Greig concluded tourism's effect on the out-migration of young people was limited. However, they did concede that it helped to attract older age groups, who may be tempted to retire to these areas because of the added facilities.

Montgomery and Murphy (1983) found similar disparities between program aspirations and results in their examination of British Columbia's TIDSA program. Although their study began before the program had run its full course, their process evaluation revealed difficulties in getting local small-scale enterprises involved and in redressing the spatial economic inequities. "Many [of the surveyed private sector] cited the high cost of documenting, preparing and submitting a project proposal as being prohibitive to most small businessmen and operators" (Montgomery and Murphy 1983, 196). There was a feeling that the system of development grants favored those large, and possibly multinational, corporations which had the expertise and man-hours to make proposal applications. Thus small-scale and local initiatives could be stillborn or overwhelmed in the application process, while outside expertise and investment benefited from the development grants. Their study also detected a spatial imbalance in the distribution of TIDSA funding, with the majority going to southern "have" areas adjacent to the two excluded metropolitan areas, while the more peripheral "have not" areas in the north and interior of British Columbia continued to fall behind. British Columbia, therefore, is having as much difficulty in redressing its spatial imbalance as Scotland has had in stemming its rural depopulation.

A problem which neither of the above studies addresses directly, yet remains vital to the concept of using tourism as a regional development tool, is the misconception that tourism is a simple technology industry. Proposals to spread tourism to undeveloped backwaters continually stress the use of abundant and free resources, such as scenery and sunshine, the need for simple labor skills, and standard construction techniques. In reality, however, that ubiquitous supply of tourist resources translates into extreme competition, especially with established destinations, and a dependency on the business expertise of developed economies.

An example of these difficulties has been provided by Diamond (1977) in his analysis of Turkey's attempts to use tourism as a route to economic development. To break into established market patterns places unknown and untested peripheral destinations at a disadvantage, so they must often place themselves "in the hands of international travel agencies holding all the bargaining power" (Diamond 1977, 552). This can lead to price cutting and the creation of loss leaders, in order to establish a reputation within the tourism market. The types of service and construction required in underdeveloped peripheral regions are often determined by foreign tastes and may be most economically provided by outside specialists. In this regard Diamond (1977, 551) notes "it has been estimated that when the Istanbul Hilton was built in 1955 [early stage of the development program] the import content was nearly 90 percent." Finally, the promotion of a new destination area calls for the kind of market analysis and advertising expertise found only in tourist-generating areas. This results in a further weakening of local control and management, and the outflow of cash to pay for such services.

Although tourism-induced development has disappointed some expectations, the fault often lies in the unrealistic nature of those expectations rather than with the industry itself. It should not be forgotten that the economies of peripheral regions are often structurally weak, so that any income or employment generated by development programs will result in leakage to surrounding areas, whether it is tourism related or not. The Tourism and Recreation Research Unit (1981) conducted a comparative analysis of income generation from various business sectors in Exmoor National Park. They found:

[The] tourist related industry is not intrinsically *weak* relative to other industries but merely reflects, as all industries do, the structure of the local economy. In fact, the income analysis suggests that many tourist-related industries perform markedly better than the other activities surveyed. (TRRU 1981, 245)

This can be seen in the sectoral comparison of gross or net income per unit of turnover (Table 14), where accommodation establishments prove to be relatively efficient ways of converting turnover into income. In fact, when the analysis is extended to include the immediate hinterland of Exmoor, the service sector and tourism-related manufacturing become more efficient generators of income from turnover than almost all other categories.

Another unrealistic expectation is that local institutions in less developed regions are capable of absorbing the developments proposed by outside agencies. Loukissas' (1982) examination of tourism development on Greek islands, for example, indicates that the scale and pace of projects can sometimes exceed local capacities to institute, and benefit from, them. This situation results in a dependency on outside suppliers and manpower, and causes undue friction where local support has been counted on. Loukissas argues, therefore, for more attention to be paid to

the local capacity to absorb development, the potential interaction between locals and tourists, and the integration of

Table 14 Income from selected industries in and around Exmoor National Park

Economic activity	National Park only				Extended Park area[5]
	Direct[1] A	Indirect[2] B	Induced[3] C	Total[4] D	Total E
	Income as a proportion of £1 of turnover				
Agriculture:					
Dairying	0.14	0.01	0.00	0.16	0.20
Livestock	0.24	0.01	0.01	0.26	0.30
Mixed farming	0.23	0.02	0.01	0.26	0.33
Manufacturing:					
Large scale	0.13	0.00	0.01	0.13	0.20
Tourism-related	0.34	0.01	0.02	0.37	0.40
Other	0.06	0.00	0.00	0.07	0.11
Contractor	0.35	0.02	0.02	0.38	0.42
Services:					
Hotel	0.19	0.02	0.01	0.22	0.36
Guest house	0.27	0.01	0.01	0.29	0.42
Bed & breakfast	0.66	0.00	0.03	0.70	0.81
Self-catering	0.29	0.01	0.01	0.32	0.43
Retail	0.11	0.01	0.01	0.13	0.22
Restaurant	0.19	0.01	0.01	0.21	0.37

Source: Tourism and Recreation Research Unit (1981, 244)

Notes: [1] Direct income is the wages, rent, and profit paid by the type of business specified. [2] Indirect income is the wages, rent, and profit paid by the suppliers of the businesses specified. [3] Induced income is the wages, rent, and profit paid by businesses as a result of the spending of income earned from the businesses specified and their suppliers. [4] The total (D) may not equal the sum of columns A–C due to rounding effects. [5] Includes income paid within the National Park boundary and adjacent areas within 15 miles of the Park boundary.

the tourism industry with the rest of the economy. (Loukissas 1982, 539)

While there may be some doubt as to the extent of regional economic gains through tourism development there is substantial evidence that tourist spending can help to maintain the viability of otherwise marginal enterprises and preserve ways of life that might otherwise disappear. Simply retaining existing employment, landscapes, and cultures may be as significant for peripheral regions as the creation of new jobs. Thus when tourism helps to supplement existing economic activities, or maintain local amenities, it is performing a supportive role in the local economy.

Cost considerations

One factor which has often been overlooked in assessments of tourism's economic return to host communities is the cost of developing local resources and catering to the visitors. Those costs include community costs such as infrastructure, crowding, and impacted services.

Since tourism often depends on an attraction which is a public good, a beach, scenery, or heritage, it is the public which must sustain many of the disadvantages and costs of the business. Visitors to a destination area will increase the costs of various public services by placing them under more pressure. An example of such costs is provided by Hawaii's 1968 estimate of the variable costs of selected public services associated with each day spent by a visitor (Table 15). In this case the cost per visitor-day was not very high, totaling an

extra 69c for the selected services. The highest individual burden for this island economy was the airport connection to the outside world, which cost an added 25c per visitor-day. The public costs were calculated by estimating the increased level of service and maintenance required to cater for the known volume of visitors, but no reference was made to the capital costs of building the airport or other infrastructure, nor to the social costs incurred as a result of the tourist influx.

Zehnder (1975) in his book *Florida's Disney World: Promises and Problems*, describes various social costs which developed in neighboring cities that could be directly attributed to Disney World, but which fell outside normal accounting procedures. He reports that the City of Orlando, Florida, was inundated by unskilled migrant workers, who came to the area seeking to build or work in Disney World. However, as often happens on such major projects, there were more candidates than openings and many found themselves destitute, without work or the means to travel home. Thus the Orlando Salvation Army, which prior to this period had found its 40-capacity lodge adequate, was forced into a community appeal for a Central Welfare and Transient Shelter costing $400,000. Furthermore, the City of Orlando itself found it necessary to hire 150 more policemen and build a new $6 million police station, to handle its spontaneous growth and the problems of prostitution, hippies, and vagrants that came with the development of Disney World. "In brief, Disney World brought social problems as well as economic benefits to the country's most publicized boom town" (Zehnder 1975, 247).

Table 15 Costs per visitor-day of public services rendered directly to visitors to Hawaii, 1968

Function	State and local general expenditure ($ millions)	Per capita annual costs	Costs per visitor-day
Highways	$38.8	$68.88	$0.189
Airports	7.4	–	0.249
Police protection	15.7	21.24	0.058
Fire protection	8.7	11.77	0.032
Sewerage	13.2	17.86	0.049
Natural resources	13.1	17.72	0.049
Local parks and recreation	16.6	22.45	0.062
Total variable cost per visitor-day			$0.688

Source: Lundberg (1976, 160)

Economics and business

As must be apparent from the above examples it is extremely difficult and time-consuming to develop a comprehensive account of tourism costs to local communities. The costs involved will run the gamut from "hard" infrastructure costs (production and maintenance of promenades, campsites, piers, and conference centers) to "soft" social costs (extra health, police, and community social services). An example of the detail and difficulties involved in assessing the net costs of tourism to a community has been provided by Heeley (1980).

Heeley examined tourism costs in the county of Norfolk, England. Norfolk is a rural county with a variety of attractions, including the Norfolk Broads (a system of lakes and rivers), the city of Norwich and a popular stretch of sandy coastline containing the resort of Great Yarmouth. Heeley examined those major components of public expenditure that could be affected by tourism

business. He examined, for example, the number of fire incidents attended by the Norfolk Fire Brigade and calculated the proportion which were tourism related. Using that proportionality he divided the county's fire service costs for 1975–6 by his tourism factor to derive an estimate of tourism's fire service cost (Table 16). Heeley combined the fire service cost with other local authority costs to develop an overall picture of tourism's contribution to the local authority "infrastructure expenditures" (Table 17). This table reveals that in 1975–6 tourism accounted for £2.7 million's worth ($US6 million) of local authority costs, or 2.2 percent of the county's total costs. These infrastructure costs were added to other local authority tourism-related expenses such as promotion, grants for festivals and theaters, and land-use planning to conserve and enhance the natural beauty of the area (Table 18). Adding these aspects of public expenditure to his infrastructure figures Heeley

Table 16 Heeley's calculation of Norfolk's Fire Brigade tourism costs, 1974–5

Fire incidents attended by Norfolk Fire Brigade, 1974–5

Classification	Fire incidents	
Hotel	17	
Guest houses	10	
Caravan/campsites	16	
Holiday camps	8	
Broadland hire craft	7	
Restaurants/cafés	8	
Public houses	6	
Shops and garages	5	
Sports facilities	1	
Entertainment centers	5	
Countryside recreation areas	9	
Total: tourist-related incidents	92	Tourism factor: $\dfrac{92}{4023} \times 100 = 2.3\%$
Total: business premises	230	
Total: private houses	1,472	
Grand total	4,023	

Local authority expenditure on Fire Services in Norfolk in 1975–6 and the cost of tourism

Employees	Premises	Supplies & services	Vehicles	Debt charges	Administration	Total	Tourism factor	Estimated tourism cost
£	£	£	£	£	£	£	%	£
1,988,016	124,168	18,904	57,104	305,440	102,920	2,767,552	2.3	63,654

Source: Heeley (1980, 526–7)

Table 17 Summary statement of net local authority infrastructure expenditure attributable to tourism in Norfolk, 1975–6

	Net costs														
Total	Per 1,000 population	Percentage of total net local authority expenditure	Local authority	Car parks	Roads	Traffic management	Public transport	Law & order	Fire	Water safety	Consumer trading	Public conveniences	Refuse collection	Public health inspection
£				£	£	£	£	£	£	£	£	£	£	£
£1,007	11.5	0.04	Breckland									500		507
£5,210	12.6	0.08	Broadland									3,100		1,157
£102,954	1,352.9	3.87	Gt Yarmouth	1,939			32,146			953		41,801	17,755	5,775
£64,728	812.1	3.29	N. Norfolk	2,674						3,538		16,893	37,411	6,811
£6,257	51.4	0.10	Norwich	6,201						939		50		6
£1,241	14.2	0.10	S. Norfolk									1,150		91
£60,086	522.0	1.61	W. Norfolk	8,503						212		14,279	35,298	1,794
£241,483	366.3	1.20%	Sub-total	19,317			32,146			5,642		77,773	90,464	16,141
			Norfolk County		1,593,354	16,150		788,949	63,654	426	12,882			
£2,475,415	3,754.6	2.30	Sub-total		1,593,354	16,150		788,949	63,654	426	12,882			
£2,716,898	4,120.9	2.20%	Grand total	19,317	1,593,354	16,150	32,146	788,949	63,654	6,068	12,882	77,773	90,464	16,141

Source: J. Heeley (1980, 560)

Table 18 Net cost of tourism to local authorities in Norfolk, 1975–6

Local authority	Net cost of tourism						
	Promotion and information services	Land use and conservation policy	Leisure and culture	Infrastructure	Total	Cost per 1000 population	Percentage of total local authority spending
	£	£	£	£		£	
Breckland		2,883		1,007	£3,890	44.5	0.10
Broadland		122		5,210	£5,332	58.0	0.25
Gt Yarmouth	56,535	2,706	184,273	102,954	£346,468	4,552.2	8.90
N. Norfolk	17,740	2,530	61,679	64,728	£146,677	1,840.4	5.20
Norwich	13,431	2,520		6,257	£22,208	182.3	0.24
S. Norfolk		204		1,241	£1,445	16.6	0.06
W. Norfolk	7,172	1,271	19,500	60,086	£88,029	133.5	1.77
Sub-total	94,878	12,236	265,452	241,483	£614,049	931.4	2.10%
County Council	9,785	1,484	8,696 (cr.)	2,475,415	£2,477,988		
Sub-total	9,785	1,484	8,696 (cr.)	2,475,415	£2,477,988	3,758.5	2.20
Grand total	£104,663	£13,720	£256,756	£2,716,898	£3,092,037	£4,689.9	2.20%

Source: J. Heeley (1980, 566)
cr. = credit

estimated that local authority costs of tourism equalled £3.1 million in 1975–6. This formed approximately 2 percent of total local authority expenditure, the proportion varying from a high of 9 percent in Great Yarmouth to a low of 0.1 percent in Breckland and South Norfolk. Approximately 88 percent of local authority spending on tourism went on infrastructural items, making this the local authority's major contribution to tourism. Heeley reports that tourism spending in the county was estimated to be £35 million ($US78 million) in 1975. When this is compared to the local authority costs of £3.1 million ($US6.9 million) it indicates that "against every £1 of tourist expenditure is a public authority cost of £0.09" (Heeley 1980, 567).

This favorable situation in Norfolk should be tempered by the fact that the analysis is incomplete, but even so it reveals some interesting discrepancies on the part of local tourism management. Heeley admits that his analysis is limited to the direct costs incurred in providing facilities and direct payments from tourists and tourist businesses. The indirect and induced earnings and costs still remain to be calculated, so it is not possible to be definite about the total tourist revenues and costs to local authorities. Despite this

limitation, the direct cost and revenue situation reveals an inconsistency on the part of local authorites:

On the one hand, the costs of supplying an adequate tourist infrastructure far outstrip those incurred on marketing, environmental planning, and leisure and cultural programmes, and *in toto* these functions appear to have an absolutely critical bearing on the prosperity of the local tourist industry. On the other hand, local government decision making in the infrastructural sphere rarely emphasizes forward or backward linkages with the tourism industry and no attempt is made to orchestrate—from a tourism point of view—this diverse set of functions. (Heeley 1980, 562)

Another point Heeley could have raised is that local people can and do use many of the tourist facilities, provided by both the public and the private sector. Under these conditions it is very difficult to calculate the exact costs and benefits of tourism to a community, via a trade-off model.

To formulate a more comprehensive and balanced decision regarding the merits of tourist development for local communities requires some form of cost–benefit analysis. Such an appraisal asks whether the community, as a whole, will be better off by undertaking a tourism project rather than not undertaking it, or by using the resources and capital in some alternative manner:

Broadly speaking, for the more precise concept of revenue to the private firm, the economist substitutes the less precise yet meaningful concept of *social benefit*. For the costs of the private firm, the economist substitutes the concept of *opportunity cost*—the social value foregone when the resources in question are moved away from alternative economic activities into the specific project. (Mishan 1972, 13)

The end of this approach is a cost–benefit ratio which compares the estimated costs and benefits of a potential project. To calculate the ratio for a tourism project would require a great deal of work and expense. The public costs of developing a tourism resource, and the opportunity costs of not developing this resource for some other purpose, would have to be assessed. Calculation of the benefits would require the development of a multiplier for tourist expenditures in the local economy. But such effort is worthwhile if the analysis forces communities to consider the potential long-term consequences of development and to realize that tourism consumes space, labor, and capital which may be better used elsewhere.

One of the few attempts to introduce a cost–benefit approach to tourism development illustrates the potential of this approach in clarifying trade-offs and exposing the actual benefits to the community at large. Bryden's "social cost–benefit approach" to hotel development in the Commonwealth Caribbean was an attempt to balance the multiplier picture of tourism development in that part of the world. He commented that:

the over-riding criticism of tourist multipliers and the use to which they have been put concerns the inference that they measure either the benefit or the potential benefit from the expansion of tourism to the economy as a whole over the longer run. The only circumstances in which this could be so are quite unreal, namely a zero opportunity cost for all the resources used directly and indirectly in tourism. (Bryden 1973, 77)

Bryden focused, therefore, on these opportunity costs, examining the central government expenditures on tourism promotion, the loss of revenue to dividends associated with foreign investment, and the shadow wage rate in the islands. His results were highly sensitive to the value of a shadow wage rate, which depended on the existence of alternative employment and consumption opportunities. Where no alternative use or employment was available the social return of hotel development was well above the minimal rate of interest on government funds (6–7 percent at that time), which was used as the dividing line between net benefit and loss. Where there were alternative and competing business opportunities the potential benefits of hotel development fell considerably. Overall, Bryden found that:

the present social rates of return from hotel development are sufficiently close to the "minimal" accounting rate of interest to suggest that net social benefits from tourism are rather small in the [Commonwealth] Caribbean. (Bryden 1973, 217)

In other words, when Bryden considered every island and attempted a more balanced evaluation of tourism's costs and benefits he found the returns were not much more than regular bank interest rates which, as we know, is a slow way to get ahead.

Bryden's social cost–benefit approach brings into focus an overall problem concerning the economic benefits of tourism. Do the "average benefits" derived from such analysis truly reflect general community conditions and show who benefits and who pays for the real cost of lost opportunities? The low social rate of return noted by Bryden is consistent with a new gain for a small group, usually developers and major facility operators, and a new loss for many in the process of change. A major problem for tourism management and planning at the community level is to determine who does benefit from its development.

The econometric techniques to measure and assess benefits are entering uncharted waters when they try to assign values to intangibles such as community pride, the value of amenities, and forsaken development opportunities. Furthermore, the emphasis on the firm or administration's investment return diminishes the role of the community and its direct stake in this industry. In an industry with a great reliance on public attractions and amenities, plus a dependence on the goodwill of local residents, the distribution of benefits needs to be more widespread and public than in the case of a traditional industry. The whole community can be viewed as shareholders and as such should participate in the dividends of public infrastructure investments and the use of public goods. Such an issue needs to be considered not only in conceptual terms but in relation to specific economic strategy.

7

Economic response strategies

To make tourism more profitable for both the industry and community requires a longer season. Businesses can develop better profit margins and more competitive prices if their committed capital investment is used over a longer period, communities can benefit from larger sales tax and longer employment periods. The focus of marketing and promotion strategies has concentrated on the shoulder seasons because the industry is in place, in the sense that establishments are open and staffed, and the weather often conducive to outdoor activities and sightseeing. If a viable winter attraction is available, such as skiing, this provides a secondary peak of activity, but a destination still requires promotion of the shoulder months if a truly four-season industry is to emerge.

To encourage out-of-season visits many destinations have developed and promoted special events or festivals during these times. Such attractions may be either traditional local festivities or artificially created events, designed specifically to lure visitors. Some have developed into national or even international events which are capable of generating mini-seasons of their own, such as Quebec's "Winter Carnival," New Orleans' "Mardi Gras," and Munich's "Oktoberfest." Even modest festivals or special events are capable of providing the necessary stimulus to travel in the off-season, providing substantial revenues to the destination community in the process. For example, Gartner and Holecek (1983) have estimated a 1980 Boat Show in Detroit had a total economic impact of $3.8 million, and, with the contribution of local residents entirely discounted, an impact of $2.5 million (Redman 1983).

The desire to stretch the season into periods of inclement weather has led to a demand for all-weather facilities and the public funds to build them. Paramount among these facilities are the convention–conference centers, but also involved are enclosed recreation centers, tennis bubbles, and protected pedestrian areas downtown. Because of its major financial and land-use implications, however, the convention option has become a political issue in many areas, and this will be examined in some detail below.

Convention market

Conventions would appear to be a natural complement to the summer peaks. There is a traditional demand for such events outside of the summer months and those involved are usually major spenders, making heavy use of hotel and restaurant facilities. Conventions and conferences have become a feature of modern life. Their growth and significance is tied to the growing importance of the quaternary sector in advanced economies. Quaternary activities correspond to the transaction of information performed by those in manufacturing, commerce, professional, administrative, and higher-level technical occupations who participate in data gathering and interpretation or decision making (Gottmann 1970). This sector of the economy has been expanding rapidly over the past 20 years in terms of numbers and influence, and since by definition their transactions involve an interchange of information and ideas, the need for meetings has increased.

Despite the economic upheaval and recessions of the 1970s, convention business boomed because face-to-face contact and up-to-date information became more important in a rapidly changing world. In 1978 *Time* magazine reported:

Table 19   Seasonal distribution of conventions

| Country | Number of conventions (date) | Jan.–Mar. | Quarterly distribution (%) | | |
			Apr.–June	July–Sept.	Oct.–Dec.
United Kingdom	12,900 (1971)	22	32	19	27
Australia	256 (1974)	11 (summer)	43	24	21

Source: Based on Cooper (1976, 15, 17).

The number of conventions has grown steadily over the past decade. This year 26 million citizens gathered in solemn or profane conclave and there spent an estimated $15 billion. That is double the amount they spent ten years ago, and twice as much as Americans allot for amusements and spectator sports. There are some 28,000 trade, professional and other voluntary associations in the US, and by year's end they will have met nearly 250,000 times. (*Time* December 18 1978, 36)

One small element of this market was Seattle, which received 572 conventions with over 330,000 delegates, who spent an estimated $65 million (Walker 1979). As a result of such business volumes, many major cities started to lobby for or construct convention centers. For example, several cities in Canada (including Vancouver, Victoria, Edmonton, Toronto, Montreal, Ottawa, and Halifax) applied to the federal government for its 25 percent of construction costs grant—a response so overwhelming that the federal government began to question the viability of so many centers. It is not alone in this regard. A *Globe and Mail* article has subsequently asked the question: "can they all (Canada's sixteen convention centers) generate enough revenue to survive?" (*Globe and Mail*, 1984, B1). It noted that the government undertook no analysis to determine market size before supporting various convention center proposals, and that the four centers in the Maritimes are in severe financial difficulty. Since this report appeared, one of these centers, in Charlottetown, has been placed in receivership (*Financial Post*, 1985).

A major justification put forward for this public investment is that it would extend the season and thus the economic benefits of tourism in those cities concerned. Since the bulk of conventions took place outside of the summer months (Table 19) there was every reason to expect convention center cities to draw more visitors in the off-season, thus making better use of existing capital investments and providing more year-round employment. However, as Walker (1979, 4)

points out in the case of Seattle, off-season demand cannot be guaranteed:

Even in Seattle, with all we have to see and do during the winter, we find it hard to sell Seattle as a convention destination. Winter belongs, for the most part, to the San Diegos and Honolulus and Acapulcos.

In October (1979) we had 35 conventions in Seattle, but the total for the next five months—November through March—will only be 37: nine in November, four in December, two in January, eight in February, and fourteen in March. (Walker 1979, 4)

Furthermore, the employment prospects associated with convention center development is also more limited than often thought. Full-time employment in such centers is limited to a few permanent administration and maintenance positions, while the majority of employees will be temporary support staff, hired for specific convention or conference needs. The employment impact on surrounding hotels and restaurants is likely to be similar, with most establishments hiring extra staff only sporadically to meet the demands of actual conventions. In fact the convention business can create a problem for the hotel industry, for it encourages weekday business but "there is no corresponding growth in weekend travel" as the delegates return home (Burt and MacKinnon 1977, 142). Thus hotels must find alternative markets for the off-season weekends, which is why many offer weekend package deals to the public.

Another concern for communities viewing convention centers as a way of extending their season is what type and size of center to build. The convention market contains a wide range of demands. The largest meetings are annual association meetings which are held on an international and national scale and can attract over 1000 delegates, plus their families. Conventions of such magnitude, however, are small in number and are courted by most major world cities. In the United States convention market of 1973, only 18 percent attracted more than 1000 delegates, whereas 58 percent drew less than 400 delegates (Cooper 1976, 11). To benefit from the high per diem expenditures associated with convention delegates, the status and publicity associated with such high-level gatherings, and possible follow-up visits by family and friends of favorably impressed delegates, many world cities have invested in major convention facilities.

To provide the facilities required and compete in an international market such cities need to meet some stringent location and site requirements. The prime locational consideration is that a destination be a "gateway city," with major airline connections to the chief delegate-generating areas around the world. "Delegates' unwillingness to incur domestic air transport costs after an international flight" (Cooper 1976, 70) necessitates that facilities be within easy reach of the gateway airport. Consequently:

In the UK, the Heathrow airport area (with a concentration of over 4,000 hotel bedrooms and aggregate meeting facilities for 6,500) has developed a substantial conference business and this trend is also evident around Gatwick [London's charter flight gateway]. Chicago, with the world's busiest airport, is also a major destination for conventions and trade exhibitions, hosting some 16,800 events in 1979 with a total attendance of nearly 8 million. (Lawson 1980, 185)

Within the city, site considerations include the availability of a large building site sufficient for the main building, possible support buildings, delivery and service area, parking, promenades, and a formal entrance. This usually requires a half or full city block. Second, the site should be central and accessible to quality accommodation and major inter-city transportation terminals—such terminals being required for domestic delegates, in the main. Third, the site should be close to major shopping and entertainment districts, the prime locations being the downtown area or major regional shopping centers. Fourth, parking space adjacent or close by is necessary because even with national and international conferences there will be local and regional delegates who travel by car and some long-distance delegates who have chosen to travel by car. Finally, proximity to recreation facilities and attractive surroundings is becoming more important, as delegates seek to maintain their exercise–entertainment regimes and cities wish to encourage sightseeing and spending within the community at large.

The costs of providing such a convention center are enormous. The anticipated 1980 costs for Ottawa's convention center and associated shopping–office complex were $US30 million, and for Vancouver's Pacific Trade and Convention Center, $US43 million. The largest cost to the destination community is the initial capital investment in the site, building, and associated parking facilities. On top of that there are the operating costs of energy used to heat or cool the buildings, plus the labor costs of the marketing and maintenance personnel. To these fixed costs must be added the variable costs associated with the actual conventions which use the facility. A convention necessitates the hiring of temporary staff and the extra public expenditures required to support and protect a visitor. The salaries of part-time staff are minor because of the low salaries paid for unskilled work; the increased use of public goods and services, however, can develop into a considerable cost factor.

A common observation of convention business is that it attracts the largest per diem spenders among all travelers, for it seems that subsidized travel and tax rebates open up the pocket books, to the benefit of major hotels and high-class restaurants. However, a survey of public services consumed by tourists in San Diego revealed "conventioneers used more services than any other activity [visitor] group, largely because they almost exclusively benefit from expenditures for the convention center and the Convention and Visitors Bureau" (Tatzin 1978, 58). Such services as major promotions to lure the convention organizers and their delegates require major expenditures in advertising and marketing personnel, on the part of the host community. Therefore, despite having the highest per capita daily expenditure pattern, convention visitors came well down the list in San Diego when a ratio of revenue to costs was compiled for the community as a whole (Table 20).

Communities do not have to enter the upper end of the convention market in order to participate in this form of season extension. The lower end of the market involves the most numerous type of conference—the corporate meeting of 30 to 100 people. These include regional sales meetings, management conferences, training seminars, and corporate participation in trade exhibitions. "Corporate meetings of various types exceed association meetings [in the United States] by a factor of between five and ten to one" (Cooper 1976, 9). Such small but frequent meetings provide a valuable

Table 20   Revenue–expenditure ratios for non-resident tourists to San Diego, California

Activity	Accommodation used	Ratio
Business	Hotel/motel	4.55
Saltwater fishing	Rental cottage	3.45
Sightseeing	Hotel/motel	3.36
Spectator sports	Hotel/motel	3.36
Sightseeing	Rental cottage	2.80
Sightseeing	Campground	2.58
Spectator sports	Rental cottage	2.50
Sightseeing	Friend/relative	2.14
Business	Day trip	2.07
Convention	Hotel/motel	1.74
Spectator sports	Day trip	1.66
Saltwater boating	Friend/relative	1.58
Saltwater fishing	Friend/relative	1.41
Sightseeing	Day trip	1.22
Spectator sports	Campground	1.00
Convention	Day trip	0.29
Saltwater boating	Day trip	0.23

Source: Arthur D. Little (1974) "Tourism in San Diego: its economic, fiscal, and environmental impacts," as quoted by D. L. Tatzin (1978, 59).

and reliable local and regional market for convention business. An analysis of San Francisco's 1970 convention business reveals that 59 percent resulted from local and regional meetings. Large urban centers can expect this type and level of business because of their position in the central place hierarchy, and only modest preparations would be necessary to facilitate the needs of this convention market. Furthermore, most of the local and regional corporate meetings can be accommodated within existing hotel and auditorium facilities.

Any community considering investing in convention centers must assess its relative appeal in a crowded and competitive market (Safavi 1971) and decide what type of convention business (large-scale associations or small corporate meetings) is more appropriate for its particular situation. The costs of this option rise dramatically when a public facility is proposed, and most public centers are unlikely to cover their operating costs. Cooper, in his review of the convention industry, was forced to concede "a centre is unlikely to make a profit or indeed cover its capital costs" (Cooper 1976, 43); while Tideman's cost–benefit analysis of congress (convention) tourism concludes:

it is clear the constant costs are the bottleneck of a congress building and of congressism in general. They cause a permanent loss for each congress building, if all the costs of investment are calculated in a correct way. Holland's most favourable congress centre (the RAI building in our capital) loses about one million dollars a year. . . . the "Netherlands Congress Building" in the Hague, built in the cheap years of the 1960s, has an accumulated loss in its fourteen years of operation of 35 million dollars. (Tideman 1982, 24)

Annual operating deficits have certainly been experienced in Canada, with Hamilton's convention center reporting a loss of $270,000 in 1983 and St John a deficit of $450,000 in 1984. Such results led the *Globe and Mail* to state "operating deficits are considered par for the course in the convention industry" (*Globe and Mail*, 1984, B1).

Despite such evidence, some still champion convention centers as catalysts to a healthier tax base and additional community assets (Burt and MacKinnon 1977; Walker 1979). The basis of such argument is that much of the generated convention revenue is underestimated because it is in the form of indirect expenditures in local hotels, restaurants, and gift shops. However, such revenue does contribute to the viability of those enterprises and enables them to pay taxes and employ staff. In addition, it is claimed that centers can be developed into multiple-use facilities, incorporating cultural and educational activities as well as conventions, thereby contributing to community amenities like a park.

The future development of convention centers may depend on the feasibility of multi-purpose options as a means of spreading the operating and capital costs of a facility. One strategy has been to incorporate trade or exhibition halls into a convention center because this

Economics and business

brings together the sales representatives and those responsible for purchasing decisions. Examples would be publisher displays for academic meetings, or equipment and drug displays for medical meetings. This addition of a sales dimension into the exchange of information enables an ever-increasing proportion of the costs to be borne by those companies renting sales space. The process goes full circle when the exhibition halls are used for a trade fair, for in this case the support industries pay the full rental and invite potential customers to peruse their wares and latest innovations. Another form of multi-purpose use is to design and operate the center as a community cultural and recreation facility. This has been done at the new Barbican Centre in the City of London, which includes three cinemas, a library, art gallery, theater, restaurant, and other daily amenities along with its convention and trade hall facilities.

Whether innovations of these kinds can make convention centers economically viable, or broaden their usage sufficiently to make financial subsidy acceptable, remains to be seen. Each case will need to be assessed on its own merits and will require more accurate means by which to measure the benefits and costs before an educated decision can be made. Whatever a community decides, it is clear that any attempt to extend the season via the convention business will not be without risk.

Farm tourism

Up to this point the strategy discussion has been most relevant to urban destinations, but there have been other efforts which are more relevant to rural and isolated areas. As was noted, the success of major development programs based on tourism has been mixed. However, when the scale of development has been better matched with local resource and institutional capacity, along the lines suggested by Loukissas (1982), tourism has been more successful in supplementing local incomes. Nowhere is this more evident than in the growth of farm tourism in certain marginal farming regions. In his summary of the Marienhamn, Finland, Symposium on Agriculture and Tourism, Dernoi reports:

Farm tourism, with all the ancillary and secondary revenue it generates, may represent a considerable percentage in the rural family's income or even assure survival of their home environment. Data taken from the conference papers shows that . . . a farmer can get an extra income of 5–15% from tourism. (Dernoi 1983, 160)

Farm tourism refers to working farms that supplement their primary function with some form of tourism business. The tourism involvement can take many forms. The most common and successful is the provision of accommodation, which can vary from small-scale operations (renting a spare room) to large-scale investments in renovating and modernizing separate farm buildings into vacation flats and cottages. Other forms of farm tourism include camping facilities, restaurants, and the sale of farm products. In Britain, farms with rivers flowing through them can obtain additional revenue by selling fishing rights to local angling clubs or hotels. In the United States, most of the "vacation farms" responding to Pizam and Pokela's (1980) national survey were engaged in some form of

Table 21   Percentage of farms offering tourist accommodation, 1979–81 (estimates)

Country	Percentage	Notes
Austria	9.8	Tyrol: 28%
		Vorarlberg: 15%
		Salzburg: 20%
England and Wales	8.0	including occasional tourism
Finland	1.3	Aland: 32%
France	3.0	
Federal Republic of Germany	4.0	
Ireland	0.2	
Norway	2.9	in some municipalities up to 40%
Spain	0.4	
Sweden	20.0	
Scotland	5.8	Highlands and Islands: up to 16%

Source: Dernoi (1983, 159).

animal husbandry. For the majority of tourists these farm vacations are synonymous with the desire for a peaceful country vacation at a reasonable price, with the farm experience being a secondary concern, so there is little direct involvement with farm operations.

Farm tourism is well established in Europe but is a relatively new phenomenon in North America. Table 21 indicates the extent of farm tourism in western Europe. Austria "can claim the highest popularity for farm tourism. According to the Agricultural Census of 1970: '26,300 out of a total of 362,000 Austrian farms let approximately 230,000 beds in about 114,000 guest rooms'" (Dernoi 1983), with much of this concentrated in the mountainous western Lander. France has an advanced national farm tourism policy, operated by the Ministry of Agriculture since 1954:

[It] introduced the *gîtes rureaux privés* by providing financial aid to farmers who wanted to use redundant farmhouses and buildings as accommodation for holiday-makers. The gîte formula, originally based upon self-catering accommodation, has now extended to five different types of facilities. . . . Overall, facilities have grown from 145 gîtes in 6 départements in 1954–5 to 28,000 gîtes in over 4,000 villages in 90 départements by 1980. (Frater 1983, 170)

In North America farm tourism is a more recent and limited phenomenon. Pizam and Pokela's attempt to construct a national sampling frame in 1977 could only identify 419 vacation farms, but since their sources were a national guidebook and state tourism agencies it is likely to be an underestimate, because many of the smaller operations rely on "word of mouth" references. In Canada the scale of farm tourism is small, but growing—especially in the Prairie provinces, Ontario and Quebec.

The location of farm tourism appears to be influenced by three factors: the level of income provided by farming, the presence of tourism resources; and the accessibility to major tourist-generating regions. Many farmers have undertaken tourism-related endeavors because of the need to supplement family incomes, and the greatest need occurs in areas where farming is a marginal economic activity. Thus farm tourism is strong in peripheral upland regions, particularly where tourism resources occur (Wales Tourist Board 1974). Opportunities to ride, fish, hunt, and hike make many upland areas attractive locations for the outdoor-recreation tourist and provide nearby farms with sufficient clientele to make some form of tourism

investment or commitment viable. The most favored location in peripheral areas of marginal farming are those with good connections to major cities. Witness the impact of the M6 motorway on England's Lake District (Robinson 1976, 47), the importance of touring caravans to tourism in the Scottish Highlands (Tourism and Recreation Research Unit 1972), and the concentration of United States vacation farms in the northeastern states (Pizam and Pokela 1980). In some cases access becomes the dominant factor, as not all urbanites seeking outdoor recreation relish or can afford long-distance travel. Some farm tourism, therefore, can also be detected close to major urban centers, with an emphasis on day-visitor activities rather than accommodation (Dartington Amenity Research Trust 1974; Murphy 1979).

The main attraction of farm tourism is that it brings tourist revenue into rural areas with minimal investment required from the farmer. It represents a symbiotic relationship between agriculture and tourism, for in marginal farming areas neither are economically viable in and of themselves, but together they can produce a profitable combination. The activity consists largely of small-scale operations, such as bed and breakfast or the roadside sale of produce, so it generally utilizes surplus capacity and labor. A proportion of this activity and its revenue generation goes unreported, but a study of farm tourism in England and Wales (Dartington Amenity Research Trust 1974) developed an estimate that between 10,000 and 15,000 farms were involved in 1974, generating a revenue of between £40 and £50 million ($US94–$117 million). This pales into insignificance, however, when compared to Austria's estimated revenue of $US1.4 billion (Frater 1983, 171).

Farm tourism's contribution to peripheral areas is not restricted to economic considerations alone for it has two other advantages for rural communities in these areas. This form of supplementary income helps to sustain farming in marginal upland areas and, in the process, perpetuates both an activity and a landscape. Visitors have a landscape image that is frequently dependent on traditional farming practices, and should that farming disappear the landscape would soon revert to scrub and bush that may not be so aesthetically pleasing.

One attempt to foster the symbiotic relationship between upland farmers and visitors in preserving a landscape is the Upland Management Experiment in England's Lake District. Attempts were made to reconcile the interests of farmers and visitors by providing financial assistance to farmers to carry out small improvements to the landscape and recreational opportunities in their area. The majority of funds were spent on developing footpaths for hikers, but other projects included rebuilding stone walls and tree planting (Countryside Commission 1976). With these small-scale projects, using local labor, it was possible to help the farmers protect their land and flocks with better walls and clearly marked paths, and the improvements enabled more visitors to enjoy the cross-country walking which is a major feature of a Lake District holiday.

Farm tourism has a further advantage in that it can be viewed as a unifying social force. Within farming families the tourism business often broadens the horizons and opportunities for the farmer's wife:

But for the farmer's wife's interest and determination, few tourism enterprises would exist. To some women, the "social" benefits of meeting a variety of people outweighed the "economic" benefits. (Frater 1983, 168)

Outside of the family, the meeting of urban and rural people has been seen as an opportunity to foster the exchange of views and promote better understanding between these two groups. Such an interaction occurs either formally through organized summer camp programs (particularly for city children) or informally through the individual wanderings and contacts of visitors. The Province of Quebec, for example, is committed to maintaining and fostering its cultural identity within a continent that has adopted the English language and many Anglo-Saxon customs. Part of its policy, therefore, is to make Quebecois aware of their heritage and familiar with their province. In this regard it introduced the "Fédération des Agricotours du Quebec" in 1976, which provided farm vacation programs throughout the province. By 1980 it was handling 4000 families with a total of 19,000 overnight farm visits (Moulin 1983).

Second homes

Second homes are distinct from farm tourism in that these accommodation units are separate from the commercial farming activity of rural areas. They are privately owned dwellings that provide self-catering vacations for their owners, and in the process bring visitors and income to the host community. The variety of physical forms and functions for second homes makes it difficult to develop a concise definition for this form of tourism. In a recent book devoted to the subject (Coppock 1977a) there are ten separate attempts to define second homes, due to its multi-dimensional character. The text illustrates some of the principal elements involved in the "second home" market, a description that statisticians and academics prefer to the popular terms of "summer cottage," "condominium," "holiday flat," and "chalet." It indicates that second homes not only take on a wide variety of forms, but that the motive for owning one often extends beyond vacation plans, and as a result the functions of these buildings may change over time. For example, a holiday home may become a retirement home, and it is the owner who decides when a property changes status from second to first home. To complicate matters further there is a wide variety of ownership possibilities in today's real estate market. Some properties may be owned outright and others shared, either by partnerships or among time-sharers.

One definition that has received relatively widespread acceptance, because of its general encompassing nature, is that of Downing and Dower (1973, 2). They viewed a second home as "a property owned or rented on a long lease as the occasional residence of a household that usually lives elsewhere." Such a definition eliminates touring caravans and trailers, boats, properties on short tenancy such as time-shares, and properties in major cities, especially within the rural–urban fringe. What it focuses on are those second homes which are either built properties, such as houses, cottages, chalets, or flats, or static mobile homes, such as caravans and trailers. These second homes are located either in the countryside or in historic and resort towns, but in both cases they are sufficiently distant from the owner's first home to qualify as tourism spending and activity.

Although there has been some uncertainty over the definition of second homes there is no such uncertainty concerning the rise and growing importance of this form of tourism. The largest number are found in North America, where the United States total for 1970 was estimated to be three million, with most located in the northeast (Ragatz 1977). In Canada there are approximately 500,000 second homes, with some three-quarters of the total located in the provinces of Ontario and Quebec (Baker 1973). Residents of North America are also the major owners of second homes in the Caribbean (Henshall 1977) and Hawaii (Farrell 1982). Following North America comes western Europe where France is reputed to have the largest number, with 1.5 million in 1968 (Clout 1977), followed by Sweden with 490,000 (Bielckus 1977) and Britain with nearly 250,000 (Rogers 1977). When one considers the proportion of households owning second homes the pattern changes dramatically, with Europe having the foremost ownership rate. In Sweden 22 percent of all households owned a second home, in Spain 17 percent, and France 16 percent (Clout 1977). In North America the comparable figures were 7 percent for Canada (Environment Canada 1979) and 5 percent for the United States (Ragatz 1970).

Upland regions with attractive scenery have been identified as a type of location sought by second-home owners (Clout 1977), and particularly popular are those within a 100–200 mile driving range of the owner's principal residence (Ragatz 1977; Downing and Dower 1973). Regions like the Peak District and North Wales in Britain, Vermont and New Hampshire in the United States, and the Canadian Shield area of Ontario and Quebec, are major magnets for this type of activity. Visits to these areas include weekends as well as holidays, with usage figures of 90 days or more being uncommon. More distant locations appeal to those seeking longer breaks from city life or work routine, and to those wishing to engage in particular recreation activities. Devon and Cornwall appeal to those wanting more reliable summer weather and a wide range of summer activities. The Scottish Highlands appeal to those interested in hunting and fishing, and in the developing ski facilities. The mild climate of British Columbia's west coast offers refuge from harsh prairie winters. Therefore, it is not unusual for Vancouver Island to play host to many prairie farmers over the winter months while their farms are caught in the grip of a Canadian winter.

Certain economic characteristics of the second-home market can make it an attractive proposition for peripheral regions. First, second homes represent a direct flow of revenue from the industrial–urban centers, providing important basic revenue for those selected regions. In addition to the initial purchase the second-home owner will be responsible for local property taxes. In some instances, notably education, their contribution will vastly exceed their use of services. Second, the revenue is widely dispersed throughout destination communities because of the numerous individual purchases of goods and services made by second-home owners. Third, the expenditure is more dependable than many other forms of tourism revenue, because of the second-home owner's commitment to the area and willingness to return year after year. This makes second-home revenue "less fickle than other types of tourism" (Henshall 1977, 76) and does not require heavy expenditure on promotion and marketing—as was the case with convention delegates.

These economic advantages can translate into considerable revenues for peripheral regions, especially for the individual rural villages and towns selected. A survey of second-home development in southwest England estimated "that the final income generated by second-home owners in the South West amounts to about £5.1 million ($US12.8 million), but noted that the major impact was confined to the local level rather than the regional economy (South West Economic Planning Council 1975, 21). In the popular second-home area of Gwynedd (North Wales) the economic benefit was more substantial, because of a smaller population base and less diversified economy. In 1974 the direct expenditure in this county was £2.4 million ($US5.6 million), and the multiplier of 0.32 compared favorably with other enterprises in the area like engineering, textiles, and wholesalers (de Vane 1975, 52).

In addition to economic advantages there are social advantages of promoting second-home ownership. The most notable is the renovation and rehabilitation of vacant or even derelict buildings, which have been left behind by the steady out-migration from rural areas. Second-home owners are more likely to empathize with the local way of life than many other types of tourist. They have selected an area as well as a home and, as we have noted, they often do so with the long-term intention of converting the dwelling into their retirement home and principal residence. Many have links with their second-home region through work, relatives, and previous residence (Downing and Dower 1973). Many are "concerned with the environmental advantages of the seaside compared with the cities . . . a better climate, cleaner air, the sea and better health" (Karn 1977, 242). Thus they form a major conservation force, not just for buildings but for the community's environment and way of life.

The development of second homes within a community represents change, and as usual there will be costs associated with this change. The foremost danger to a destination area is that its supply of suitable properties and housing will not keep pace with the demand for second homes. The most favorable situation occurs when the outsiders purchase vacant or surplus land and accommodation. Once such surplus has been used up the price of land and houses can rise dramatically, and the local rural population probably will not be able to compete with affluent outsiders in the resulting real estate market. The rise in housing prices in Victoria on Vancouver Island during the late 1970s was attributable in part to the large number of Albertans purchasing second homes, using their increased income and equity from the enlarged oil revenues of that province. The popularity of second homes in North Wales has gone beyond raising real estate prices toward one of market and community dominance. According to Dafydd Williams, General Secretary of the Welsh National Party, Plaid Cymru:

Second homes were no longer confined to isolated dwellings without electricity or water; there were now whole villages given over to them. Among the areas of the former rural district councils (RDCs) second homes represented 31.5 per cent of all homes in Teifiside RDC, 20 per cent in Llyn RDC and 15.1 per cent in Cenmaes RDC, and in individual villages the proportion was even higher. (Coppock 1977a, 200)

Additional real estate problems could arise for the host community if second-home ownership started to deplete the local housing stock and removed much of it from their market. Renovations and redesign of properties for a second-home situation could make the housing stock more appropriate to distant and more affluent tastes, thereby effectively removing a section of the housing stock. A market orientation to distant urban centers can lead to outside advertising only, so that locals can only look on as properties change hands via national or outside real estate agencies, leaving the local community with little or no cash injection after the initial purchase.

Such changes in the real estate market can lead to cultural and social problems. The second-home owner is an outsider, and even if he does possess some previous links to the region, he has been exposed to other ideas, priorities and a city life. In North Wales:

The expansion of second homes was not only [considered] socially unjust; it was also a serious threat to the Welsh language and to the sense of national identity which that language helped to maintain. . . . Those buying second homes came from a dominant culture which had all the advantages of

mass communication, and this and English education were sufficient to bring about a shift in the linguistic balance in the very strongholds of the Welsh language. (Coppock 1977a, 201)

In Canada, where many second-home owners are from the United States, the main concerns have been national pride and the loss of development control. The Americans were often the first to realize the recreational potential of many isolated areas, and being the first they naturally selected the best areas, such as waterfront or view lots. "The spectre of foreigners buying up the best recreational and agricultural land leaving only a limited amount available for Canadian ownership, is worrying Canadians in all provinces" (Cutler 1975, 19). Although there is plenty of land still available, the real irritation is that United States residents and other non-local buyers have a disproportionate share of the better recreational land because of their pioneering efforts and higher bids. Cutler considers:

The question that must be asked now is whether we have arrived at the point at which this friendly invasion should be allowed to continue without restraint. (Cutler 1975, 21)

Most provincial governments feel the time has come for some stronger lease control over Crown or government-controlled land, which constitutes most of Canada's territory, but they have been wary of interfering with private land sales.

Another area of concern with regard to the social consequences of second homes is in the area of conservation. The desire of second-home owners to maintain the type of environment and quality of life they perceive as being desirable can run counter to the wishes and interests of the local community, especially the young. There is a fine line between conserving a way of life and stifling its development opportunities. While such opportunities are scarce in peripheral areas they are not unknown. It is possible for conflict to arise between supporters of the status quo, including second-home owners and recently retired immigrants, and the younger indigenous population who wish to capitalize on new development and employment opportunities. The author is not aware of any documented cases of such conflict, but has witnessed or heard of several instances where the potential exists. For example, a Cornish farmer complained about his local rural council being "taken over" by the bankers and lawyers who had retired to his district. These professional people had both the time and inclination to

Figure 26   Aesthetic despoliation of coastal areas by uncontrolled trailer camps

Economics and business

Table 22 Percentage distribution of recreational subdivisions of 1000 acres or more

State	Percentage
Florida	24.1
Texas	12.9
California	11.6
Arizona	6.6
New Mexico	5.8
Pennsylvania	3.8
Colorado	3.6
North Carolina	3.1
Missouri	3.0
Arkansas	2.2
Remainder of the United States	23.3

Source: Data compiled from OILSR files, HUD, 1981, as quoted by Stroud (1983, 305).

run for office and as a result were in a position to decide on local issues and priorities in the farming community. In the discussion of Professor Cribier's (1983) paper on retirement to French coastal resorts she described the activity as "middle-class hedonism," where Parisians remained unaware of, or unconcerned about, local employment conditions and problems.

Most of the preceding discussion has referred to housing conversions and renovations within towns or villages, but in many areas the prime type of second homes are static trailers or caravans and purpose-built structures in a rural setting. These developments create environmental concerns, especially when the infra-structure and planning is inadequate to accommodate them. Questions of siting and density of development are particularly germane to waterfront areas, where a good site for the individual home owner may ruin the view of many others, and where the magnetism of a favored location may result in development densities which exceed its carrying capacity, resulting in soil erosion and run-off problems. Figure 26 illustrates the type of aesthetic despoliation which occurred in Britain, before stricter controls on coastal land use were imposed. In North America where the wilderness calls, but lakes beckon, the resulting strip development along lakefronts has often upset the natural balance of surrounding areas (Priddle and Kreutzwiser 1977). The removal of reeds and grasses to increase access for swimmers and boaters has increased erosion and reduced bird and fish populations. The poor design or inappropriate location of septic tanks has resulted in spoiled groundwater and polluted lakes; and some

accessible lakes have become so popular that they are completely ringed by second homes, as is the case with Lake St Joseph in southern Ontario and Shawnigan Lake in British Columbia.

In the United States the demand for second homes exceeds the supply of existing or vacant properties so real estate developers have created recreational subdivisions to meet this excess. These consist of land areas "divided into at least 25 lots for the purpose of sale as part of a common interstate promotional plan" (Stroud 1983, 303). Most of the large recreational subdivisions are found in the sun-belt states, but others are located in scenic areas of the Rocky and Appalachian Mountains (Table 22).

These recreational subdivisions have the same locational trends as the second-home market they are designed to serve, except for one significant exception. They seek inexpensive land, accessibility to the freeway system and proximity to major urban centers, but "the absence of governmental regulations may be the single most important determinant in site selection" according to Stroud (1983, 307). This translates into recreation subdivisions seeking scenic and accessible land within *rural counties* where land is not subject to strict development controls. The result has often been environmentally disastrous.

Too often recreation subdivisions have been con-structed in sensitive ecological areas in peripheral regions, where a lack of government legislation allowed the short-term revenue interests of a developer to supersede long-term environmental and economic considerations. Stroud provides the example of the Rio

Rancho Estates, occupying 91,000 acres of semiarid, rolling cattle range 11.5 miles northwest of Albuquerque, New Mexico, where

The physical layout of the development took no cognizance of the natural terrain as developers superimposed pre-determined grid road patterns over rolling hills and branching arroyos. Roads were bladed everywhere whether they were to be used or not [in the immediate future]. Sandstorms and gullying have resulted. Septic tanks and wells are used on individual lots except for a small core area; the tanks may degrade groundwater quality and individual wells may lower the water table in this water-short region. (Stroud 1983, 311)

In the wetlands of Florida's southwest coast is the Deltona Corporation's Marco Beach, which is a 19,500 acre recreation subdivision where

A grid pattern is used within the network of finger canals. Even though dredge-and-fill permits have been blocked, thousands of acres of valuable wetlands have already been destroyed. Clustering of development has not been employed and storm buffers and shoreline stabilizers including dunes, beaches and barrier islands have been used for development. The result has been severe beach erosion. (Stroud 1983, 311)

If a rural community in a peripheral region is to benefit from second-home development it must strive for balance. There is a need to develop strategies which satisfy the aspirations of potential second-home owners and the needs of local communities. Coppock (1977a, 213) outlines two potential solutions.

The first is to concentrate second homes in holiday villages. These can take the form of small-scale subdivisions, augmenting existing settlements, or they could be planned retirement communities. In either case, such concentrations of development would protect the environment by providing proper and adequate infrastructure, particularly sewage and waste disposal and water supply, and would probably save land. It permits the construction of recreational facilities that local communities could not afford or justify on their own. However, the United States experience with recreational subdivisions suggests that such solutions require careful and skilled planning if the right social, economic, and ecological balance is to be achieved.

Coppock's second solution is to provide only accommodation for short lets, or to grant ownership permits only on the condition that a property should be let to others, when not required. The first option would keep ownership in local hands and, in effect, create a supply of self-catering rental units. The second option would provide more traditional second homes, but with greater occupancy levels and more revenue generation for the local community. But if the symbol of ownership and a place of one's own is so important will prospective owners accept such conditions?

To help determine which strategy is most appropriate for a community will require information concerning the supply and demand characteristics of the second-home market in its region. It is a complex and emotional issue in rural areas and only some of the major elements have been discussed here. The clearest need is some form of national recreational survey which can identify those areas which are vulnerable or inappropriate for second-home development. Such an approach is already underway in Denmark and Sweden (Lundgren 1980).

Summary

Successful economic strategies for destination communities will require consideration of exogenous forces, community benefits and development scale in addition to the more direct concerns of resource availability and market opportunities. A community should never forget it is entering a competitive international market which leaves it susceptible to outside economic and natural forces. Since it often sells public goods there is a greater need than normal to demonstrate either direct economic benefits or indirect revenue and amenity impacts. Furthermore, given the evolutionary nature of destination development and its link with the tourist market each community should realize there comes a point at which local capacities can be exceeded and tourist products jaded. Finally, the increasing cost of development increasingly dictates that communities search for more multi-purpose approaches to facility investment and pursue small-scale incremental growth that can match local resources and institutional capacities, thereby minimizing leakage and the loss of local control.

Section 4

Society and culture

Tourism is a socio-cultural event for the traveler and the host. Part of travel's attraction is the opportunity to see different areas of the world and observe "foreign" cultures and ways of life. International travel brings the residents of urban–industrial societies to less developed nations and cultures. The contrast between resident and visitor under these circumstances can be startling, due to differences in language, cultural values, economic development, and politics. Such contrasts can also occur with domestic tourism, however, as urbanites pour into their coastal and rural hinterlands in search of recreation and relaxation. This domestic travel brings people of different backgrounds and lifestyles together, and can lead to conflict concerning land use and economic priorities in the destination areas.

The relationships between hosts and guests in destination areas can be characterized by four major features according to a UNESCO study (1976). First, they involve transitory relationships. Visitors are only in a community for a short period, so any interaction between hosts and guests has little chance to progress beyond casual and superficial levels. Second, there are temporal and spatial constraints to visitor–host inter-action. Visits are usually seasonal and non-repeated events, so the hospitality business often becomes exploitative to take advantage of this situation. Tourism facilities and services are frequently concentrated in a few locations, due to the locational pull of outstanding attractions and the destination community's desire to minimize the disruption of other activities. Third, with the development of mass tourism visitor–resident meetings lack the spontaneity associated with indi-vidual schedules. Most contacts are now arranged via package tours, planned attractions, or even "arranged"

meetings. Such meetings are controlled events and often become commercial arrangements. Fourth, when visitors and residents meet it is generally an unequal and unbalanced experience. Residents often feel inferior when they compare their situation to a visitor's apparent wealth, and can become resentful at the contrast. Furthermore, the visitor is on holiday and enjoying novel experiences while for the resident such events and meetings have become routine, and represent work not fun.

These characteristics have been examined by sociologists and anthropologists in their investigations into the effects of tourism on the social relations between hosts and guests, and on the cultural integrity of destination communities. The social impacts involve the more immediate changes in quality of life and adjustment to the industry in destination communities. The cultural impacts focus on the longer-term changes in a society's norms and standards, which will gradually emerge in a community's social relationships and artifacts. There is some doubt as to whether tourism is a cause or symptom of change in this rapidly evolving world. Cohen, for one, has challenged the popular notion that tourists are a major factor of socio-cultural change, or that their impact is necessarily a negative transformation of destinations:

This view prevails particularly in the areas from which tourists originate, where people are aware of tourism, but not of other factors of change in popular destination areas; it is often not shared by the people of the area itself, whose attitudes to the consequences of tourism are left unexamined. (Cohen 1979b, 28)

The values and attitudes of researchers and tourists from the industrial and affluent tourist-generating countries are often different from those of the residents

117

in less developed and less affluent societies. Consequently, a discrepancy can develop between their
evaluations of tourism's impact and those of the host
population.

Since the purpose of this book is to examine tourism
development issues and planning options in industrial
nations it focuses on the issues and strategies emerging
in the domestic tourism of those parts of the world. Close
attention will be given to the problems and views of
residents as well as the industry, since the principles of
participatory democracy in the west make it mandatory
to examine the issues raised by social and anthropological research from a community perspective.

An industry claiming to be in the "hospitality"
business can find its product planning and marketing
strategies laid to waste through bad service and a
hostile reception from local residents. It is crucial to the
tourism industry's long-term survival, therefore, to
develop a better understanding of its local image, and
its impact on the host community, and to consider the
long-term effects of its development plans. It will also
need to consider the authenticity of its product because
after years of travel experience more visitors now wish
to "get behind the scenes" and learn more about foreign
cultures and ways of life. To provide such authenticity
and still maintain the daily routine of a destination
community is one of the great challenges facing the
more popular destinations.

8

Hospitality and authenticity issues

The introduction of outside ideologies and foreign ways of life into societies that have been relatively closed or isolated can lead to "changes in attitudes, values, or behavior which can result from merely observing tourists" (de Kadt 1979, 65). This demonstration effect is unavoidable because tourists generally possess greater financial and leisure-time affluence than many local residents, and their vacation experiences are based frequently upon conspicuous consumption. The demonstration effect can be a benefit if it encourages local people to adopt and work for the things they lack, because in the process this helps their development. However, in many Third World destinations it has created resentment, as local residents find themselves unable to emulate the lifestyles and products they are witnessing.

The members of society most susceptible to the pressures of the demonstration effect are the young people, who may feel dissatisfied with local opportunities available to them and are prepared to imitate the lifestyle of visiting tourists as a way of seeking something better. Boissevain (1979) reports how the young people of Gozo, a small island close to Malta, have welcomed the opportunity to view the outside world through their tourist contacts. One result of this exposure has been a change in the traditional local gatherings at Sunday morning markets:

Just a few years ago both young and old met there for hours to exchange news as much as to shop. Now mostly older people go to It-Tokk [a market], for the youths meet in the evenings at the bars. Tourism is thus also helping to drive a number of wedges between the generations. (Boissevain 1979, 87)

In addition to creating generation gaps the demonstration effect has contributed to the continuous out-migration of young, educated workers. Young, well-educated people are not satisfied with the menial or "limited prospects" employment commonly associated with tourism, and view emigration to the urban-industrial centers of tourist-generating regions as their best route to the tourists' standard of living.

As the demonstration effect illustrates, two contrasting situations can evolve from tourist development, representing the separate polar points along a social interaction continuum. At one extreme tourism-induced social change can lead to *development*, representing socio-economic advances in the community, an improvement in the quality of life indices, and overall net social benefits. At the other extreme, change can lead to *dependency*, represented by economic growth which leaves an underdeveloped social structure or reinforces existing social discrepancies. In this latter situation a few members of the destination community are gaining from the tourism development, but the majority are not participating in or benefiting from the experience.

An illustration of the dependency situation is provided by Kent's (1977) analysis of Hawaii's tourism industry, which he describes as a "new kind of sugar." He relates how Hawaii's tourism industry is closely controlled by major companies, where everything is done to ensure tourists use their facilities, leaving little spillage for the small-scale and local entrepreneur. As part of tourism's new total approach to development, plans include new resort-company towns, such that:

The wheel of history spins full circle. In the same way that the old plantation aristocracy held agricultural workers in a state of feudal dependency through ownership of the houses they lived in, modern resorts will be able to threaten rebellious workers with outright eviction from their company-owned homes. (Kent 1977, 193)

Society and culture

His overall assessment of such confined socio-economic development is that old industries and values have been replaced by nothing of substance:

For the working people of Hawaii, the widely acclaimed "age of abundance" has never materialized; tourism has only brought the same kinds of low-paying, menial, dead-end jobs that have always been the lot of the local workers. (Kent 1977, 182)

To maximize the socio-economic development potential and minimize the discontent and out-migration of the young requires a broader community involvement in the industry and its rewards. Such involvement will require the support of residents, because how they react to proposed developments and the social impact of many visitors will be the key to the "hospitality" atmosphere of a destination.

Community attitudes

How a community responds to the opportunities and challenges of tourism depends to a large extent on its attitude to the industry. Attitudes are personal and complex variables, but in terms of community attitudes to tourism, three determinants can be identified. First, the type of contact which exists between resident and visitor can have a bearing on a resident's reaction to, and support of, the industry. Second, the relative importance of the industry to individual and community prosperity will be a factor. Inconvenience becomes more tolerable if some compensation is evident. Third, a tolerance threshold in resident receptiveness can be expected, in terms of the volume of business a destination can handle.

Three *contact situations* have been identified by de Kadt (1979, 50), each having its own influence on local values and attitudes. First, when the tourist purchases a good or service from a resident. Second, when the tourist and resident find themselves side by side at an attraction, such as a beach or golf course, or local activity, such as a festival or nightclub. Third, when the two parties come face to face with the object of exchanging information and ideas. De Kadt considers the first two instances are far more common than the third, meaning that transitory and commercial exchanges take precedence in most cases over the opportunity to increase mutual understanding.

In industrial nations where domestic tourism is predominant it is often difficult to distinguish tourists from residents during such transitory and commercial meetings, which results in a low profile for the industry in many communities. MacFarlane's (1979b) comparative survey of social interaction in several tourist destinations reveals the level of perceived contact can be moderate. He found approximately half of the residents surveyed reported little or no personal contact with tourists. The limited contact between visitors and residents has also been observed in a survey of British residents (British Tourist Authority 1975), but this survey goes further and notes that the people most negatively affected in their everyday life were:

(1) People living and working in the center of tourist destinations.
(2) People living in small tourist towns "where there's nowhere to hide from the tourists".
(3) Students and old-age pensioners who are dependent on cheap accommodation and are unable to meet the inflated prices in popular destinations.

These observations would indicate that the type and level of contact between visitors and residents is spatially selective. Those who live close to the tourism activity will be most aware of the industry and feel the full impact of its traffic and sales disruption. Those in the suburbs, meanwhile, will be largely unaware of the industry and will seldom come into contact with visitors. Smith (1980) has illustrated a spatial-attitude link in her model of tourism and regional development (Figure 27). She contends that if visitor expectations and needs can be met in a core zone then the tourists will seldom need to leave this area and penetrate adjacent residential neighborhoods, thus preserving the privacy and separate lives of local residents. If the core zone becomes inadequate, spillage and development into adjacent residential areas will result, bringing more direct, and possibly unwanted, contact with local residents. From Smith's model it is apparent that those who live further from the core will be able to avoid personal contact with the industry if they so desire, even though they may be benefiting economically through indirect and induced earnings.

Due to the different types of contact, certain residents can be expected to develop much stronger attitudes to tourism than others. Those residents with a *commercial stake* in the business, whether they be employers or employees, are likely to have more definite and positive attitudes towards tourism than those with little or no direct involvement. It was Pizam's (1978, 10)

Figure 27 Diagram of a tourist region
Source: Smith (1980)

CORE contains those attractions and facilities that made the community a tourist destination.

DIRECT SUPPORT ZONE houses the local residents and various functions required by the community. These consist of stores, recreation and government offices serving the people, plus support services for the tourism industry.

INDIRECT SUPPORT ZONE of the hinterland, which incorporates the area affected by the multiplier effect, and involves the investment and jurisdictional realm of the host state or province.

contention that "entrepreneurs saw tourism as having many more positive impacts on the quality of life on the Cape [Cape Cod, Massachusetts] than the residents did, and these impacts were not restricted to the economic type only." Entrepreneurs also attributed better police and fire protection, plus more recreational facilities, to the presence of tourism. Murphy's (1980b) cross-sectional analysis of decision-making groups in three English tourist centers found a similar disparity.

He found that the decision-making groups, represented by the business sector and local administration, had a more positive attitude to tourism than the residents (Table 23). Interestingly, however, it was the local administration, represented by councillors, planners, and other senior administrative personnel who

appeared more enthusiastic about the industry and its potential for the community. They were the strongest advocates of tourism's economic advantages and had a higher attitude profile than the industry representatives. (Murphy 1980b, 366)

One reason why residents have consistently lower attitude ratings for local tourism, compared to other groups, is that they are often unaware of its economic significance and overall contribution to their community. The British Tourist Authority (1975, 4) observed "many residents are unaware of just how tourism benefits an individual who is not directly employed in the tourism industry." Its survey found the public was largely ill-informed concerning tourism's contribution both to the national and local economies. This is a common problem, demonstrating a general weakness in the industry's public relations, when it fails to explain its role and contribution to those local people whose cooperation and goodwill are essential.

When Murphy analyzed his data from a different perspective, another social–spatial dimension emerged in community attitudes. His discriminant analysis of the three English tourist centers found a strong link between the relative importance of tourism to the community and resident attitudes. For example, Torquay's dependence on tourism and the distinct seasonal profile of this resort generated strong reactions. While the majority of respondents were positively disposed toward the industry, some were highly critical. One resident went so far as to state "Torquay and the tourist industry make sure I keep my place, and that I and many more like me are kept in reserve for low-paid jobs" (Murphy 1981, 194). Here the seasonal nature of a resort created either "seasonal employment" or "seasonal unemployment" depending on one's point of view and economic circumstances. In contrast the more balanced economies of York and Windsor provided a less conspicuous industry, which generated less emotional responses and more moderate attitudes. While many of the residents of York and Windsor were favorably disposed to tourists, some still had reservations about the industry itself. They noted that those engaged in tourism seemed to be prospering but questioned how much benefit the community at large was receiving, which reveals again how the degree of involvement colors attitudes to the industry.

The third determinant of community attitudes is linked to the *scale of the industry* and its associated *volume of business*. As the industry grows, not only does the quality of social interaction change, but residents come under increasing stress as they begin to compete for space and resources within their own home communities. Some degree of stress is inevitable in an industry which asks residents to share their environment and culture with strangers, but research has revealed there are some constant irritants which commonly mold attitudes.

The most frequently quoted irritant for residents is congestion, particularly with respect to traffic and parking, but also in terms of longer shopping lines and the loss of a favorite spot in the local restaurant or pub (Table 24). In some cases the problem of congestion outweighed all other perceived disadvantages, particularly in the smaller and more popular destinations. Second to congestion is a concern that as tourism grows in importance local councils begin to give it preferential treatment. Here some residents felt that the character of their community was being changed for the convenience of visitors rather than for local people. The growth of motel strips and the advent of fast-food chains have been linked to tourism demand, and some residents felt they were losing control over the form and function of their own community (MacFarlane 1979b). Another worry associated with tourism development is that property values will be inflated, particularly those in or adjacent to Smith's core zone, and taxes will be raised as local councils invest in additional infrastructure (Young 1973, 113). Residents are concerned also about the growth of litter and vandalism, commonly associated with tourism development. Residents of Britain appear to be particularly sensitive to this problem, and the industry should perhaps take more responsibility for the refuse and antisocial behavior it sometimes generates.

In the surveys referred to above, the overall attitudes toward tourism ranged from slightly negative (Cape Cod), through neutral (Torquay), to slightly favorable (Stratford, York, Lake District). From this somewhat limited sample it is apparent that no tourist destination is widely enthusiastic about the industry, and in some cases the residents appear to be disillusioned with this activity.

If the industry is to improve its community relations it must find ways to maximize the positive features of its development and minimize the problems. An obvious place to start is reducing the social stress and irritants associated with increasing business volumes, by separating functions and placing limits on development. But much more can be done to demonstrate that

Table 23 Local attitudes toward tourism in Torquay, Windsor, and York (1977)

Attitude score	Residents	Decision makers	Local authorities	Tourism sector
1.0–1.9 (unfavorable)	132 (21%)*	4 (5%)	2 (5%)	2 (5%)
2.0–2.9	270 (42%)	24 (28%)	4 (9%)	20 (48%)
3.0–3.9	206 (32%)	43 (51%)	25 (58%)	18 (43%)
4.0–5.0 (favorable)	29 (5%)	14 (17%)	12 (28%)	2 (5%)
	Chi-square = 39.03 p = 0.000		Chi-square = 18.94 p = 0.003**	

Source: Murphy (1980b, 361)
Notes: * % of respondents; ** more than 20% of cells have fewer than 5 cases.

Table 24 Negative tourism impacts identified in resident surveys

	Stratford, Ontario[1]	Niagara-on-the-Lake, Ontario[2]	Prince Edward Island[3]	Cape Cod, Massachusetts[4]	Corpus Christi, Texas[5]	Sleat, Scotland[6]	Lake District, England[7]	Northumbria, England[7]	Torquay, Windsor, and York[8]
	%	%	%	11 pt scale means	7 pt scale means	%	%		%
Congestion (traffic and parking)	47	55	20	–4.05	–0.63	50	40	25	36
Preferences to tourism/increasing commercialism	25	19	11	–	–1.30	20	–	–	–
Taxes, inflation of property values	5	6	12	–2.66 (higher prices)	–	–	–	–	33 (economic problems)
Litter, vandalism	–	–	4	–3.51 (litter) –2.70 (vandalism)	–	27	27	29	24 (aesthetic problems)

Sources: [1] R. N. MacFarlane, "Social impact of tourism: resident attitudes in Stratford," unpublished M.A. thesis, Department of Geography, University of Western Ontario, 1979. [2] G. V. Doxey, *Tourism in Niagara-on-the-Lake, Ontario: A Case Study of Resident–Visitor Interaction,* Toronto, York University, 1974. [3] J. C. Birch et al., *Tourism Impact Study for Prince Edward Island,* Cambridge, Mass. Abt Associates, 1976. [4] Pizam 1978, 8–12. [5] Thomason, Crompton, and Kamp 1979, 2–6. [6] J. E. Brougham, "Resident attitudes towards the impact of tourism in Sleat," unpublished Ph.D. thesis, Department of Geography, University of Western Ontario, 1978. [7] British Tourist Authority 1975. [8] Murphy 1980, 355–67.

benefits pass to the community as well as to industry personnel. The industry's contribution to the community's economy and amenities must be demonstrated in such a way that residents will be more willing to accept the seasonal inconveniences and irritants. If such benefits cannot be demonstrated then the community should start to ask itself "what is going on?"

Resident–visitor relations

The growing awareness of tourism's ability to create social stress and negative community attitudes toward the industry has led to the creation of several resident–visitor social relationship models. One direction taken by the theorists has been to focus on the stress factor and seek a threshold level between acceptance and rejection of the industry. The approach has much in common with the carrying-capacity concept, but tends to be more abstract because one is measuring the intangibles of human stress and attitudes. Young illustrates this view, believing "there is a saturation level for tourism in a given locality or region, and if that level is exceeded the costs of tourism begin to outweigh the benefits" (Young 1973, 111). Doxey has taken this idea a step further with his "irridex" model, which identifies the cumulative effect of tourism development on social interrelations. The other direction taken by the theorists places more emphasis on the type of contact between residents and visitors, and takes into account that stress can be more bearable if the residents' involvement brings economic or other benefits. In this regard Butler has proposed a more complex model of resident–visitor relations.

Doxey (1975) noted that the existence of local tolerance thresholds and hosts' resistance to further tourism development were based on a fear of losing community identity. Based on his observations in Caribbean and Canadian tourist destinations, he developed a model that shows a direct link between increased community irritation, or stress, and continual tourism development (Figure 28).

In the early stages of development visitors are likely to be greeted with enthusiasm by local residents. The new industry brings employment and revenue, plus the early visitors (explorer types) are appreciative of local customs and lifestyles. This state of "euphoria" is particularly noticeable in areas where there are few alternative forms of employment, and when the level of tourist activity is not overwhelming. As the volume of visitors increases, contact between resident and visitor becomes less personal and more commercialized, and visitors demand more facilities built specifically for them. The industry is now taken for granted and local people develop a more "apathetic" attitude to the activity. If development continues it may exceed community tolerance thresholds because of increased congestion, rising prices, and its threat to traditional

"IRRIDEX"

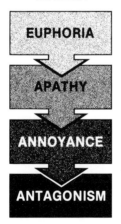

EUPHORIA — Initial phase of development, visitors and investors welcome, little planning or control mechanism.

APATHY — Visitors taken for granted, contacts between residents and outsiders more formal (commercial), planning concerned mostly with marketing.

ANNOYANCE — Saturation points approached, residents have misgivings about tourist industry, policy makers attempt solutions via increasing infrastructure rather than limiting growth.

ANTAGONISM — Irritations openly expressed, visitors seen as cause of all problems, planning now remedial but promotion increased to offset deteriorating reputation of destination.

Figure 28 Causation theory of visitor–resident irritants

ways of life. Then apathy can turn to "annoyance," as residents feel their community is being changed around them and the costs of accommodating the industry are beginning to exceed perceived benefits. But annoyance pales into insignificance if development continues and leads to "antagonism." At this stage open hostility to tourism facilities and visitors can occur, as local residents perceive it to be the cause of all their economic and social problems. The murder of affluent white tourists in some undeveloped countries and firebombing of second homes can be seen in this category.

The final two stages indicate local residents have perceived changes to their lifestyle and identity which they will not tolerate. Doxey notes the need to distinguish whether the causal factors for this deterioration are dimensional or structural changes. In Niagara-on-the-Lake they were principally dimensional changes, such as crowding and traffic jams, which could be overcome through physical planning and management. In Barbados they were structural changes, where the nature of its society was being changed by outside investment priorities, alien ideologies, and politics. Structural changes are more difficult to control and remedy, requiring political decisions at the highest level before any effective management can be applied.

Doxey's model suggests a unidirectional sequence, where residents' attitudes and reactions will change over time within a predictable sequence. Butler, on the other hand, contends that a community's emerging attitude toward tourism is likely to be more complex, and will be affected by the varying degrees of contact and involvement its residents have with the industry.

Butler (1975) identified two groups of factors that can influence visitor–resident relationships. First, the characteristics of visitors will have a bearing that extends beyond the physical impact of their increasing numbers. Butler indicates that the tourists' length of stay and their racial and economic characteristics need to be considered as well as their number. He observes that "a Canadian tourist in the United States is likely to have little cultural impact while the same individual may have a significant impact in Polynesia" (Butler 1975, 86). Thomason, Crompton, and Kamp (1979) report that prolonged-stay (winter) visitors to Corpus Christi, Texas, were generally welcome and local community groups were supportive of this form of tourism. Second, a destination's own characteristics will help determine its ability to absorb the growing number of visitors. Characteristics like its level of economic development, the spatial distribution of its tourist activity in relation to its other economic activities, the strength of its local

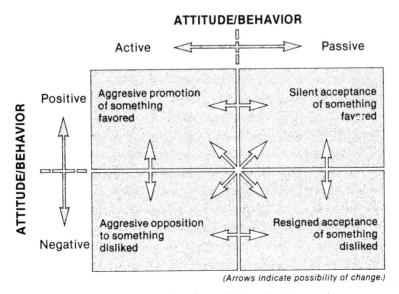

Figure 29 Attitudinal/behavioral attributes of inter-cultural perception
Source: Bjorklund and Philbrick, as cited by Butler (1975)

Table 25 Stepwise discriminant analysis of local groups toward tourism[1]

Step	Variable entered	Wilk's Lambda	Between-group F ratios		
			Bus.–Admin.	Bus.–Res.	Admin.–Res.
1	Occupation	0.747	0.08[2]	15.54	19.23
2	More leisure facilities	0.615	0.42[2]	16.04	15.21
3	Burden on the rates	0.557	2.48[2]	12.30	10.02
4	Attract more people	0.509	2.70	11.45	7.81
5	Number of benefits	0.474	2.68	10.57	6.44
6	Better-kept town	0.453	2.77	8.77	5.51

Source: Murphy (1983, 10).
Notes: [1] N = 152; variables = 17. [2] Not significant at p = 0.05.

culture, and political attitude will shape how well a destination can mold and manage its tourist product and visitors. Large metropolitan areas, with their tourist product concentrated in and around their cores are able to handle millions of visitors with less disruption than small rural communities handling a few thousand visitors.

In addition to visitor and destination characteristics Butler considers resident reactions will be more complex than those envisioned by Doxey. Butler contends that the attitudes and behavior of residents, in turn, may be expressed via active or passive behavior (Figure 29). "The resulting combination of responses allows four reactions to occur. It is quite possible that all four options can take place in an area simultaneously" (Butler 1975, 88). With this model, combinations of attitudes and reactions to tourism become possible and understandable. Businessmen who are involved with tourism are likely to be favorable and aggressive in their support, through Chamber of Commerce activities and personal promotion. Lobbyists, such as conservation or neighborhood protection groups, could be unfavorable and aggressively opposed to certain tourism developments, using letters to the editor and protests to the council as their expressions of dissent. In general the public is likely to be passive and silent because they derive some personal benefit from the industry, because it has no direct bearing on their lives, or because they see no way of reversing the process.

Murphy's (1983) discriminant analysis of group responses to local tourism revealed significant differences can exist between the residents, business sector, and administration. This more detailed analysis of community attitudes in the three English tourist centers revealed that the business sector, administration, and resident groups could be statistically differentiated on the basis of their occupations and different perceptions of tourism's impacts (Table 25). The residents had different views to the businessmen and administrators from the beginning of the stepwise analysis, but the opinions of the business sector and administration could not be separately identified until the last three variables were entered. Although the groups could be separated statistically, considerable overlap existed between the three groups (Figure 30). This suggested no group was sacrosanct, particularly the administration, which had members from both other groups and often tried to balance the wishes of the business sector and the electorate. The findings of this study suggested that although varying attitudes to tourism could be expected in many destinations, the opportunity to develop cooperation and trade-offs was still present. For example, the residents revealed a wide variety of constructive opinions, "reflecting their extensive range of individual [travel] experiences and demonstrating the fallacy of treating them as a tight-knit group of anti-developers" (Murphy 1983, 12).

To develop such cooperation and trade-offs, however, will require communication. A discussion of community problems and priorities should precede development, and areas of compromise should be the sort to produce a tourist product that is both economically viable and socially acceptable.

Authenticity

The motives for pleasure travel are many, but a common reason is curiosity. "Curiosity leads the traveler to

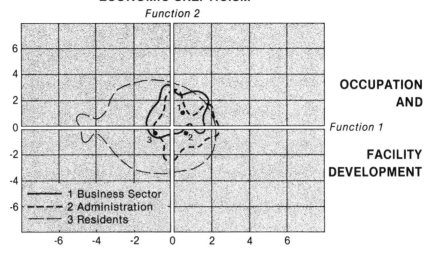

Figure 30 Distribution of decision-making group views toward local tourism
Source: Murphy (1983)

search for all kinds of experiences in all parts of the world. To see other people, other places, other cultures and other political systems is a prime motivational force for travel" (Hudman 1980, 36). Within this curiosity is the search for something different. "The discovery of new worlds has always renewed men's minds [and] travel has been the universal catalyst" (Boorstin 1975, 79). Therefore, a major component of travel motivation has been the cultural novelty of various destinations. Cultural tourism can take on many forms. Ritchie and Zins (1978, 257) have identified twelve aspects of local culture that can attract tourists to particular destinations:

(1) Handicrafts.
(2) Language.
(3) Traditions.
(4) Gastronomy.
(5) Art music, including concerts, paintings, and sculpture.
(6) The history of the region, including its visual reminders.
(7) The types of work engaged in by residents and the technology which is used.
(8) Architecture giving the area a distinctive appearance.
(9) Religion, including its visible manifestations.
(10) Educational systems.
(11) Dress.
(12) Leisure activities.

Despite man's insatiable curiosity and the significant cultural tourism potential this has generated for particular destinations, some observers feel that the challenge of exploration and the chance to experience foreign cultures have been compromised by the development of the tourism industry. One of the severest critics is Boorstin who, as an historian, feels that travel in the old sense of the word has been emasculated into tourism:

The traveler was active; he went strenuously in search of people, of adventure, of experience. The tourist is passive; he expects interesting things to happen to him. He goes "sight-seeing". . . . He expects everything to be done to him and for him. (Boorstin 1975, 85)

As part of the modernization and industrialization of travel, tourists now see more tourist attractions than the real countryside and way of life in foreign lands. In Boorstin's eyes the modern tourist seldom sees a living culture, "but usually specimens collected and embalmed especially for him, or attractions specially staged for him" (Boorstin 1975, 102). A natural progression in this process can be development of tourist attractions that "serve their purpose best when they are

127

pseudo-events. To be repeatable at will they must be factitious" (Boorstin 1975, 103). Thus development of tourism can lead to a loss of authenticity in the travel experience.

The degree of curiosity and desire for authentic experiences will vary according to the type of tourist. Boorstin believes the search for authentic experiences is limited to "travelers," the elite type of tourist who has the time and interest to explore how other cultures operate. Others consider that most people, including the modern mass tourist, have some degree of interest in foreign places and people, which remains an important motive for travel (MacCannell 1976).

The degree of authenticity that remains in destination areas will depend on its priorities and ability to host the growing number of visitors. In the early stages of development most destinations can provide authentic cultural experiences because the explorer types of tourist make few demands and are prepared to adjust to local ways. When the number of visitors increases, including charter tourists, a destination needs to modify its approach and planning if it is to accommodate this larger market without dramatically altering its social-cultural patterns. The priorities at this stage will determine the degree of authenticity a community offers in its cultural tourism. There will undoubtedly be some compromise to aid the industry and to protect the community, by packaging tourist events and attractions at times and places convenient to both visitors and residents.

Cohen (1979b, 26) has developed a conceptual framework illustrating a dual interpretation of the term "authenticity," which rests on whether it is being assessed by the tourist or host community (Table 26). The ideal situation is when both the destination and tourist view an event or attraction as authentic (situation No. 1). But Cohen shows an event can be real for one

party while it appears staged or false for the other, and a situation can develop where even a real experience is not appreciated as such by tourists (situation No. 2). His example of this is the Thai villagers, who dress in traditional native costume while going about their daily lives and are viewed as staged exhibits by many of the visiting tourists. Another would be the disillusioning experience many first-time observers of the parliamentary process have received, when witnessing either raucous debating or somnolent legislative proceedings (Figure 31). In the first case some tourists have learned to expect manipulation from previous trip experience, in the second some institutions have been elevated by the public psyche to a level that is often beyond their real capabilities.

The most common situation facing popular destinations is one where local events and attractions require some form of staging, in order to serve the visitor more efficiently and to permit non-tourist functions to continue in and around the tourist activity. One option is to be open about such staging and allow the tourist to be aware of it, which Cohen refers to as "overt tourist space" (situation No. 3). The other is to create events and attractions that will appear real to most tourists when in fact they are artificial or packaged creations, a product which Cohen describes as "covert tourist space" (situation No. 4).

Examples of overt tourist space can be seen in the growing number of heritage museums designed to show tourists a traditional way of life that has either disappeared or been adulterated, and in staged performances of traditional dances or ceremonies. A prime example of such contrived situations in North America would be the renovation and reconstruction of Colonial Williamsburg, Virginia. An outdoor museum has been created by resurrecting an old city within a new one (McCaskey 1971, 52), where staff recreate the

Table 26 Types of touristic situations

	Tourist's impression of scene	
Nature of scene	Real	Staged
Real	(1) Authentic	(2) Denial of authenticity (staging suspicion)
Staged	(4) Staged authenticity (covert tourist space)	(3) Contrived (overt tourist space)

Source: Cohen (1979b, 26)

Where MLA* means Much Larking About

'It's got it all . . . frequent frightening scenes, occasional crudity, coarse and suggestive language . . . but is it theatre?'

Figure 31   Exposure to the democratic parliamentary process
Source: Norris = *The Vancouver Sun*
*MLA really means Member of Legislative Assembly, BC's seat of government

atmosphere of colonial times by wearing period costume and acting out the daily lives of early settlers, using the technology and language of that era. In Canada a similar reconstruction has taken place at Upper Canada Village, near Kingston, Ontario. This settlement is even more contrived than Williamsburg because it is an assembly of historic buildings and artifacts from surrounding areas, including some scheduled to be submerged by the creation of the St Lawrence Seaway. In England a focus for such contrived settings has been the nation's industrial heritage. Industrial structures and machines have been made the theme at Ironbridge (Inglis 1975), while in the North of England Open Air Museum, at Beamish, an attempt has been made to recreate that area's way of life at the turn of the century.

The staged nature of the above examples is generally accepted by the tourists and destination communities, because they are based on genuine components and events and they have been assembled to provide more convenience and satisfaction for both parties. But where the contrived setting is artificial in terms of content and location the level of criticism increases, as in the case of Boorstin's "pseudo-events."

Boorstin considers that the development of mass tourism has spawned a new type of tourist—one who is satisfied with superficial and contrived experiences, traveling in group situations and expecting everything to be arranged for his convenience. To accommodate this type of tourist, many destinations have created artificial events and attractions designed to amuse the tourist and provide him with memorable photographs. Boorstin feels

These attractions offer an elaborately contrived indirect

experience, an artificial product to be consumed in the very places where the real thing is as free as air. They are ways for the traveler to remain out of contact with foreign peoples in the very act of "sightseeing" them. They keep the natives in quarantine while the tourist in air-conditioned comfort views them through a picture window. They are the cultural mirages now found at tourist oases everywhere. (Boorstin 1975, 99)

Pseudo-events such as changing of the guard ceremonies at attractions wishing to establish a link with Britain, the creation of bizarre attractions based on natural freaks or man's imagination can be viewed as regrettable kitsch, but there is no denying they have a definite market.

These grossly contrived situations have four common, and in Boorstin's eyes, damning, characteristics. First, they are not spontaneous or natural events, but are planned and staged, such as Nanaimo's annual bathtub race across the Straits of Georgia. Second, they are designed to be reproduced so they can occur at times convenient for the tourist rather than when is normal or appropriate. A good example of this is the massive Bavarian-style "cuckoo" clock in Kimberley, British Columbia, where a Bavarian caricature, in place of the standard cuckoo, can be encouraged to appear at any time by inserting a coin—but if you wait for the hour to strike you can see him for free. Third, their relationship to authentic events or reality is ambiguous, as is the case with some staged attractions that claim to represent the Amish lifestyle in Lancaster County, Pennsylvania (Buck and Alleman 1979; Hovinen 1982). Finally, and most worrisome to Boorstin, they may become a self-fulfilling prophecy because over time their representation of authentic events can take on the appearance of authenticity. Heenan (1978) presents an example of this in terms of the evolution of Hawaii's "Aloha Week." At first it catered almost totally to local citizens, but later attention shifted to attracting outsiders as a way of improving Hawaii's poor October business. "In recent years, however, planners have seen the need to re-establish waning local interest while continuing to attract mainland visitors" (Heenan 1978, 32).

Authenticity becomes more contentious when a destination tries to conceal the staging process. The objective of such covert action is to arrange events and attractions so that visitors feel they are getting behind the scenes and temporarily experiencing real life or circumstances in the host community. The rationale for this deception is to save the community from coming to a complete halt while functioning as a host to thousands

or millions of guests, by providing an area or diversion to quickly explain the workings of a local activity. However, some observers feel ill at ease with this trickery, especially when they liken tourist motivation to that of pilgrimages:

The motive behind a pilgrimage is similar to that behind a tour: both are quests for authentic experiences. Pilgrims attempted to visit a place where an event of religious importance actually occurred. Tourists present themselves at places of social, historical, and cultural importance. (MacCannell 1973, 593)

Any attempt to stage the authenticity of an event or attraction can become tantamount to sacrilege, in MacCannell's view, when it leads a tourist to believe he is witnessing a real event while he is in fact being manipulated into accepting a fake.

MacCannell equates various states of staged authenticity with a continuum of front and back settings in social relationships (MacCannell 1976, 100–2). At one extreme is the *front setting*, a formal meeting place for hosts and guests. In a home the host would put on a display of neatness and prosperity for guests and receive them in a reception or living room, where all the finest furnishings are kept. At the other extreme is a *back setting* where the hosts are engaged in their daily chores or personal relaxation, and prefer not to have guests enter these work areas or sanctums. Within the home setting these areas would include the kitchen and the den.

Tourists who are in search of an authentic experience move along this continuum, hoping to penetrate behind the frontal show settings into a back setting where the real, day-to-day living takes place. MacCannell illustrates how modern tourists are commonly led into believing they have penetrated back settings of society when they are really being shown a staged facsimile:

Tourists commonly take guided tours of social establishments because they provide easy access to areas of the establishments ordinarily closed to outsiders. . . . The tour is characterized by social organization designed to reveal inner workings of the place; on tour, outsiders are allowed further *in* than regular patrons. . . . At the same time, there is a staged quality of the proceedings that lends to them an aura of superficiality, albeit a superficiality not always perceived as such by the tourist. (MacCannell 1976, 98)

MacCannell feels that attempts to show visitors the inner workings of stock exchanges from enclosed observation balconies, or the workings of an industrial plant via bus tours and occasional displays, leads to superficial exposure and certainly not a personal experience of the trading floor or shop floor. While MacCannell is not so elitist or scornful in his view of modern tourism as Boorstin, he feels uncomfortable with staged attractions. MacCannell considers the tourist's quest for authentic insights is being prevented by the impenetrable layers of staged reality separating him from his true objective.

Such concerns have been supported by Papson (1981) who has added his own term "spurious reality" to describe the situation. He fears that reality has become spurious in many destinations because their events and attractions have been created or imposed by sources outside of everyday community existence, not least of which are senior levels of government whose main interest is economic opportunity. His examination of tourist events and historic sites in Nova Scotia and Prince Edward Island indicated that the policies of these two provincial governments created a redefined social reality. "This is not to say that reality is falsified, but rather it is contrived, self-conscious, and alien to everyday reality. As such, reality becomes spurious" (Papson 1981, 233). For evidence he cites the creation of pseudo-events in Nova Scotian communities, encouraged by the Department of Tourism's incentive grants, organizational seminars, and promotion. The purpose of these events is to bolster the economy of local communities through the likes of lobster, clam, and strawberry festivals, and numerous craft fairs. Even real historical sites have received similar promotional and development efforts, so that "historical props" have been added to encourage the tourist to visit and stay longer. For example, within the "Historical Properties" area of Halifax two men dressed as town criers "are used to create a sense of the past, provide an historical encounter, and serve as background for photographs" (Papson 1981, 231).

Acculturation

Destination communities are beginning to question not only the short-term implications of modifying or staging their culture to suit tourism's needs, but also the long-term results of such strategies. Will the development of staged attractions and pseudo-events lead to the self-fulfilling prophecy situation as Boorstin fears, and result in the irreversible cultural change of traditionally closed societies? One theory which out-

lines the possible dangers for such societies is the acculturation theory (Nunez 1977).

The acculturation theory states that when two cultures come into contact for a length of time an exchange of ideas and products will take place. This exchange process, however, will not be even, because the stronger culture will dominate and begin to change the weaker culture into a mirror image. The relative strength of a culture is based on its socio-economic conditions, its population size and the type of contact it seeks. In the tourism literature most studies that have illustrated this theory have noted a gradual weakening of traditional Third World cultures, influenced by the tastes of relatively affluent tourists. Varley (1978, 103) found that "the types of accommodation and consumer goods demanded by visitors [to Fiji] require the supply of modern standardized products." Thus, Fiji's tourism development not only exposed islanders to increasing numbers of foreigners but also to their products and ways of life. Consequently, it is no surprise that a conference workshop on "the impact of tourism on small developing countries" concluded:

There may be conflicts between (a) attempts to conserve "traditional" landscapes and lifestyles and (b) efforts aimed at economic development and improved standards of living. (Commonwealth Geographical Bureau 1982, 2)

Symptoms of acculturation, however, are not restricted to Third World destinations; for similar problems and trends can develop within the domestic tourism of industrial nations, when previously closed traditional communities of peripheral regions are exposed to tourism's cultural consequences. Reiter (1977) reveals how the politics of centralized planning has changed an isolated, close-knit, and self-contained rural community in France into a commercialized resort, when it found one local politician eager to embrace and promote its economic development strategies. The presence of a local ally has enabled the national government in Paris to transform La Rochelle into "a redefined commodity for the use of outsiders with superior status" (Reiter 1977, 145) by selling communal land in that area of the French Alps for ski development and vacation chalets. Pi-Sunyer (1977) indicates that the cultural shock and capitulation is aided by the speed at which some isolated areas suddenly become popular destinations, using as his example a Catalan maritime community in northern Spain.

In both the above examples tourism has provided a

Society and culture

route to development, but in the process it has brought into focus a host of social and economic ills that previously lay beneath the surface. Farrell (1982) provides a good example of this in his analysis of Hawaii's changing socio-economic milieu. He considers there have been two patterns of evolution within the islands. One, affiliative in character, emphasizes local culture and lifestyles even at the expense of slower economic development; the other welcomes assimilation and the symbols of a dominant mainland culture. Within these conflicting approaches to development "tourism may trigger what is really fundamental and deep-seated disquiet," but at present "most hostility is directed toward the industry in the abstract and the tourists who symbolize it" (Farrell 1982, 224).

Two symbols of tourism's contribution to the general acculturation process presently underway within industrialized nations everywhere are the growing standardization of accommodation and changes in language usage. The hotel industry has been consolidating and expanding its operations through the development of a chain or franchise approach. Dunning and McQueen's (1982) survey of major transnational hotel corporations reveals that a considerable proportion of their marketing and development has been directed toward industrialized nations (Table 27). The logic behind this approach is to remove the uncertainty

many psychocentric tourists have concerning their night's rest, at the end of a long and probably arduous touring day. This is achieved by presenting a constant standard of service and facilities regardless of location, but it reduces the accommodation component of travel to a common denominator—one which normally reflects the familiar conditions of home.

Language, as a social vehicle of communication, is a vital element of cultural survival, and examination of patterns of linguistic loyalty can illustrate the degree of social assimilation and ethnic loyalty present in a society (Cybriwsky 1970). In the tourism market of social and cultural contacts the degree to which a native language is retained can be a key indicator of the extent of local acculturation. The loss of native language is a major concern to Welsh nationalists regarding the rise of English second homes in North Wales. Between 1961 and 1971 the proportion of the population speaking Welsh dropped from 26 percent to 20 percent (Coppock 1977a, 201).

White (1974) has proposed three ways in which tourism could lead to changes in language patterns. First, through *economic change* where tourism positions exceed the number or skills of a local labor pool, necessitating the hiring of immigrant labor. A shift toward use of the immigrant's language as a common language may occur, exerting pressure on local

Table 27 Number of hotels abroad associated with leading transnational corporations, 1978

| Transnational corporation | Country of origin | No. of associated hotels abroad | | Percentage in developed countries |
		Developed countries	Total	
Holiday Inn	United States	67	114	59
Inter-Continental	United States	28	74	38
Hilton International	United States	33	72	46
Sheraton Hotels	United States	34	64	53
Club Méditerranée	France	30	56	54
Trust House Forte	United Kingdom	37	53	70
Novotel	France	27	45	60
Travelodge	United States	31	34	91
Ramada Inns	United States	25	33	76
Hyatt International	United States	6	26	23
Western International	United States	13	26	50
Southern Pacific Hotel Corporation	Australia	15	25	60
PLM Hotels	France	2	24	8
Dunfey Hotels	Ireland	24	24	100
Crest Hotels Europe	United Kingdom	18	18	100

Source: Based on Dunning and McQueen (1982, 72)

residents to speak this new language in order to facilitate business and social contacts. Second, through the *demonstration effect*, where residents aspire to achieve the status of visitors, and are prompted to imitate their language as well as their lifestyle. Third, through *direct social contact*, which may require residents to converse in the tourists' language in order to fully participate in commercial and social transactions.

White examined these three factors in his study of the Romansh language in the Graubunden canton of southeast Switzerland. This area contains some of the prime Swiss Alps tourist destinations, including St Moritz, Pontresina, and the Swiss National Park. Between 1880 and 1970 the proportion of residents in this area using Romansh as their first language declined from 76 percent to 41 percent (White 1974, 14). During the same period the use of both German and Italian increased dramatically. The decline was much faster in those communes where tourism activity was dominant, leading White to declare that "the mechanism of language change in the whole study area over the last eighty years is inextricably tied up with tourism" (White 1974, 23).

Analysis of the links between this language decline and tourism's development indicated the dominant factor was economic change. White noted that where accommodation was based on small-scale, locally owned and operated enterprises the Romansh language declined slowly, indicating that direct contact and the demonstration effect had minor impact. In contrast, where accommodation was mainly provided by large hotels and foreign companies, which required a great deal of immigrant labor, the Romansh language declined severely in the face of such economic change. White considered that:

the forms of tourism based on hotel accommodation pose a greater threat to the social and cultural outlook and life of the host community than other forms based on "lower" grades of tourist provision. (White 1974, 31)

Interestingly, he concludes the development of large-scale hotel operations provides

evidence for tourism being a factor in breaking down local socio-cultural features and replacing them with a pattern of greater socio-cultural homogeneity between tourist-despatching and tourist-receiving areas. (White 1974, 35)

This reiterates the comments made about the growth of hotel chains and franchises, outlined above.

As a socio-cultural event for both the traveler and the host, tourism should consider the needs of both parties. Up to this point the emphasis has been on the customer and his convenience, but local disillusionment with the industry indicates that the feelings of residents can no longer be ignored. Destination areas have been inconvenienced by the congestion and debased by certain staged events and attractions, plus there is growing concern over the acculturation process of tourism. If tourism is to merit its pseudonym of being "the hospitality industry" it must look beyond its own doors and employees to consider the social and cultural impacts it is having on the host community at large.

9

Social and cultural strategies

It is evident from the preceding review of social and cultural issues that most destinations have not reached Doxey's annoyance or antagonism stage in their relationships with visitors, but that the threat of passing into these undesirable situations cannot be ignored, for some warning signals are emerging. At present such signals reflect local inconvenience and dissatisfaction with the emerging tourist image, rather than distress over changed social structures or the loss of cultural identity. The planning challenge becomes one of ensuring that present minor irritations do not blossom into issues that could threaten a community's socio-cultural objectives and viability as a destination.

Social carrying capacity

One guide to the development of appropriately scaled tourism that has been suggested is the creation of a social carrying-capacity approach for each destination. Young (1973, 124) in discussing the negative local impacts of tourism states "one obvious solution is to influence national tourist policy so that the flow to each particular region is optimal—neither too high nor too low—and to convince the policy makers that beyond a certain level further increases are counter-productive." The limits of local tolerance for tourism may be described as a social carrying capacity because exceeding this threshold will have detrimental effects on the industry, since an unfriendly atmosphere will reduce a destination's attractiveness. D'Amore (1983, 144) has defined social carrying capacity for tourism as "that point in the growth of tourism where local residents perceive on balance an unacceptable level of social disbenefits from tourism development."

A social carrying-capacity concept offers two useful functions to tourism planning. First, it presents the philosophical stance that every destination has a finite supply of resources, including hospitality. This aspect is frequently overlooked in the early stages of development when the residents' early enthusiasm is expected to continue, regardless of the added pressures being placed on the host community. Second, it provides a framework within which to assess the relative social impacts of tourism developments. An exact gauge of tolerance levels is not expected because of the dependency on residents' perceptions of the industry and its impacts, which can vary considerably. However, significant advances have been made in perception and attitude surveys that permit the development of general opinion ratings, and in the area of recreation planning, where social carrying capacity has been used to determine user satisfaction with the landscape and various activities (Lucas 1964; Stankey 1971).

The relevance of social carrying capacity's links with public support for the industry can be seen in Mings' (1980) review of New Zealand's tourism picture between 1969 and 1978. He identified several aspects of the industry's development that generated strong public support in this region of the South Pacific, during a time when other nations were witnessing rising anti-tourism sentiment. A major factor in New Zealand's favor was that the proportion of visitors to indigenous New Zealanders was relatively low compared with many other destination areas. Mings reported (1980, 26) that "in 1978 the ratio of visitors to New Zealanders was 130:1,000; while figures for other selected areas were appreciably higher (Spain, 391:1,000; Canada, 626:1,000; Switzerland, 970:1,000; and the Bahamas, 3,691:1,000)." This meant that New Zealand's social carrying-capacity levels had not been threatened at the national level, and nor were they threatened at the local level, thanks to two factors. First, because many of the primary tourist attractions were located away from major population centers the opportunity for visitor–resident conflict was substantially reduced. Second, the need to develop alternative sources of overseas earnings through the attraction of foreign visitors had been stressed repeatedly in the media and by the government, as New Zealand's traditional overseas food markets disappeared. In this case the residents' threshold level was not under pressure, and the separation of visitor–resident travel patterns plus the acknowledged economic significance of tourism added to its acceptability.

Social carrying capacity not only functions as a measure of social sensitivity to tourism development, it can offer guidance to tourism policy. D'Amore (1983) has used it in this regard to develop guidelines for tourism development in several small British Columbia destinations. After considering which conditions were conducive to socially sensitive tourism development and those which were inappropriate, he identified nine guidelines that are not just applicable to the British Columbia situation but to all aspiring destinations.

D'Amore's first guideline is that the residents of destination areas must be shown the socio-economic significance of the industry through promotional campaigns. He advocates that promotional efforts go beyond attempts to instruct residents to smile and tell visitors to "Have a nice day." To encourage residents to share their resources and amenities requires that they must be made aware of the economic and amenity advantages that come with the industry—yet this is seldom done. It would be easier to make residents smile and welcome tourists if they had something to smile about, such as "demonstrated" economic benefits and more amenities.

His second guideline states that tourism planning should be based on overall development goals and priorities identified by the residents. D'Amore feels that if residents can maintain their unique lifestyle and fulfill their own aspirations, then visitors can enjoy individualized areas that have not been altered to suit tourist expectations. Under these circumstances the chances of exceeding local social carrying capacity will be diminished, because development will reflect the needs and desired pace of change of local residents and not those of the industry.

Farrell's observations relating to the frantic development of the Waikiki district in Honolulu raises the same concerns over outsiders determining local goals. "The question which comes to mind immediately is 'Do a few persons in corporate board rooms [off the island] have the right to engineer major migrations from the mainland when need, beyond providing reasonable growth and shoring up agriculture, cannot be established?'" (Farrell 1974, 205). The same considerations apply to accommodation, where it is helpful to plan and create hotels and condominiums in terms of "uniqueness of place, site, and scale requirements and to create a sense of identity, besides considering the more obvious requirements of materialistic function and economics" (England 1980, 54). Such an approach would maintain the *genius loci* of a destination and ensure that tourism facilities and functions blended into the local landscape, as well as the economy.

The third guideline suggests that promotion of local attractions be subject to resident endorsement. Promotion of a tourist image helps to determine what type and number of visitors will be attracted and what their expectations will be. As was noted earlier there can be considerable variance between the local image as presented by tourism agencies and that perceived by the residents themselves. Many tourist attractions and gift shops around the Great Smoky Mountains National Park portray Cherokee Indians as wearing feather war bonnets and living in tepees, when this was never part of their culture (Figure 32). This commercial image of a stereotype Indian has angered many Cherokee people and caused a great deal of bitterness toward the industry (Gulick 1960). Such discrepancies not only occur when there are cultural differences between hosts and guests but when domestic tourism brings townspeople into rural environments. Pets and livestock don't mix and the image of quaintness and "a country bumpkin" is not appropriate for modern farming communities.

The fourth guideline calls for coordinated public and private efforts to maintain the integrity and quality of local opportunities for recreation and relaxation. Residents in remote areas often view their recreation opportunities as compensation for the lack of access to urban amenities, and as a consequence they consider any deterioration of these opportunities a serious matter. Local tourism development must avoid the dangers of over-harvesting local fish and wildlife. D'Amore reports "there is considerable resentment of

Figure 32 Cherokee Indian displays near Great Smoky Mountains National Park

visitors canning or otherwise processing large quantities of fish to take home" from Campbell River, British Columbia—a famous fishing resort. Overton records how in Newfoundland the

game laws were enacted to protect and define the caribou as a tourism resource, but considerable conflict was generated between the "poor settlers" engaged in the fishery (who relied on caribou as an important source of food) and the state (which acted largely in the interests of the tourism industry). (Overton 1980, 40)

Similarly, local residents must be left some summer recreation outlets of their own. D'Amore reports strong tourism resentment in communities where tourists were beginning to dominate the use of local lakes. In one case the competition forced local wives to claim a lake campsite on Thursday night, while the husbands followed in car pools on Friday evening. In Cornwall local residents resort to using small, inaccessible, and unpublicized coves in their search for beach recreation; or forsake the coast altogether and head inland away from the tourist-clogged beaches and resorts.

The fifth guideline calls for greater involvement of native people in the development of local tourism so that their traditions and lifestyle will be respected. Within developed nations there are certain groups that are attempting to retain their cultural identity in the face of an overwhelming national acculturation process. In North America many native Indian and Inuit (Eskimo) groups have avoided major involvement with mass tourism because they feel most tourists do not respect or understand local ethnic traditions and values. D'Amore reports how the Haida Indians have problems with tourists on the Queen Charlotte Islands, taking photographs of local life and sacred sites without permission. Smith (1977a) relates how the Eskimo women of Kotzebue, Alaska, refused visitors permission to photograph their traditional butchering process. When such appeals went unheeded, they were forced to erect barricades to shield their work from prying eyes or to haul the carcasses to the privacy of their home for processing—destroying the social aspects of this function.

A study by the Native Brotherhood of British Columbia (1980) helps to explain the native Indians' degree of limited commitment to the industry. It agrees with a government committee on tourism development that native Indian history, culture, arts, and crafts would be of great interest to tourists but cautions that some of the major cultural events such as rodeos, dancing, and potlatches cannot be incorporated into a tourism product:

These socially oriented activities are intended for Indian people only, and intrusion by non-Indians would be most unwelcome. While the specific reasons for this attitude differ somewhat from area to area, the common thread is that Indians fear that intrusion by non-Indian people into their communities to view and participate in these activities would ultimately lead to a reduction in their quality of life. (Native Brotherhood of BC 1980, 42)

There are, however, some events held by Indian groups which are not so personal and can be designed to appeal to a broad tourist market. Examples of Indian carving are included in the Ksan Village at Hazelton, British Columbia, and displays of native dancing are held during the Penticton Peach Festival in the Okanagan Valley. Such events should be viewed as economic ventures, designed to enhance native income and employment opportunities, rather than as social events.

The British Columbia native Indians have not turned their backs on the industry entirely, for some reserves are strategically located across prime tourist routes or adjacent to major attractions. The study found that several bands had developed some small-scale businesses, but there were only 25 such native-owned businesses and they were predominantly campgrounds and craft stores. These types of businesses were favored because they required few business skills, were labor intensive, would help alleviate the high Indian unemployment rates, and were the most viable option on reserves that were in remote locations

The sixth guideline recommends that local capital, entrepreneurial ability, and labor be invested in local tourism development. D'Amore recommends such action on the grounds that it will permit a greater degree of local control over the direction of tourism development and that the use of local resources will increase employment and economic benefits to the community. He notes that where residents have the impression that tourism is in the hands of outsiders, in the form of big companies and hotel chains, local people feel more alienated from the industry.

D'Amore's call for more local investment and control is supported by Getz's (1983) observations concerning tourism planning in Canada, where he feels the planning has been "top-down." The federal and provincial governments have introduced development strategies which have treated communities as resources to be developed or exploited for their tourism potential, and he hopes "perhaps the sad experience of numerous megaprojects in Canada is gradually encouraging a shift from big plans and top-down policies to more local small-scaled tourism planning" (Getz 1983, 8). Getz's observations can also be applied to Scotland where he has examined the impact of tourism in the Highlands (Getz 1982). In his assessment of the situation in the Aviemore area he considers:

Ownership and management of business and facilities are dominated by in-comers, and this may lead to local resentment. Attitudes of locals and newcomers differ in certain respects, possibly leading to conflicts over such issues as conservation and growth. (Getz 1982, 80)

In response to this situation Getz (1982, 11) recommends "providing financial assistance which favours those born locally, to enable them to set up tourist and other businesses."

The seventh guideline recommends that opportunities be provided to obtain broad-based community participation in tourist events and activities. It should not be forgotten that it is the residents' home which is being put on display and the residents who must act as hosts, whether they are directly involved or not with the industry. Local tourism is more likely to complement resident lifestyles whenever a wide range of community members are involved in the organization or provision of services, for under these conditions the interests of the community and industry can become more compatible. Visitor–resident interaction need not be limited to a business setting, for with appropriate encouragement and planning the social aspects can be fostered in smaller-scale tourism. D'Amore suggests the possibility of bringing together the resident retirement community and visiting retirees. This holds out much promise in some of the smaller destinations. He also relates how the Penticton hospital established a clinic, staffed by a rotating roster of doctors, specifically for visitors. An average of 90 patients per day utilized the clinic's services during the summer months, a community gesture that indicated Penticton was interested in the visitors' welfare and not just their money.

The eighth guideline suggests destination areas adopt or refine themes and events that reflect their history, lifestyles, and geographic setting. D'Amore feels residents can expect to gain from such themes and

events a sense of identity and pride in their community, since local lifestyle and customs are being reinforced. He cites the case of Kimberley as an example of this and the preceding guideline. "Kimberley provides the best example [of those centers surveyed] of widely-based community support and involvement" (D'Amore 1983, 146), much of this support revolving around its adopted theme of becoming the "Bavarian City of the Rockies."

Kimberley is located in the Selkirk Range of the Rocky Mountains and its major employer, the Sullivan Mine operated by Cominco Ltd, is scheduled to be phased out by the year 2000. This notice of closure gave the community an opportunity to consider its other resources and work together to develop them. It decided that surrounding mountains offered the potential for ski resorts and adopted the development theme of a Bavarian city to make Kimberley distinctive from its competitors.

Accordingly, commercial buildings and homes have been decorated in a Bavarian style and the downtown core converted into a pedestrian plaza highlighted by a giant Bavarian clock (Figure 33). Whether or not one agrees with the community's selected theme and subsequent "ersatz" architecture, there can be no doubt that it has won the support and endorsement of many residents:

As volunteers, many local people are involved in tourism. For example, senior citizens hold teas and slide shows for bus loads of visiting seniors; ski enthusiasts help clear the downhill area and the trails used both by locals and tourists; residents organize two annual festivals that attract many visitors. The fact that the directors of the BC Winter games, held in Kimberley in 1980, obtained a thousand volunteers is further proof that the town lives up to a reputation for getting things done. (D'Amore 1983, 146)

The ninth, and final, guideline calls for more work to mitigate local growth problems before proceeding with any further increases in tourism activity. It has been noted that tourism is an agent of change and many community complaints concern congestion and increased housing and living costs. In growing communities it is often impossible to determine the exact causes of change or increasing costs, 'but it is clear that increased numbers of tourists will exacerbate any shortages. It becomes essential that the needs of permanent residents are addressed prior to, or in conjunction with, additional tourist facilities. Otherwise, local people will tend to associate growth problems and

Figure 33   Kimberley's Bavarian-style clock and town center

other problems with tourism, and may develop a resentment toward the industry.

D'Amore cites two examples of tourism development proceeding faster than local residents feel is appropriate. The residents of Queen Charlotte City, facing a scarcity of building lots and rising house prices, thanks to an upsurge in population, were shocked to hear that its ferry links to the mainland were about to be expanded. The residents feared that increased access for tourists would result in increased congestion, even higher prices, and possible health hazards. Many of the visitors to this area come in recreation vehicles which block the narrow streets; their needs for food and gas place added strain on a hard-pressed freight service, raising prices in the process; and there are no disposal stations to handle their waste products, so many campers dump their effluent into open ditches or creeks. Given these prospects, and recognizing the disbenefits to both the resident and the visitor, the province's Ministry of Tourism lobbied against the proposed ferry changes and was successful in having them scaled down. Less success has been achieved in

Pemberton, where residents expressed resentment over a perceived tendency of the council to cater to visitors first and residents second. The locally funded convention center was approved by residents, but they objected to being charged rentals to use facilities their tax dollars helped to create. This they viewed as a form of double billing. Furthermore they are becoming concerned that lakeside motel and campground developments will effectively alienate residents from nearby beaches.

The social carrying-capacity guidelines advocated by D'Amore seek to balance community aspirations with the type and pace of tourism development undertaken. It is apparent that while such an approach offers no specific planning methods because the circumstances and opportunities will vary at each destination, it does offer a conceptual framework that can reduce visitor–resident tension. By considering the social ramifications of various proposals in terms of a community's social carrying capacity for change and development it should be possible to make resident and industry objectives more compatible.

Society and culture

Concentration and dispersion

The social carrying-capacity concept provides a framework for tourism planning within the community, but within that framework communities can develop two basic spatial and alternative planning strategies— the concentration or dispersion of tourist facilities. The choice depends on local conditions, and need not be mutually exclusive.

Concentrating tourism development in core areas or specific tourist zones has become a common strategy in popular destination areas. Such a policy provides a means by which the facilities and services for tourists can be isolated from other, and possibly incompatible, land uses. In effect it creates a new service industry zone, which if planned and coordinated as a whole can offer local tourism the benefit of industrial linkages (attractions, retail outlets, parking, and access to inter-city links) while creating a new employment and commercial center for the community. This planning approach, in effect, formalizes Smith's model of the tourism core (Figure 27).

Examples of this type of planning can be seen most clearly in the tourism development taking place in many inner city areas, adjacent to the central business districts. These areas have witnessed a flight of industry to more spacious and less expensive locations, leaving behind prime waterfront sites, historical and industrial artifacts, vacant buildings, and high unemployment in surrounding residential areas. Various cities have attempted to convert these relics into new zones of service industry, designed to serve both visitors and residents and generate employment opportunities suited to the central city's new role in the post-industrial age. The focus on tourism-related functions is not intended to be the sole means of reviving such economic backwaters, but tourism is proving to be a feasible economic option with desirable environmental and social side effects. In some cases careful planning has enabled tourism to complement and interact with other activities of the city, producing a return to the tradition of mixed land uses and functional interaction within a small area.

Evidence of this strategy can be seen in the St Katharine's Dock redevelopment in central London. An abandoned dockyard area has been revitalized with the construction of a trade center, luxury hotel, a collection of historic vessels, and pubs and shops scattered amongst renovated and converted ware-houses. It is estimated that these tourist attractions and facilities have created more than 1700 jobs and contribute £1.25 million ($US2.5 million) a year in property taxes to the local authority (English Tourist Board 1981a, 50). In Victoria, British Columbia, an old harbor district has been renovated on the premise that tourism revenues would support the cost of conservation and development. In this case the city has attempted to reduce congestion in the downtown core by diverting tourist flows into this adjacent backwater, and to expand its tax base in the process (Murphy 1980a). In the United States, several inner-city re-development projects have embraced a tourism theme and successfully changed the image of decay and decline in those areas. In Baltimore's Inner Harbor area (Figure 34) vacant warehouses and unused wharves have been replaced by a trade center, convention center, science museum, planetarium, and aquarium, converting this underutilized waterfront into a vibrant leisure–tourism focus for the city. Baltimore's Inner Harbor attracts "over 10 million visitors a year to an area which was completely dead 15 years ago [and] not only generates income for the city, but has helped to project a new image of Baltimore to the outside world" (Beioley 1981, 25). In Lowell, Massachusetts, a depressed textile town has built upon the strength of its industrial heritage rather than raze and redevelop. The creation of a state Urban Heritage Park followed by a National Historical Park has preserved the heart of Lowell's industrial area, by interpreting its heritage and providing recreation facilities based on the industrial canal system:

The centre of Lowell has been transformed. New businesses have sprung up [around the parks], buildings have been restored, the canals have been landscaped and in 1981 some 350,000 people [were expected] to visit the town and look around the mills and museum or take guided tours. (Beioley 1981, 11)

Injecting new economic life into inner-city areas by expanding the tourism core into these areas can create some problems. The employment created through tourism and related service activities is generally low paid and seasonal, and may not be suitable for all displaced blue collar workers—especially the men with trade skills and union traditions. The successful development of a leisure–tourism complex may dis-place marginal uses and small businesses that serve the local area or nearby downtown commercial core. The growth of the tourism core may lead to the intrusion of

Figure 34 Baltimore's tourism-oriented Inner Harbor

commercial activity and traffic into surrounding residential areas, straining the relationship between the community and industry. These costs need to be weighed against the benefits of increased economic activity for the city as a whole, and are illustrative of the overspill costs associated with a successful concentration strategy.

The City of Westminster, London, is a good example of the costs associated with a concentration strategy. In this case there was no derelict industry or dockland to replace, but older housing facing a future of conversion or redevelopment. This provided an opportunity for the accommodation sector to locate close to the major attractions of central London without the associated high land costs of the core. By 1974 Westminster contained 39 percent of London's hotel bedspace and there was pressure for more tourist accommodation zoning. The continuous growth of hotels in a residential area, however, brought on the types of social stress predicted in Smith's model. Once the more obvious sites and locations had been developed for hotel accommodation the industry started to penetrate stable residential areas, raising land and house prices in the process and leading to the demise of local facilities such as the corner store. In order to protect its residential component and existing character the City of Westminster City Plan (1978, 113) sought "to ensure that any new hotels or major visitor facilities . . . are located in areas of non-residential character within the Central Activities Zone." This zone represents the commercial heart of Westminster, encompassing such major visitor attractions as Westminster Abbey, the Houses of Parliament, the theater district around Piccadilly and the Strand, and the shopping magnets of Bond Street and Oxford Street.

If a concentration strategy leads to local pressure or threatens to create social stress in some parts of a destination the alternative policy of dispersion becomes a more viable option. The dispersion of tourism throughout a destination is seen as a way of spreading the load and benefits throughout the whole community. Such a policy does not mean a mixing of tourism and residential land uses, since this would simply exacerbate existing tensions and the overspill problems outlined by Smith; rather, it seeks to spread the tourism industry along existing transport networks and to other commercial nodes throughout the destination region.

London provides a good example of dispersion strategy because of the growing congestion and social pressures in central boroughs such as Westminster. A major theme in London's tourism plans has been the diversion of tourists, especially second-time visitors, away from its internationally renowned attractions to other features of the region. Many potential and actual attractions that could provide new tourist itineraries have been identified in the suburbs and commuter zone (Greater London Council 1974). Since these attractions are dispersed and frequently single items, they have been linked and organized into some form of day-trip tour. Examples of raising the interest in and access to outlying tourist attractions can be seen in Figure 35. One of the most popular out-of-town tours is that connecting central London with Hampton Court and Windsor Castle. The tour spends half a day at each royal palace, providing a day outing for a visitor staying in central London. To encourage the use of public transport and thereby provide back-haul or off-peak business for rail and bus systems, certain outlying attractions have been promoted:

One example is the development of a day long circular trip north of London to St Albans and Hatfield. St Albans offers a cathedral and an excavated Roman town, while nearby Hatfield has the stately home of Hatfield House. Both could accommodate more visitors, especially during the week when domestic trips are reduced. (Murphy 1982, 20)

In addition to spreading visits throughout the region, London would like to develop more tourist accommodation in suburban and outlying areas. Such a process is already underway with the development of a hotel complex near Heathrow Airport, and there are hopes to increase hotel development in areas such as Richmond and Windsor.

Similar efforts to disperse tourism throughout a destination area, in order to reduce central congestion and benefit outlying areas, can be seen in a variety of locations. In metropolitan Los Angeles the suburban city of Long Beach has been using its foreshore oil revenues to diversify its local economy, by developing tourist attractions to divert some tourist traffic away from the traditional magnets of Disneyland and Universal Studios. Rather than compete directly with these internationally renowned child-oriented attractions Long Beach has attempted to offer a more adult-oriented alternative. It has started to build a tourist attraction based on man's technological achievements,

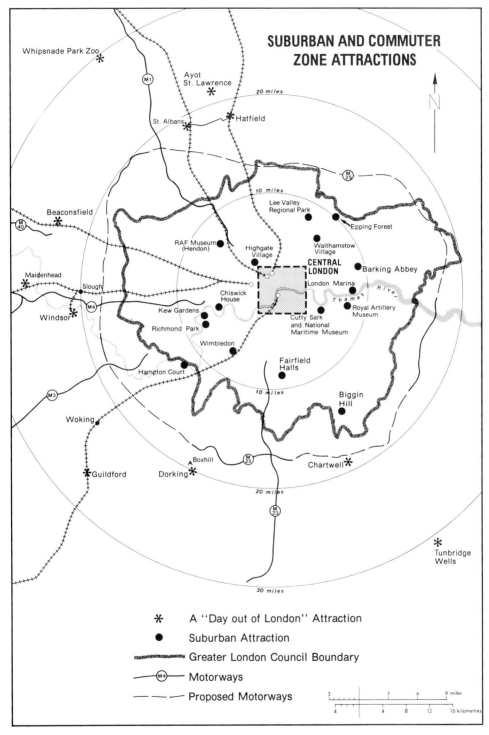

SUBURBAN AND COMMUTER ZONE ATTRACTIONS

Whipsnade Park Zoo

Ayot St. Lawrence

20 miles

St. Albans   Hatfield

M1

Beaconsfield

M40

10 miles

Lee Valley Regional Park

Epping Forest

Maidenhead

Slough

M4

Windsor

RAF Museum (Hendon)

Highgate Village

Walthamstow Village

CENTRAL LONDON

Barking Abbey

London Marina

Chiswick House

Kew Gardens

Richmond Park

Wimbledon

Cutty Sark and National Maritime Museum

River Thames

Royal Artillery Museum

Hampton Court

Fairfield Halls

Biggin Hill

M3

10 miles

Woking

M25

Boxhill

Guildford   Dorking   Chartwell

20 miles

M23

Tunbridge Wells

30 miles

✳   A "Day out of London" Attraction

●   Suburban Attraction

〰〰〰   Greater London Council Boundary

—M4—   Motorways

— — —   Proposed Motorways

3   3   6   9 miles

4   4   8   12   16 kilometres

Figure 35   Regional dispersion strategies in London

Society and culture

including the *Queen Mary* liner and Howard Hughes' *Spruce Goose* seaplane.

On Vancouver Island, British Columbia, the capital city and major destination of Victoria is becoming sensitive to tourist volumes and development proposals, while the remainder of the island possesses underutilized facilities and resources. Consequently the provincial development plan calls for "broadening the existing appeal and seasonality of the [island] region . . . with efforts made to disperse visitor concentration occurring in Victoria" (Province of British Columbia 1982, 140). The intent is to coordinate public and private investments to develop the island's scenic attractions and recreation opportunities, provided by its maritime and alpine resources, to complement the urban heritage attractions of Victoria. Rather than have Victoria remain a terminal destination this strategy hopes to convert it into a gateway for an island vacation.

It is apparent from the examples cited above that a concentration and dispersion strategy are not necessarily mutually exclusive, but that elements of each can be adopted in order to gain the maximum development within the social carrying capacity of a destination area. It is not being suggested that congested core areas have their business substantially reduced, as this would also reduce employment and amenity opportunities for local residents; but, rather, it is suggested that when such areas approach capacity thresholds future growth and development be diverted to surrounding areas.

The combination approach has been recommended by Getz (1982) in his assessment of development alternatives in the Spey Valley, Scotland. A growth center strategy based on concentrating development in and around the ski resort of Aviemore would take advantage of economies of scale and the spread effects of a growing urban–economic center, but could cause increased social and economic problems in this small town. A complete dispersal policy would prevent further development in Aviemore but encourage growth in all other settlements throughout the valley, utilizing local labor and avoiding the social/cultural problems associated with large-scale projects. However, the difficulty of developing year-round facilities and custom in these small settlements would limit potential employment and income benefits. A compromise strategy of developing Aviemore into a year-round resort within its social–environmental constraints and channeling complementary development to outlying communities where social and environ-

mental conditions permit would provide the best of both options. In this regional example, and that of Vancouver Island, planners are attempting to diffuse local social tensions by promoting a regional tourism product that offers a more comprehensive package and is likely to be more rewarding to both the visitor and resident.

Pace of change

Residents are not only aware of the amount of tourism activity in their community, they are also sensitive to the changes this industry brings to their lifestyles, employment opportunities and future options. If development in the industry is slow and cumulative it is often perceived as being less threatening. Under such circumstances it can be accommodated by local resources, including investment, and with local labor. If, on the other hand, it involves a major and sudden change brought on by a large-scale project, this can be perceived as threatening because of its magnitude, impacts on surrounding land uses, and frequent dependency on outside funding and labor.

Examples of the negative social impact of dramatic change are most apparent in Third World situations, where a rapid infusion of visitors has affected local standards and priorities. LeFevre (1977) ties the rapid growth of tourism in previously quiet backwaters to the construction of jet airports which suddenly connected tropical islands to burgeoning international air routes. This close bond between international airlines and tourism development resulted in foreign-owned and designed resort–hotel projects that were frequently alien to the local populace. Not only did an airport bring in thousands of strangers with new demands and customs, it became a gateway to the outside world for native people. Cowan notes more Cook Islanders took advantage of their new airport connection to leave than tourists came in, during the early months of its operation. He feels that as the process of modernization continues "more and more Cook Islanders will become absorbed or assimilated into the industrialized society of New Zealand, leaving behind a disrupted social structure in the traditional villages and a demographic imbalance of very young and very old people" (Cowan 1977, 81).

The link between pace of change and tourism-induced social stress is not confined to Third World countries, for similar problems can arise in small and isolated communities within developed nations. In a study of three North Carolina coastal towns, Peck and Lepie (1977) examined a rapid-growth situation (Oriental), a slow-growth development (Bath), and a transient situation (Harkers Island) consisting of weekend and special events tourist traffic. They examined each community in terms of its "power structure," particularly in terms of land ownership and project financing; the "pay-off" with regard to the benefits and opportunities for self-advancement offered by tourism; and the "trade-off" which compared the shift away from traditional agriculture and fishing activities to commerce, plus the revisions of social norms and mores involved in the process. They concluded "the *rate* of cultural change induced by tourism affects the integration of the community" (Peck and Lepie 1977, 171), integration being the social harmony between local residents and their social relationships with visitors.

In Oriental it was noted that those on limited or low income felt victimized by price increases made to take advantage of the more well-to-do newcomers, and by the tax increases needed to provide an infrastructure for a new retirement community (Sea Vista) which brought little direct benefit to residents. In contrast, tourists were hardly visible to the residents of Bath, because of their small number and spatial separation of tourist and local functions. Indeed, Peck and Lepie felt tourism in Bath served local residents more than outside visitors because local facilities and attractions were still community-oriented. On Harkers Island most visitors were "pass-through customers" who interfered with local life during the occasional weekend or special event, but in the process had little lasting effect because most of their supplies were brought in from the mainland by outside middlemen.

Peck and Lepie noted that the source of regulatory power associated with the rate of social change had an important bearing on how well communities adjusted to the development of a tourism industry. A great deal hinged on whether it was local residents who were the prime agents of change or external sources. Strong local power bases associated with slow change tended to direct tourism development toward compatibility with local activities and lifestyles, and fostered more integration of newcomers (who were small in number) into the established social network.

Cultural strategies

Two cultural factors requiring planning consideration are the authenticity of a cultural experience on the part of the visitor and the long-term cultural viability of a destination area in the face of mass tourism. The two are related because they involve the presentation and preservation of a destination's cultural heritage, but the role tourism will play depends to a large extent on local sensitivity and attitude regarding the indigenous culture. While tourism is certainly an agent of change it is not alone in this regard, and tourism may well be the most visible symptom of cultural change rather than the prime cause. Most of the world is gradually being assimilated into a consumer goods economy, linked together by a growing communications and transport network. The general result has been increased acculturation, where traditional cultures of isolated areas have absorbed or borrowed facets of the dominant urban–industrial cultures, moving us towards an "homogenized world." Modern tourism may be an agent of this process or a bastion of resistance to uniformity and conformity, depending on the direction of its management and marketing strategies.

Boorstin and MacCannell's concern over the authenticity of the modern tourist's experience is shared by the industry, and is not simply an academic question. Wahab (1975, 49) claims "the genuine environment always attracts more tourists than the imitation . . . the creation of 'artificial' environments, similar to those which the tourists have at home, does not promote tourism in the long term." Thus a destination area would be well advised to retain those elements which made it distinctive, and to present its cultural heritage in such a way that would be both meaningful for themselves and convenient for the visitor.

Rather than ridicule staged tourist attractions as pseudo-events and tourist traps, Buck (1977) has looked beyond their alleged sideshow qualities to develop a more balanced assessment of their role. Using his experience of the Old Order Amish culture in Lancaster County, Pennsylvania, Buck feels there can be distinct advantages in developing attractions which can educate visitors and relieve the pressure on sensitive residents. He considers that tourists gazing at museum displays, making the rounds of farmers' markets, and photographing prepared scenarios and animated Amishmen in a wax museum is preferable to having these same people harassing real Amishmen and playing amateur anthropologist. Although the tourist attractions of Lancaster County varied in quality and taste, Buck felt many were "valid and responsible attempts to present aspects of Amish life and culture and at the same time to remain sensitive to Amish distaste for things worldly, secular, and outside their strict traditional and religious credo" (Buck 1977, 31).

Despite these advantages of staged attractions and the general good intentions of the industry, Buck feels that more could be done to explain and protect the cultural heritage of a destination. He recommends that the industry move from a *laissez-faire* position on attraction development to one of self-imposed respon- sibility and policing. There is a need to establish a quality control for the attractions and tourist image of a destination area, and who better to set the standards than the industry which is affected by an area's overall reputation and image. But Buck reserves his strongest criticism for those scholars who have mocked past efforts at staged authenticity. He feels that "anthro- pologists, sociologists, journalists, and historians share with tourist attraction enterprises a common interest in the presentation of authentic statements about historic and/or exotic places, peoples, and cultures" (Buck 1977, 32). Instead of being negative, such experts should share their insight and experience with the private sector in order to foster a greater awareness and appreciation of another culture.

The epitome of scholarly involvement in a staged tourist attraction can be found in the Polynesian Cultural Center, located in the small community of Laie, an hour's drive from the prime Hawaiian tourist destination of Waikiki. It is a recreation of Polynesian cultures which is owned and operated by the Church of Jesus Christ of Latter-Day Saints, commonly known as the Mormons. The center was established with a threefold purpose, according to Stanton:

1) to preserve the culture of the Polynesians;
2) to provide employment for students of Brigham Young University—Hawaii Campus;
3) to provide direct financial aid to BYU—Hawaii (Stanton 1977, 193)

It is a "reconstruction of the exotic, more popular elements of Polynesia and puts 'on stage' for the visitors selected aspects of Polynesian life" (Stanton 1977, 203). In addition to showing aspects of Hawaiian culture, it also illustrates the material culture and performing arts of other Polynesian cultures, bringing employees from Fiji, Tahiti, Samoa, and Tonga to demonstrate their culture. This tourist attraction fulfills the cultural tourism expectations of most visitors and has become the second most popular tourist attraction in Hawaii. Just as important from the community's point of view, however, is the fact that the center has increased the income and material welfare of Laie without interfering with the daily lives of the people. "Students attend grade school, a college functions effectively, the bank opens and closes; in general people work *away* from the prying eyes of the tourist" (Stanton 1977, 203).

Most modern tourist attractions are staged to some extent, but the term "staged" need be associated no longer with poor taste or deception. There are many examples of quality staged attractions which provide the tourist with a condensed exposition of a cultural heritage that is both informative and stimulating, but not necessarily complete in every detail—much like a good lecture. It is up to the student/visitor to pursue the details and nuances at his own level and pace. Such an arrangement is convenient for the resident as well as the visitor. It reduces the need for tourist exploration and disturbance of the local community, and can provide a forum through which local people can take pride in demonstrating their culture and retain old crafts and customs in the process.

Examples of quality staged attractions include the reconstructed trading post at Fort Steele, which provides a good illustration of pioneer life in western Canada, without interfering with the daily routine of nearby Cranbrook. The renovated *Queen Mary* offers an example of a multi-purpose attraction. In addition to revealing the features and history of this past transport era, the vessel's huge size has permitted the inclusion of associated uses. These include a luxury hotel, a shopping plaza, and a marine exhibition developed by Jacques Cousteau (Figure 36). The North of England Open Air Museum, at Beamish, has been described as a "people's museum" (Cole 1979). Centered around Beamish Hall, its open-air displays allow visitors to relive the life of industrial England at the turn of the century.

The acculturation problem is not so grave within the tourist flows of industrialized nations since the cultural differences between host and guest are not so extreme; but differences still exist, and in the interest of both destination communities and the tourism industry they should be respected and maintained. The major cultural differences emerge when foreign nationals

Figure 36 Staged attractions of Fort Steele (pioneer days) and *Queen Mary* (technological exhibit)

arrive, with a different language and heritage compared to the host population. In most cases these visitors are on some form of package tour and oriented to urban areas or major attractions, where it is easier to manage the interaction process and the indigenous population is familiar with commercial exchange and trade. The most vulnerable destination communities in industrialized countries are those small rural communities, where physical and cultural isolation is being eroded by improved accessibility and the outward pressure of explorer types of tourist. These destinations offer the appeal of quaintness and being off the beaten track, but can retain such qualities only if they remain minor destinations and operate within their own social and environmental capabilities.

The task facing tourism management in terms of the acculturation problem is to protect the more isolated and non-commercialized communities from abrupt changes in their lifestyles and values. Tourism in most instances will be seasonal and small scale, so it is possible to minimize its disruptive nature and develop it so that it complements and supports existing activities and institutions. It has already been noted that tourism agencies in Europe and North America are promoting farm tourism to aid the marginal profitability of such businesses and communities in upland areas, but when the attraction of such areas becomes too strong it may be necessary to dilute this appeal and spread it over a wider area. Such has been the case in the Yorkshire Dales area, which, in addition to the natural beauty of its farming landscape, became a Mecca for those seeking "Herriot's country." This popular literary work and its subsequent mass exposure on television brought thousands of inquisitive visitors, many from North America, who would not normally have placed this rural area on their itinerary. The Yorkshire Tourist Board's answer to this was to capitalize on the interest, but spread the demand across as wide an area as possible. So while publicizing the Dales and their previously unheralded tourist appeal the exact location of Herriot's practice remained a mystery, and visitors were encouraged to explore the villages and small towns on their own and to make their own decisions regarding the characters and locations in the books.

An important aspect of culture, both for the host community and the industry, is the quality and uniqueness of local architecture, historical buildings, and monuments. These inanimate objects reflect the history of the hosts, and are a major tourist attraction according to Ritchie and Zins (1978). Thus it behoves tourism planning to conserve such assets and, where possible, ensure that additional facilities blend in with existing architectural styles.

Britain's historic stately homes have utilized their tourist appeal to help defray the costs of upkeep and the burden of taxes. Foremost among these has been Woburn, owned by the Duke of Bedford, and opened to the public in 1954 in order to assist in paying off a £5 million ($US14 million) estate death duty. Since Woburn was off major tourist routes and distant from major attractions, the Duke of Bedford felt obliged to supplement the appeal of the house with other attractions, including a safari park. These were designed to develop Woburn into an appealing day-trip destination for local people and visitors from London. In similar manner, Lord Montagu of Beaulieu has focused attention on his stately home in the Hampshire countryside. In 1981 more than 200,000 visitors came to Beaulieu not only to look around the house, but to visit his National Motor Museum. These two examples illustrate uses which can be made of the extensive grounds associated with historic country houses, and the individual characters of their owners, but they are not alone in seeking ways of combining tourism and conservation. Many other country houses, some quite small and historically insignificant, have attempted to blend history and recreation.

Well-planned tourism is able to support and encourage the efforts of scenic and historic conservation in Europe (Dower 1975), and has provided the economic justification for much heritage conservation in Canada. A Canadian travel survey revealed that 29 percent of Canadian tourism spending was attributable to visiting historic and cultural sites (Galt 1974). This figure was higher than the so-called "all-Canadian leisure pastimes" of boating, hunting, skiing, and sports watching combined (*Canadian Heritage* 1982).

As small communities develop into more popular destinations the need for additional facilities, especially accommodation, becomes necessary, and modern buildings begin to rise next to historic monuments or outstanding attractions. At this stage it is crucial that the *genius loci* be preserved. According to England (1980, 49), the need is "to ensure that the new is woven delicately into the pattern of the old in order to produce an effect of unity, homogeneity and compatibility"—compatibility with the local culture and architectural style. England feels that certain tourist villages or resorts around the Mediterranean have developed the right degree of place identity, scale, and panache in their design to fit into existing environments. He stresses, however, that successful tourism architecture does not always have to be muted and constrained. Quoting Morris Lapidus, the designer of Miami Beach's famous Fontainbleau Hotel, he says:

Don't take these Miami Beach Hotels seriously, they are built for fun . . . to introduce a sense of excitement. . . . I want to build what man wants. . . . I am not trying to build monuments; my hotels are not built to impress architects but to make people enjoy themselves, and be economically viable for the people who built them. (England 1980, 53)

It is not only the planner and architect who is considering ways in which to blend tourism into a local economy and lifestyle with the minimum disruption and maximum return. The people living in isolated communities of industrialized nations are not without ideas and strategies of their own, for they are educated, experienced tourists in their own right, and part of the self-government system. As a result they are capable of adjusting to the new tourism phenomena without unduly disturbing the old lifestyle and values.

In this regard small communities which face a seasonal invasion of tourists can provide an alternative to the assimilation consequences of the acculturation process. The independent and self-reliant community should not be viewed automatically as being the weaker submissive culture, but should also be viewed as a community capable of accommodating visitors while not sacrificing its other functions and interests. This is more akin to the cultural drift theory, which claims that the host population adjusts to the needs of visitors when they are present, but returns to its previous lifestyle on their departure (Collins 1978). In this way a community maintains a cultural distance between itself and visitors, establishing separate business and family relations.

An illustration of self-adjustment along the lines of the cultural drift theory can be seen in Jordan's (1980) participant observation of life in Vermont Vacation Village (pseudonym). This village had been in the tourism business, or "selling its culture" as Jordan puts it, for more than 50 years, and on summer-season weekends visitor populations of 900 or so outnumbered the locals by a three to one margin. In order to survive as a farming community yet take advantage of the tourism market the village has developed a distinctive annual calendar, with specific events for the visitor and the resident (Figure 37). The balance between its two business interests has led to a summer and fall season for the tourist activity, and a winter and spring season for local residents and their farming practice.

The *summer season* starts in June, picking up momentum during the school vacations and ends on the Labor Day weekend, which comes in early September. The tourist season ends with the closing of camps, the beaching and stacking of boats along the lakeshore, and the closure of the Tourist Information Booth. There is a definite end to this part of the tourist season because on September 15 the local post office terminates its extensive summer postal delivery to the various summer cottages and campgrounds, the two village stores cease to restock national newspapers and magazines, and food on grocery shelves is often past the recommended expiry dates.

The *fall season* consists of five mini-seasons, two of them oriented to the residents. In chronological order they are as follows. The "leaf season" occurs in late September when people from the cities drive through, or stay for a day or two, to see and photograph the colorful autumn leaves. Although it is a short-lived season it can account for 10 percent of tourist revenues. The "harvest days" are not connected with the agricultural harvest which is already completed, but with the "harvest of another crop"—the tourists who collect arts and crafts, enjoy auctions and folk festivals. "Harvest Days are a period of hectic activity for those natives involved (local craftsmen, writers, and painters), and for some as much as 75 percent of their annual income as craftsmen may be realized" (Jordan 1980, 39). This frantic period is followed by what the locals call "Days of Grace," when there are few visitors and the winter weather has not come early, enabling the residents to relax in relative comfort. But the tourist season is not over for the year, for next comes the "hunting season," the most unpopular period of tourist activity:

Hunters are considered to be the most unprofitable, even dangerous type of tourist and there is little inter-personal contact. . . . Hunters are unprofitable because their expenditures are slight. Ammunition, whiskey, hunting licenses are generally purchased before they get to the Village, and only the costs of food and the rent for cabins goes to the Village. These amounts are judged to be inadequate in consideration of their behavior, when by day they terrorize the neighborhood with their careless gun fire or, by night, when their loud drunken parties are disruptive. (Jordan 1980, 39–40)

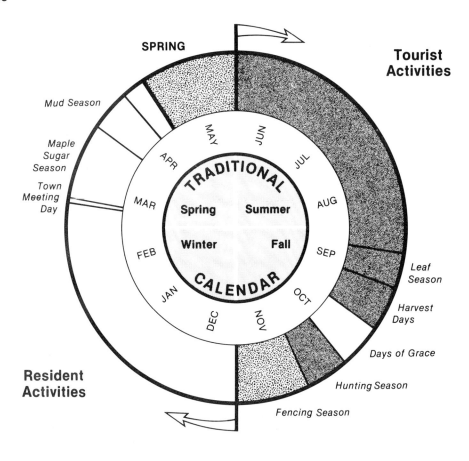

Figure 37 The
Vacation Village
calendar
Source: Jordan (1980)

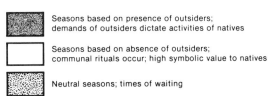

The "fencing season" is primarily a farming activity, repairing broken fences, preparing snow fences to control the drifting, and generally getting ready for winter.

The *winter season* is a community time since there are no nearby ski resorts and winters can be very severe. Winter is an ordeal in Vermont, and local residents attempt to make the best of it. For example, winter, not summer, is the season for weddings, and the village comes together in order to face the elements:

Three winter events reinforce the group identity with the village: Town Meeting Day, Maple Sugar Season, and Mud Season. The first two are Vermont "holy days", secular yet with elements of a traditional, even scared [sic], past inherent in them. Mud season is simply an intensified testing at the end of the long winter. (Jordan 1980, 41)

The "Town Meeting Day" is considered by Jordan to be "the most important single annual date in the calendar," when local people and their representatives discuss the operations of the town during the past year and prepare a budget for the coming year. Jordan notes:

although almost 25 percent of the taxes are paid by summer people (second-home owners), none are invited, expected, or wanted at the annual town meeting. Town Meeting Day is an exclusive communal ritual and a boundary-maintaining device to separate natives from outsiders. (Jordan 1980, 42)

The winter season melts into the *spring season* sometime in late April or early May. This is a waiting period when local residents prepare for the next tourist season. Spring represents calving time for the dairy farmers, and spring cleaning and painting for the tourist business.

In summarizing his experience of living in Vacation Village, Jordan feels the residents have developed a dual personality. "Sometimes the natives seem to want to keep Vacation Village, themselves, and all of Vermont a secret, as during Maple Sugar Season and Town Meeting Day.... At other times, they seem willing to participate in the phoney-folk culture" (Jordan 1980, 52). Thus these residents of a rural but accessible destination area have organized their lives so they can take advantage of the tourist interest in their community during the summer and fall months, but return to their traditional farming ways in the off-season. While Jordan, as an anthropologist, may regret the pseudo-event atmosphere of periods like "Harvest Days" he is forced to admit that economic factors make it necessary for this small town to continue to accommodate its tourism business—as long as a balance can be maintained.

Although it is a sample of one, the experience of Vacation Village suggests small communities can engage in tourism activity and control their own destiny. Accepting and developing tourism on its own terms, using it to supplement and complement their lifestyle has enabled Vacation Village to operate as a tourist destination and farming community for over 50 years.

Part of its tourism involvement is staged, such as the "Harvest Days," but most genuinely reflects the community's resources and way of life—reflecting a balanced position.

Summary

The socio-cultural problems of destination areas in industrial nations are essentially ones of irritation over the inconvenience tourism brings to local life, and the perceived changes to traditional beliefs and behavior as the commercialism and consequences of mass tourism calls for more packaging of local culture. At present, the irritants and stress noted in destination areas have not poisoned the hospitable atmosphere, but the potential for danger is there according to Doxey. Butler's more detailed model of social interaction and a growing number of case studies show that communities can build more tolerance for the industry, and their visitors, if they can see more individual and community benefits arising from the interaction. Likewise, communities can adjust their lifestyles and offer authentic glimpses of their culture if local people become more involved in developing and designing the local tourist product.

Local involvement is seen as one way of controlling the pace of development, integrating tourism with other activities and producing more individualistic tourist products. The industry needs to move beyond its patronizing "smile campaigns" to address the real issues of congestion, authenticity, and acculturation. By focusing on a destination community's heritage and culture in the development of its tourism product the industry will not only present a truer picture of a destination, it will become an ally of many public interest groups. Furthermore, by emphasizing the individual character of a destination, tourism can become a vital force against the world-wide homogenization of culture.

Section 5

Planning and management

Tourism issues have been subdivided into sections up to this point for the purpose of exposure and explanation. Such systematic divisions, however, are artificial in the complex and interrelated activity of modern tourism; they conceal the significance of sectoral and spatial linkages, they fail to acknowledge the overlap of physical, social, and economic forces on a destination's tourist product. In dividing its subject the text has reflected the fragmentation problem facing tourism and those communities which intend to become involved with it. The lack of coordination and failure to investigate competitive or complementary opportunities have reduced the effectiveness and rewards of destination planning. Some type of coordinating framework is necessary to develop tourism's potential and its contribution to the well-being of host communities.

Tourism's potential for economic and amenity development has been seized upon by various levels of government, but the result has been top-down planning and promotion that leaves destination communities with little input or control over their own destinies. While the result of such centralized planning has been rapid growth and widespread development in industrial nations, the impacts on host communities and spillover effects were seldom considered or appreciated. As a result, tourism development frequently failed to live up to its promised expectations and many communities have begun to develop jaundiced attitudes to this panacea growth industry. Tourism, like no other industry, relies on the goodwill and cooperation of local people because they are part of its product. Where development and planning does not fit in with local aspirations and capacities, resistance and hostility can raise the cost of business or destroy the industry's potential altogether.

If tourism is to become the successful and self-perpetuating industry many have advocated, it needs to be planned and managed as a renewable resource industry, based on local capacities and community decision making. To achieve these objectives will require a more balanced approach to planning and management than has existed in the past. More emphasis is needed on the interrelated nature of tourism development, in terms of its component parts (physical, economic, and social considerations), its spatial implications (accessibility, routing, and intervening opportunities), and evolutionary pattern (development stage and competitiveness). More balance in the decision-making process is required between those with the funds (governments, big business, and banks) and those who have to live with the outcome and are expected to provide the hospitality. More local input and involvement at the planning stage will give destination communities a greater stake in the industry and create a more responsive partnership. Finally, the new approach to tourism development must combine planning (the initial goal and development strategy) with management (day-to-day, season-to-season operational decisions), because the ability to adjust to changing market or seasonal conditions is of paramount importance in such a competitive business.

With these observations in mind, this section proffers an alternative to past tourism planning methods. It notes how the traditional economic emphasis of post-war planning and promotion is giving way to a more comprehensive assessment of tourism's development potential and impacts. There is a growing awareness of

153

Planning and management

the industry's dependency on and responsibility to the host community, and an increased ability to plan in a more integrated manner at the local and regional scale. Consequently, it is advocated that future planning and development be undertaken from the perspective of a community industry—one that is responsible to the community it is selling.

To achieve this community emphasis in planning and management it is proposed to develop the industry within an ecological framework. This approach will enable the integration and development of the industry's components to a scale that is more in harmony with a destination area's physical and human capacities. Furthermore, it will be flexible enough to consider destination areas, with their specific priorities and problems, at various planning levels, thereby permitting different planning emphases, but all with the common goal of developing a viable and appropriate community tourist product.

An advantage of this proposed ecological approach to tourism planning is that it can fit in with existing systems theory and planning being used in urban and regional development strategies. Under these circumstances tourism's needs and impacts can be integrated into local and regional planning, to be considered along with those of other activities. This would acknowledge that tourism has become an important component of modern lifestyles and that every community is or can be involved in this industry. Furthermore, the systems approach to planning is incremental, relying on continuous monitoring before proceeding to the next stage. This flexibility allows for management to be linked with planning, permitting adjustments to changing circumstances.

10

Tourism planning goals and methods

The post-war tourism boom lured many nations and individual communities into the business with little forethought concerning a viable tourism product, the social and environmental consequences of development, or the spillover effects in surrounding areas. Instead, the approach to tourism development was essentially myopic, both in terms of its economic objective and planning scale. The pursuit of economic benefits has seldom been accompanied by concern over lost opportunities or trade-off situations. Planning for these economic objectives has been conducted by individual entrepreneurs or individual communities, with little regard for potential impact on others.

Too often the pace of growth and burgeoning opportunities resulted in *ad hoc* responses to changing market conditions and local opportunities, rather than to coordinated strategies working toward preconceived individual and community goals. The outcome of this frenzied activity and patchwork planning has been inconclusive at best, if we are to believe the titles of various academic surveys. Titles like *Tourism: Blessing or Blight?* (Young 1973), *Tourism: Passport to Development?* (de Kadt 1979), and *Tourism: The Good, the Bad, and the Ugly* (Rosenow and Pulsipher 1979) indicate the contentious nature of post-war tourism development. It is evident that tourism has the potential to become a destructive force as well as a benefit for destination communities. Furthermore, 30 years of mass tourism experience has led to a more cautious approach to development by existing and potential destinations.

One reason for caution is that the period of unending growth appears to be coming to an end, and individual or community planning and investment mistakes cannot depend on a general rise in activity to minimize or obliterate such errors. The immediate cause of the slowdown in tourism growth is the recession, but in spite of these difficult times the industry has proved to be remarkably resilient. A recent survey of tourism in OECD nations revealed "tourism is holding up." International tourist arrivals were up by 0.7 percent between 1981 and 1982, and receipts in real terms fell by only 0.3 percent (OECD 1983). By themselves these figures do not appear impressive, but when one recalls how many other industries have suffered severe declines in activity and revenue generation over the same period, holding tourism at the same high level can be viewed as a success.

Such resilience lends credence to the view that tourism has taken hold on our lives (Yankelovich and Lefkowitz 1980) and become a component of the post-industrial age. In fact, tourism is probably maturing, entering a natural period of stability after its rapid post-war growth, as new economic circumstances and demographic trends revise travel needs and patterns. This has major implications for both existing and aspiring destination areas, for it means the industry is entering uncharted waters. One implication noted in the OECD report is that while "the recession has not kept people from traveling, it has changed their destinations and shortened their stay in some countries" (OECD 1983, 29). Such changes can lead to more emphasis on domestic tourism within the tourism-generating nations of western Europe and North America, along with international travel to their sunbelt neighbors. Existing and potential destinations in these areas will need to prepare for new travel patterns and demands brought on by changing economic and life-cycle circumstances.

The response to changes in the tourism market will require increased input and involvement by the community at large. In addition to using public goods, the industry increasingly requires public funds for infrastructure, facilities, and marketing. Residents of industrial nations are accustomed to being consulted on development proposals that affect their community and wallet. Furthermore, as experienced travelers and witnesses to 30 years or more of mass travel these residents have developed some degree of expertise and experience concerning tourism. To ensure that tourism development maximizes local benefits while minimizing its disruption and negative impacts requires the establishment of goals for this industry.

Goals for tourism

Planning is concerned with anticipating and regulating change in a system, to promote orderly development so as to increase the social, economic, and environmental benefits of the development process. To do this, planning becomes "an ordered sequence of operations, designed to lead to the achievement of either a single goal or to a balance between several goals" (Hall 1970, 4). Thus all planning requires goals to provide a frame of reference for the detailed physical planning and day-to-day management decisions.

Goals are abstract and continuous concepts, intended to provide general direction rather than specific guidelines. To be effective, goals must be feasible and have general support. In tourism this means a community's proposals must be realistic and attractive to tourists in a competitive market place. To develop a satisfactory tourist product and acceptable image requires the cooperation of many sectors, including the public, so the wider the support for its goals the more successful will be the industry.

For tourism in industrial nations the goals need to be a subset of overall community objectives, since it represents but one of several activities within most local economies. Cities frequently look on tourism as a way to bolster their retail and service sectors, and derive greater returns on their cultural and recreational investments. Toronto, for example, attracted 20 million tourists in 1979, who spent over $US1 billion. Many of them were attracted to the city by its museum, science center, zoo, art galleries, and other facilities (Wall and Sinnott 1980). Small communities in rural areas are interested in diversifying their economic base and providing employment for their women and youth, who cannot find work in the traditional primary activities.

Slocan Valley in the British Columbia interior is one region hoping to reduce its dependency on lumber and mining by developing tertiary sector employment in tourism, plus provide more local amenities in the process (Hall 1982).

The exception which proves the rule, concerning the development of tourism as one of several activities, occurs when tourism has become the dominant activity—as in a resort. Under these circumstances the community goal becomes one of reducing the dependency on tourism, with its seasonality and low-wage limitations. Many resorts are attempting to entice manufacturing or research establishments to their scenic and amenity-rich areas, but find it difficult to overcome the problems of isolation and lack of industrial linkage. Some have experienced success, however, in catering to the growing retirement market. The presence of retired people helps to even out the seasonal peaks, and provides major revenue and capital infusions as the elderly bring their pensions and equity to the destination community (Karn 1977; Forward 1982).

To date, most tourism goals and planning have been oriented toward business interests and economic growth. The prime motive for tourism development and planning has been commercial and economic gain, both on the part of the private sector entrepreneurs and governments. Entrepreneurs, companies, and major land owners have provided for a growing market; local governments have encouraged growth and development through the provision of leisure and cultural facilities (Heeley 1981; Lundgren 1983). Senior government interest and support has been motivated by the employment, taxes, and foreign currency which tourism can create. Tourism has been used as an agent of economic development in depressed peripheral regions and as an export activity.

The United Kingdom Ministerial Guidelines of 1974 reiterated tourism's role in the government's balance of payments and regional development policy. This was followed by an experiment in using tourism growth centers to stimulate regional development. Growth points, such as Bude/Wadebridge in Devon and Scarborough in Yorkshire, were suggested as focuses for tourism development that could induce positive spin-off effects in surrounding areas (English Tourist Board 1978b, 1978c).

In the United States, the 1981 National Tourism Policy Act created the United States Travel and Tourism

Administration whose basic mission "is to promote US-inbound tourism as an export" (Edgell 1983, 429) and thereby assist in reducing the national travel budget deficit. In Canada, several provinces have joined forces with the federal government in an effort to encourage more domestic tourism and develop attractions of international standing. Again the prime purpose is to reduce a hemorrhaging travel deficit, and to spread tourism revenues into underused peripheral regions. Table 28 illustrates the variety and location of various Travel Industry Development Subsidiary Agreements (TIDSAs) across Canada.

In the *laissez-faire* atmosphere of western societies and a tourism industry dominated by small businesses, economic considerations have been slow in relinquishing priority to other concerns. But the very success of past development has necessitated relating tourism's economic, social, and environmental impact with wider public interest objectives. One example of this gradual modification in an economic approach to destination planning can be seen in Gunn's (1979, 191–4) treatise on designing tourist regions in North America. His first goal is to provide for "user satisfactions" on the grounds that it is the tourist who must be attracted and satisfied if a destination is to develop and prosper. His second goal is to provide for "increased rewards to ownership and development" for those entrepreneurs who risk their capital in destination development, for without such venture capital the industry would be stillborn. The third goal is "protection of environmental resource assets," such as historical and archeological sites. While Gunn's first two goals remain distinctly business-oriented his final goal recognizes the symbiotic relationship between a successful tourism industry and a protected environment—the early stirrings of a renewable resource philosophy.

Communities must start to appreciate the fragility of certain resources and protect their resource base if they are to develop a long-term industry. Potential tourist attractions can be spoiled by industrial development or urban renewal, while established amenities may be destroyed through over use. Dearden (1983) maintains that too many resource industries have developed the capacity to harvest and sell to a fine art, but unfortunately this expertise frequently exceeds their capacity to grow or replenish consumed resource stock. He reports that British Columbia's "1982 herring quota was reached in just 36 hours of fishing" (Dearden 1983, 76). This reveals a serious neglect of the fish stock,

and leads to a situation where it is no longer possible to provide an adequate investment return—which was Gunn's second goal. Likewise, the British Columbia lumber industry is rapidly running out of accessible mature timber, thanks to over-harvesting and under-planting. It is vital, therefore, that a resource-based industry like tourism does more to protect its interests in scenic landscapes, wildlife protection, and heritage conservation.

McIntosh (1977, 151) goes further than Gunn, encompassing his goals for tourism development within a community framework. This permits some form of local control and direction to be placed upon the still business-oriented emphasis. His first goal is to "provide a framework for raising the living standard of local people through the economic benefits of tourism." Second, to "develop an infrastructure and provide recreation facilities for both visitors and residents." Third, to "ensure that the types of development within visitor centers and resorts are appropriate to the purposes of those areas." Finally, to "establish a development program that is consistent with the cultural, social and economic philosophy of the government and people of the host area."

This concern for community input and self-determination can be seen in the recent planning objectives of destinations which are either being overwhelmed by tourist volumes or are considering a greater commitment to this activity. Those national parks in Britain which receive large numbers of visitors have created plans to tackle the problem of reconciling tourist traffic with the preservation of a local environment and way of life. For instance, the Snowdonia National Park Plan (1977, 3) attempts to integrate tourism with the economic and social well-being of local people. Among its objectives it includes several of the goals suggested by McIntosh:

i) to maintain the *traditional* pattern of agriculture,
ii) to encourage those forms of tourism with the greatest *local benefit*,
iii) to create jobs at most of the *existing* settlements within the Park, and
iv) to *safeguard* the identity of *local communities* by seeking to retain and develop the cultural heritage. (Snowdonia National Park 1977, author's italics)

Even in North America, where free enterprise and minimal government interference are still championed, there have been occasional stirrings of a more

157

Table 28 TIDSA and related multi-sector agreements in Canada

Location	Funding (Fed./Prov. share), and term	Primary objectives
Newfoundland	$13.3 m. (90/10), 1978–83	facility upgrade to increase length-of-stay and number of visitors
Prince Edward Island	Tourism component: $10 m., Comprehensive Development Plan, 1969–84	facility upgrade destination area approach heritage attractions tourism to be developed in harmony with the Island's social and economic needs
Nova Scotia	$13.8 m. (80/20), 1977–82	destination area development to create employment opportunities by extending tourist season, increasing number of visitors and expenditures per visitor throughout the province
New Brunswick	$14.7 m. (80/20), 1975–80	to increase number of visitors and lengths-of-stay through improved resource planning and facility development
Quebec	$76.0 m. (60/40), 1978–83	increase of information centers improvement of Provincial Parks development of special cultural and historic heritage projects to create attractions destination areas
Ontario	Tourism component: $4.0 m. (50/50) Economic Development Agreement 1980–83	facility and plant upgrade and development of destination areas to address tourism's seasonality and the changing travel markets
Manitoba	$20.0 m (60/40), 1979–84	establish programs to enhance destination areas and to facilitate the establishment of non-governmental organizations in tourism industry
Saskatchewan	Tourism component: $11.5 m. (60/40) Multi-sector Subsidiary Agreement for Qu'Appelle Valley 1974–84	upgrade of facility and increase in destination area attractions to increase visitor numbers and lengths of stay
Alberta	no TIDSAs signed	
British Columbia	$50.0 m. (50/50), 1978–83	infrastructure upgrade, planning, destination area and ski resort development
Northwest Territories	Tourism component: $600,000 (60/40) Community Economic Development Agreement 1979–81	improve facilities to create destination area enhance tourism activity
Yukon	Tourism component: 1) $400,000 (60/40) Renewable Resource Agreement 1979–82; 2) $6.0 m. (85/15) 1980–82	improve facilities to create destination area, enhance tourism activity

Source: Montgomery and Murphy (1983, 185–6)

community-oriented approach to development. In British Columbia, where recent emphasis has promoted tourism in small resource-based communities, an attempt has been made to develop socially acceptable guidelines for future expansion (D'Amore 1983). In the Yukon, with its small population, a planning team of consultants and government planners was able to reach most residents through the distribution of a brochure/questionnaire and public meetings, to obtain their views and input for its 1978 tourism development strategy (Graham 1979). Despite such public participation, however, the prime goals remain oriented to the development aspirations of the government and industry rather than the communities involved. Such levels of participation would fall into Arnstein's (1969) "tokenism" category. They involve consultation with the public but provide no opportunity for residents to become partners in the decision-making process.

Planning

With the goals of tourism development expanding to incorporate environmental and community considerations it is not surprising that the process of implementing those goals has also changed over time.

Planning in tourism has undergone considerable refinement and adjustment in response to the changing scale and complexity of the industry—in much the same way as government involvement changed in form. The early considerations were economic or physical plans associated with a particular project or facility. First it was considered necessary to make some rudimentary market assessment and then to design the physical plant. In this way planning became an isolated and site-specific venture, with little or no concern about possible spin-off effects on adjacent areas or environments. One of the most successful post-war ventures of this kind was Walt Disney's Disneyland theme park. Disney engaged the services of the Stanford Research Institute in 1952, "asking them to locate the best area, taking into consideration where the freeways, and population growth patterns, were going to be. We wound up with a little more than 300 acres of orange groves in Anaheim, California" (Elder 1980, 1). The site considerations and difficulty in obtaining financing for such a unique concept absorbed all the planning attention, but Disneyland's success and magnetism created some unforeseen and unpleasant side effects. Elder, who works for the Disney organization, contends:

If Walt could have turned back the clock to the early 1950s, and started all over again, he obviously would have acquired more land—much more land than those first few orange groves. As Disneyland grew in popularity, and number of attractions, so did the surrounding area, until adjoining Harbor Boulevard became practically a "neon jungle" of motels, gas stations, restaurants, and other tourist support facilities. It was an artistic nightmare. (Elder 1980, 1)

Gravel (1979), who has developed a model of tourism planning's evolution (Figure 38), gives such early planning the title "operations research" and contends there was little change in approach until the 1960s. The only refinement of note in these early planning attempts was the adoption of computer technology which permitted the analysis of more econometric data, but which in itself was not a fundamental change in method for it was primarily a technical innovation. Throughout this early era Gravel contends most plans adopted a "non-integrated approach," focusing on a specific market or site with little attempt to consider the wider implications of proposals and projects.

The turning point, according to Gravel, came with strategic plans like Labeau's *La Consommation touristique belge: son évolution passée et future* in 1965. This report argued "that measures of tourism must make use of direct and indirect methods because of their complementarity." This recognized the importance of external ramifications and where possible the need to accommodate them. With this approach, tourism planning began to consider the regional and environmental context of its development proposals and so began what Gravel calls the "integrated approach."

One aspect of the planning process, however, was slow to change and that was the "once-over" planning method whereby a tourism plan was formulated by a state or province at more or less regular intervals, usually every five years. At the end of each planning period the plan was considered to be obsolete and in need of major revision, thus the process started over again. The epitome of such planning was the tourism master plan.

A "master plan" is a comprehensive detailing of guidelines for development. It is the outcome of (i) defined goals and objectives, (ii) the collection and analysis of market and resource data, (iii) the development of strategy alternatives, and (iv) the political decision-making process. Its development has been

influenced by the introduction of more flexible land-use techniques (such as structure planning, or systems approach to planning) and by a growing awareness of the socio-economic impacts of development schemes (as shown by cost–benefit analysis). (Baud-Bovy and Lawson 1976, 15)

The result is a more elaborate planning sequence, and with it a major commitment of time and money by public authorities, as is shown in Figure 39. Such master plans have been alternately supported and criticized. Some observers maintain such a planning solution places public bodies in a stronger position to consider and control private development schemes, while others hold that master plans are often too rigid, inflexible, and unrealistic.

As tourism and recreation have changed in scale and emphasis, new tourists and recreational products have to be considered. New conditions in either the generating or competing areas, plus changes in accessibility, can alter the flow and pattern of visitor arrivals. Changes in a country's priorities and objectives can alter exchange rates or reduce public funding. All of these can have a strong influence on planning policies. Thus the latest trend, according to Gravel's model, is a move toward systems planning where the

process is a continual one aimed at partial development, constant monitoring, and revisions. The scope of the plan evolves over time and it is hoped such flexibility will enable it to adjust to changing circumstances, producing long-term results which are more complete and of superior quality than a series of separate master plans.

Ontario's Tourism and Outdoor Recreation Planning System (TORPS) is an early example of this type of planning. It was developed by that province to examine recreation and leisure travel and the various supply options which could be developed to accommodate both domestic and visitor demands. A private proposal using a systems approach is the Product's Analysis Sequence for Outdoor Leisure Planning (PASOLP) developed by Baud-Bovy and Lawson. A diagram of the PASOLP method is given in Figure 40, which indicates the complexity of this type of approach. Note it still includes the term "master plan," but now this aspect is not the final step for it is followed by an impacts phase, where the socio-economic and natural side-effects can be monitored and the plan changed if its external

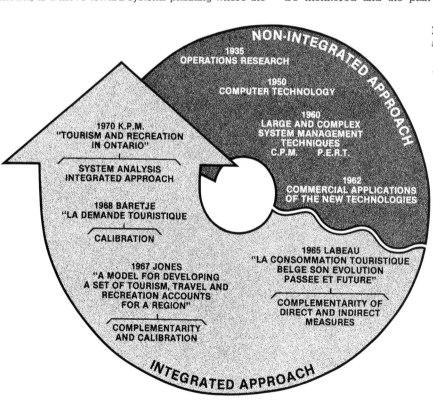

Figure 38 Evolution of approaches to tourism planning
Source: Gravel (1979)

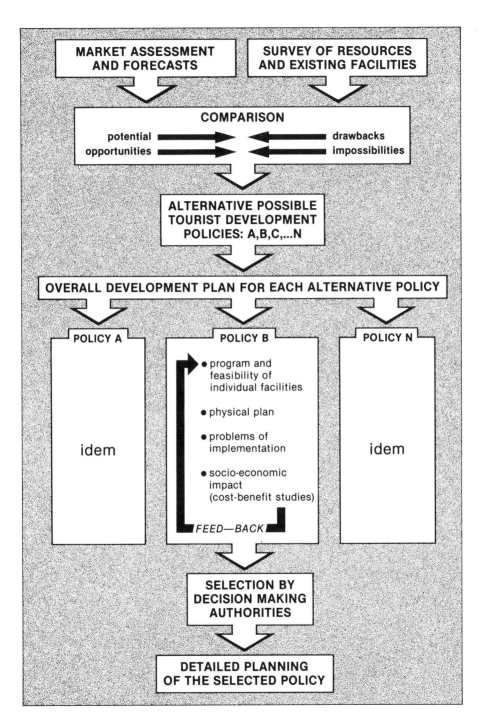

Figure 39   Standard master plan process
Source: Baud-Bovy and Lawson (1977)

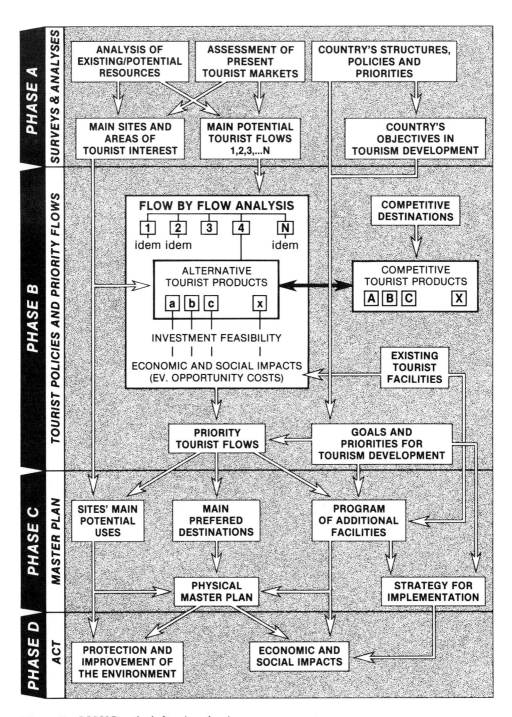

Figure 40   PASOLP method of tourism planning
Source: Baud-Bovy and Lawson (1977)

effects are proving to be negative. This overall monitoring and feedback process is more evident in Figure 41, which outlines the total planning process (Baud-Bovy and Lawson 1977, 139–44).

The monitoring, feedback, and flexibility of systems planning is also evident in the move to expand the planning concept to incorporate management. "Effective management of tourism will involve a range of techniques including marketing and publicity, information and interpretation as well as planning controls and traffic management" (English Tourist Board 1981a, 82). This acknowledges that tourism involves people as well as places, and that planning a facility in harmony with its environment is only part of the success story. Management is also required to make visitors aware of the attraction, help them get the most out of their visit and thus ensure a goodwill ambassador. It can also channel their movements so as to spread the load or protect sensitive areas. As the Disney resort developer observes:

After dealing with nearly 300 million people, at Disneyland and Walt Disney World, however, we've learned probably as much as anyone about anticipating, and meeting, the needs of people. In our book, that's what master planning and attraction development is all about—planning for the needs of people. (Elder 1980, 1)

Examples of management plans can be seen in the national park and heritage coast plans of Britain, the national park plans for Canada and the United States. Indeed, a recent comment concerning bear control in the Yellowstone and Glacier National Parks is indicative of the new trend: "We call it bear management," says Glacier ranger Bob Morey, "but 90 percent of it is people management" (*Newsweek* 1982, 18).

Integration of visitor considerations into the planning and management process is finally bringing a human perspective into the development process but to date it is largely restricted to only one component—the visitor, and the needs and desires of local residents tend to be subsumed in the interests of local businessmen and administrations. An examination of Baud-Bovy's diagrams reveals no opportunity for citizen participation yet the residents of a destination area are the ones operating on the shop floor. Residents must put up with the congestion, put on the "smiles," and live with the physical development, but have little or no say in the decision-making process that will inevitably affect their community and way of life. Development and planning

in isolation from the community at large cannot continue if the industry is to develop in harmony with the capacity and aspirations of destination areas. To become a self-renewable resource industry and agent of hospitality will require more citizen participation in the development, or non-development, of a destination.

Tourism and the planning process

The move toward a more balanced goal formation and planning within a community setting has prompted some preliminary attempts at integrating tourism into local plans, but so far with limited success. Heeley (1981, 74) reports that the British statutory planning reforms "created larger and more powerful authorities which, allied with the trend towards corporate management and organization within local government, promised to root tourism more securely within the local government machine." However, after reviewing the actual planning experience he concludes tourism has received "little heavy-weight expression in the post-reorganization authorities," a feeling supported by the observations of Veal (1975) in the Midlands and Palmer and Probert (1980) in South Wales.

In Canada the emphasis has been to integrate tourism planning into a provincial strategy of general economic and social development. The province of Ontario created a "Framework for Opportunity" strategy which focused on seventeen "development zones," each with its own identity and potential (Ardagh 1977). These zones cannot be contiguous in such a large province, so they are linked by touring corridors and bound together by hinterland environments. In British Columbia the provincial tourism strategy is based on nine major tourist regions and is designed to facilitate regionally distinctive themes reflecting the economic and physical diversity of the province (British Columbia 1979). In both provinces a major concern is the coordination of tourism development with existing economic activities and a multitude of administrative boundaries. In British Columbia alone there are:

Seventeen provincial ministries (of which Fisheries, Forestry and Highways are particularly important), 15 federal departments/agencies (including the Canadian Government Office of Tourism which is responsible for promotion and the Department of Regional Industrial Expansion which is responsible for federal economic development programs), 13

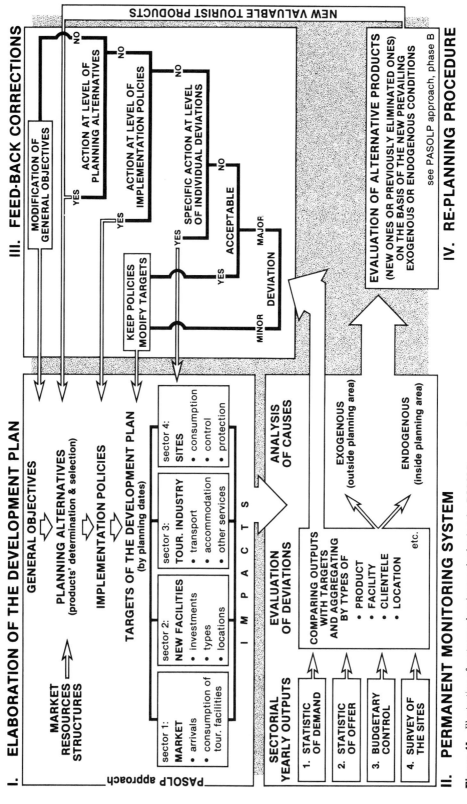

Figure 41 Illustration of systems planning method using the PASOLP approach
Source: Baud-Bovy and Lawson (1977)

major industry sectors, 9 tourism regions and numerous municipalities and special interest groups intimately involved in the tourism sector. (British Columbia 1979, 5)

It is not surprising, therefore, that the Canadian Tourism Sector Task Force called for a focusing of planning responsibility within a single government department, with a definition of respective tourism roles for all government levels (Powell 1978). This in fact echoes Heeley's (1981, 74) sentiment that "although tourism is so clearly ripe for some corporate treatment, there are few signs of holistic approaches being adopted."

In response to the need for a more comprehensive and integrated approach to tourism planning at the local level, two tourism consultants have proposed a community emphasis to tourism planning. Rosenow and Pulsipher (1979, 63) believe a principal advantage of possessing a place that residents believe is special is "that planning can begin from an agreed-upon point of reference. Consensus, always elusive in land-use planning, is more attainable when special qualities have been commonly recognized." Consequently, they have developed a personality planning process which attempts to identify the elements that make a community unique and assist in formulating specific action programs to enhance that uniqueness and its tourism appeal.

The process involves four steps. First, the delineation of distinctive community features, including its historical and natural resources, ethnic and cultural features, and dominant landforms. Second, the plotting of critical zones. These are areas where the visual quality is especially important, such as entrance routes, major travel corridors and areas which attract large numbers of people. These critical zones are seen as "the community's public face" (Rosenow and Pulsipher 1979, 67), and may be equated with MacCannell's front setting. Third, the establishment of use objectives within each critical zone. These may involve preservation, modification (development that is compatible with the zone's appearance), or enhancement (altering or concealing obtrusive elements). Fourth, the formulation of specific action programs based on the use objectives. These can include such things as zoning, the purchase of scenic easements, landscaping, and the preservation of historic buildings or dominant landforms.

In practice the specific action programs can be as varied as the individual community's resources and creativity. Rosenow and Pulsipher provide an example of this planning process at work in Heber Valley, a mountain valley near Salt Lake City, Utah. They conclude in this case study that public input is essential:

The people who must live with the planning decisions should be involved in their formulation, particularly since many action programs resulting from personality planning are not community or public sector efforts: they must be implemented through the initiative of individual landowners or citizens. (Rosenow and Pulsipher 1979, 81).

With such a planning process a community can retain its own sense of place and develop it according to its own priorities and capacity.

From this short review of tourism's planning goals it is evident that although the industry's focus has been changing it is still far short of establishing itself within the general planning framework of industrial nations. It needs to continue to restructure its priorities so that environmental and social factors may be placed alongside economic considerations. The growing emphasis on a community responsibility should continue, since this industry uses the community as a resource, sells it as a product, and in the process affects the lives of everyone. The more comprehensive regional approach to planning must continue if the fragmented industry and its market, which both cross so many political, geographic, and administrative boundaries, are to be coordinated into a meaningful tourism product and experience. What is needed is some framework which can pull these general trends together and permit tourism to be integrated into established planning practices and policies.

11

Tourism as a community industry*

Planning for tourism has changed and evolved along with the industry since the Second World War. It has developed from a site-oriented and physical emphasis into a more regional and systems approach. Part of the systems approach includes a management concept in recognition of visitor and resident perceptions and their bearing on a successful travel experience. This process of evolution will continue as tourism enters a new phase, with different demands and priorities.

The tourism industry is entering a stage of maturity after its 40 years of rapid expansion and development. There has been evidence of a slowdown in growth rates during the 1970s, part of which may be attributed to the recession, but part of which can be linked to changing demographic profiles and consumer preferences. The days of novelty and naivety on the part of the tourist have disappeared. Tourists now expect and demand more because they are experienced travelers. They will be satisfied no longer with second-rate attractions and accommodation, nor with poor service and rudeness. It is a buyer's market and there are many destinations and alternative experiences from which to choose. Increasingly one hears the call for quality, hospitality and value for money—and all of these require careful planning and management.

It is not only the industry which is facing maturity, for the mass tourism experience has taught destination areas many hard lessons. In this competitive business changing circumstances or fashions can quickly erode an established market. A destination needs to protect the integrity and attraction of its own product, plus guard against the action and rivalry of competitors. This is forcing destinations to look beyond their own situation and consider joint ventures with other destinations in

*Based on P. E. Murphy (1983), "Tourism as a community industry," *Tourism Management*, 4, 180–93

order to create a more coordinated and appealing product. The key lessons emerging from the past 40 years are quality, flexibility, and coordination.

The residents of destination areas have received their instruction as to the benefits and problems associated with the industry. This activity, like all others, has its costs to society and the environment. In economic terms it brings low-paid and seasonal employment in the main, with most of the benefits traditionally flowing to a limited number of businesses. The environmental and cultural conservation interests of the industry have not prevented over-exploitation and destruction of the physical and cultural landscape. Socially, the number of visitors can exceed the capacity of local communities to absorb and benefit from the interaction.

The evidence suggests that tourism is an established part of our lives and is unlikely to retreat into its past as the exclusive pursuit of a privileged few. The maturity of the industry and destination communities will require more comprehensive and balanced planning, that can take into account both the issues and options which have emerged since the Second World War. One possible direction for such planning would be to view tourism as part of a destination community's ecosystem.

Ecological approach

An ecosystem is "any area of nature that includes living organisms and non-living substances interacting to produce an exchange of materials between the living and non-living parts" (Odum 1970, 262). Tourism would fit into such a system, since it involves destination areas, where visitors interact with local living (hosts, services) and non-living (landscape, sunshine) parts to experience (consume) a tourism product. There is an interdependence in the system because neither can succeed without the other; the natural resources of the community require industry involvement to inform, transport, and accommodate visitors; the industry needs social support from the destination community to fulfill its hospitality function. The interaction of these components produces an exchange of revenue between various sectors, that, if properly managed, can lead to the creation of a renewable resource industry.

The important characteristics of an ecosystem approach are its flexibility (in that it can be applied at any scale) and the concept of reciprocity between its living and non-living component parts. For tourism, with its multiple planning scales and symbiotic relationship between prosperity and a healthy environment, such features appear to be most appropriate. However, "before interfering any more seriously with existing complex living relationships an effort must be made to understand them" (Tucker 1970, 23) and one of the more informative ways for tourism is to focus on the community setting of ecological systems.

An ecological community is a group of a few or many species living together in a locality. Such communities may be classified on a hierarchical basis, with each possessing its own ecological potential or its own carrying capacity, representing the number of organisms and activities the local ecosystem can sustain. The carrying capacity of each community depends not only on its scale and resources but also on its seasonable periodicity and stage of development.

The spatial and temporal characteristics of an ecological community have particular relevance to tourism planning. Their relatively static nature provides a tangible entity for both the expert and the layman; for the expert it is an area to study and plan, for the layman it is often home and a matter of survival. The hierarchical nature of the ecological community enables planners to select the scale most pertinent to their analysis and management purposes. The temporal perspective enables the significance of tourism's seasonality to be incorporated into planning. The seasonal periodicity associated with ecological communities helps to make us more aware of the importance of an "off-season" for the regeneration of both physical and social environments. In the longer term there is a link between the evolutionary cycle of a resort and the self-regulating tendencies of an ecosystem.

A model of an ecological approach to tourism

planning is presented in two stages in Figure 42 (A and B). Like all schemas it is a simplification of complex processes and no proportionality or relativity should be implied.

The spatial perspective with its associated hierarchy is represented by the community scale boxes of Figure 42A. These are discrete jurisdictional systems, each with their own priorities and goals, and their size is indicative of their scale of operations. The physical, economic, social–cultural, and exchange components of the community's ecology are portrayed as continuums to illustrate their continuous nature and have been joined to show they are interrelated. The negative and positive signs represent situations where a component is undeveloped or over-developed with regard to the community's tourism carrying capacity. An ecological balance would be achieved at some mid-point where all the components can function without being threatened.

Different goals have been associated with each planning level in Figure 42B, representing the divergent interests which exist at various community levels. At the national scale the main concerns are economic and social issues, such as the balance of payments and socio-economic problems of depressed peripheral regions. The tourism goals at this level are primarily conceptual and are manifested by policy statements, intended to conserve and develop tourism resources which will enhance the attraction of a national tourist product and depressed regions in particular. At the regional level, concern over environmental capabilities and route carrying capacities comes to the fore. To apply national directives and policies in the field requires recognition of regional constraints and the multiple demands placed on a regional ecosystem. The general goals of the national level are replaced by more specific objectives using ecological and systems models to determine the relevant trade-offs and consequences. At the local level the implications of physical development and the wishes of residents become more important. Local issues include concern over the site impact of proposals and the neighborhood effect of such developments, which are essentially questions of local physical and social carrying capacities. But above these considerations is the challenge to the *status quo* which all change represents, and whether the public considers a proposal will produce net improvements over existing conditions. At this level, widespread participation in the decision-

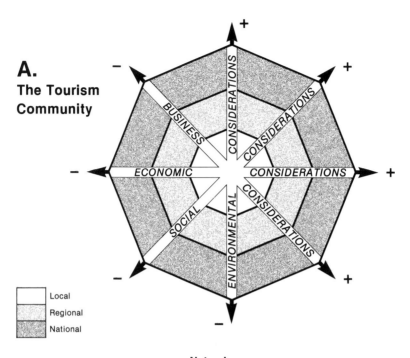

A.
The Tourism Community

BUSINESS CONSIDERATIONS

CONSIDERATIONS

ECONOMIC CONSIDERATIONS

SOCIAL

ENVIRONMENTAL CONSIDERATIONS

Local
Regional
National

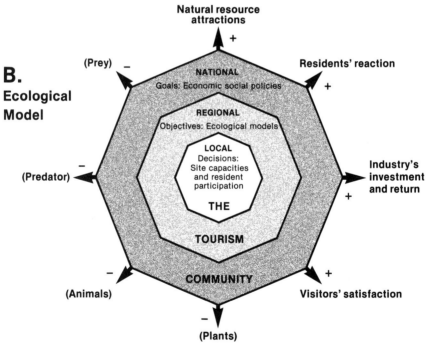

B.
Ecological Model

Natural resource
attractions

(Prey) −

Residents' reaction

NATIONAL
Goals: Economic social policies

REGIONAL
Objectives: Ecological models

LOCAL
Decisions:
Site capacities
and resident
participation

THE

TOURISM

COMMUNITY

(Predator)

Industry's
investment
and return

(Animals)

Visitors' satisfaction

(Plants)

Figure 42   Ecological model of tourism planning

making process is either a statutory or practical necessity. Although the economic considerations have been emphasized at the national level this does not mean they become insignificant at the local level. Indeed as we saw in an earlier chapter individual communities are concerned about the level of economic return they can expect from this industry, and several have looked to multiplier studies to give them some guidance in this area. Acceptance of a multi-level approach to tourism goals and planning, however, helps overcome the parochial nature of many such studies and permits a more balanced assessment of the situation. In this way it answers one of Hanna's questions on page 95.

The components selected for study and consideration in the model are those which are relevant to both an ecosystem and tourism alike, and their functional relationships are examined in more detail in Figure 42B. From an ecological perspective the key elements are a community's resource attractions, which reflect its natural and cultural heritage. These are the basis of tourism activity, needing to be protected and conserved if the industry is to fulfill its renewable resource potential. They can be equated with the plant life of an ecosystem, since this forms the basis of the food chain which if over-harvested can lead to loss of life and general physical degradation.

The residents' reactions to tourism incorporates Doxey's concept of local attitudes changing with the scale and form of tourism development. Development can lead to euphoria or antagonism, the general objective being to achieve a balance of development that brings economic and amenity benefits within acceptable levels of commercialism and congestion. Residents are equated with the animals of the local ecosystem. They are part of the community's general attraction and are expected to be hospitable, yet they also need to go about their daily lives while they are part of the community show.

The industry's investment and return reiterates Gunn's concern that as a business tourism must make an acceptable profit. While Gunn's comments related to individual entrepreneurs this continuum refers to the community as a whole. If the community is to be put on show, selling its natural resources and heritage, it should be able to identify a satisfactory level of return for its efforts and inconvenience. In this case the industry has been likened to the predators of an ecosystem. It feeds on the plants and animals by selling the landscape, amenities and culture of a destination. A predator is not an evil creature in the natural world for it keeps the system in balance. Likewise, the industry makes a contribution to a destination community if it husbands local resources and provides tangible benefits (such as revenue and amenities) in the process.

Visitor satisfaction should be a goal for every tourist destination, for customer satisfaction is vital to the survival of all businesses. If a destination's tourist product delivers what was promised in the image and pleases the visitor, the exchange will bring immediate revenue and future business through word of mouth recommendations. The visitors can be equated with prey in an ecosystem, because the predator industry has fed on them directly and the community gained from them via indirect and induced earnings.

Not only do visitors pay for the privilege of visiting a community, they are increasingly being asked to pay a premium. In York, England, local residents are admitted free of charge into the city's Heritage Centre while visitors must pay an entrance fee. China is reputed to be discriminating against foreign visitors in their tourist charges for transportation, food, accommodation (*Vancouver Sun* 1982). In this way we see the stirrings of a demonstrated economic return for community facilities and public goods, and in most cases the visitor is prepared to accept a nominal fee to see or use a quality attraction.

While not everyone would like to equate the tourist industry with predators and the visitor as its prey, this analogy is well-founded within the ecological community concept. In many cases a community's major attractions are public goods like the landscape, cultural heritage, and community facilities. To these the industry has added supplemental and supportive facilities to encourage the visitor to stay longer and spend more money. Visitors are prey because the community, especially the tourist industry, feeds on them and the revenue they bring. They are asked to pay higher prices during the prime seasons, but their reaction to this is general acquiescence as long as they are satisfied with their visit, particularly in terms of value for money.

A tourism example of providing value for money while operating within an ecological framework is provided by Walt Disney World, Florida:

Planning for WDW followed ecological considerations. The 27,000 acre area was defined by two, primary, natural drainage channels, with a ridge between them. These channels immediately identified the most buildable parts of

Planning and management

WDW—the Magic Kingdom would be located on one naturally high ground, and Buena Vista [a recreation community] on another.

The planning goal was to make most of the dry season areas dry all year around; and to achieve this, a sophisticated drainage system was designed and built to keep three-fourths of WDW dry, year-round without unduly lowering the water table and thus adversely affecting the total ecology of the area. (Blake 1972, 38)

To achieve a balance with nature the scale of development was kept in proportion with the environmental capacity of the area. Thus, the Magic Kingdom amusement park occupies only 100 acres, and Buena Vista 4000 acres out of the total 27,000 acres, which represents an area twice the size of Manhattan. Furthermore, disruption of the environment has been minimized by processing and controlling the effluent and other by-products of the development projects. For example,

a modern incinerator that cleans its own stack emissions; a tertiary sewage treatment plant that removes 97 percent of suspended solids; a "living farm" of trees and plants to filter waste water "naturally" after it leaves the sewage plant; and a gas-fired jet engine energy plant that recycles waste heat and uses it to cool many of the structures at WDW. (Blake 1972, 32)

The delay and expense of ecological planning has not prevented Disney World from becoming a profitable business venture, and it has enabled the development of a sensitive environment to the benefit of all concerned.

For a destination area to compete and prosper in the competitive world of tourism all four components in Figure 42A must attain a state of mutual interdependence and coexistence. If any of the four develops out of proportion, or becomes disenchanted with the process, the ecological community will retreat from its climax equilibrium state. Thus, an important aspect of the ecological community model is the concept of balance between the various components and scales. Increasingly, researchers and planners are referring to the stewardship of resources and the need to balance tourism's demands with a community's other needs and priorities (British Tourist Authority 1975; Romeril and Hughes-Evans 1980). But in most cases such thoughts are expressed in terms of a single community or level (as in the case of Disney World) without acknowledging the hierarchical scales and functions of ecological and tourism systems, thereby omitting some important interdependencies of both systems.

Krippendorf's (1975) treatise *Die Landschaftsfresser* (*The Landscape Devourers*) illustrates the growing link between tourism and an ecological setting, but in this case too the ecological community's full hierarchy and balance of components is incomplete. Krippendorf's experience as Director of the Swiss Tourist Association revealed the environmental dangers of uncontrolled tourism development which he describes as "crudely chomping into the landscape" (Zimmerman 1980, 31) destroying the very features which first attracted it. He proposes 23 strategies "for a human and environment-oriented tourism policy," with his first proposal being the "maintenance of decent, humane living conditions" where the "care and protection of the landscape must invariably be accorded priority over the economic and technical expediencies of tourism." He suggests this broader approach to tourism planning be implemented on a large scale, with regional planning representing the minimum acceptable level of "decentralized concentration."

Krippendorf's proposed focus for tourism planning at the regional level or higher excludes the local level, the coalface of the industry. The familiar urban arenas of tourist activity, the individual lakes and valleys, have been discounted in the drive for coordination and a rational regional policy. But such a strategy reduces concern for the building blocks of a regional perspective and excludes the local population from a decision-making process involving their particular community.

It is the municipal level which must implement regional plans (Canada) or structure plans (England), hold public hearings, zone the land and live with the outcome—good or bad. The political dimension of this decision-making process has been underrated generally by planners and developers. They have failed to give adequate weight to the short-term horizons of elected representatives and the growing involvement of interest groups—particularly those concerned with environmental issues. Rose in his review of the "philosophy and purpose of planning" quotes Buchanan:

Statutory land planning may be a vital element, but it remains only one element in any effective organizational planning system. Until this is more widely understood we shall make little progress. (Rose 1974, 53)

The lack of sufficient consultation and planning at the local level has certainly contributed to the delay and demise of many projects and policies proposed by central planning authorities. An ecological community approach maintains that a planning system must extend down to the micro-scale of local government. Integration cannot be terminated at an intermediary level, as advocated by Krippendorf, nor left solely in the hands of "experts." It must be complete in terms of both scale and input.

Management of physical and social resources to lead to an improved quality of life can be extended to a local area situation through the use of techniques such as gaming simulation. Loukissas (1982) reports on the successful utilization of this technique during a Man and the Biosphere (MAB) project "Ecology and rational use of insular systems," held on the Greek island of Skopelos. He shows that participants (laymen who make decisions or researchers from specific disciplines) "more quickly assimilated large amounts of information about the geography, history, economy, and other aspects of an area or situation through gaming than [via] more traditional approaches" (Loukissas 1982, 10). The technique was able "to take into account many relevant elements such as political, economic, and psychological factors and integrate them" without the vagueness associated with theoretical discussion.

Public participation

The community emphasis of the ecological community model indicates that as the scale of planning decreases more public participation should be expected and encouraged. Planning experience in other fields reveals that informed and able citizens are willing to participate in decisions regarding the development and future of their communities (Coppock and Sewell 1977; Sadler 1978). The same public has considerable tourism experience, both as hosts and visitors, providing a reservoir of information and enthusiasm if properly tapped. Runyan and Wu believe that:

The inclusion of complex impact considerations in a tourism planning process strongly implies relatively wide community involvement in impact assessment. Increased involvement in estimating complex impacts contributes to the reliability of the estimates. Such involvement also serves as a constructive vehicle for appraisal of impacts by individuals and groups other than those which are "expert," a body of interests most planners feel should be included in a planning process.

The strength of professionals lies in forecasting relatively simple and quantitatively definable impacts; the wide involvement allows a look at more complex impacts, their comparison with those that are relatively simple, and an appraisal of the combination. Although resident involvement can significantly increase the time and effort required by professionals to complete a project, the payoff is impact information of increased reliability and usefulness. (Runyan and Wu 1979, 451)

The call for participatory planning is a criticism of the business and physical orientation of past tourism planning and its failure to keep abreast with developments in urban and environmental planning. Goodman describes the move towards community planning as:

A system of community socialism (as opposed to either private enterprise or centralized socialism), in which the economic institutions would grow from the smaller government units in society, is a model which would allow social outputs to be determined by the people most immediately affected by them. (Goodman 1972, 217)

Input from concerned community groups could provide a balance to the short-term objectives of the business sector, and possibly encourage greater variation and local flavor in future projects which would be a welcome change from the growing homogenization of present development. Past experience with public participation in other planning areas indicates "participation on a mass scale is an idealistic dream. In a representative democracy, it is impractical and unnecessary; in a political culture with a tradition of elitism, it is out of the question" (O'Riordan 1978, 153). Thus in many instances it has been found that the process has been institutionalized (O'Riordan 1978; Tozer 1981) or even conservative in approach (Kasperson 1978; Burton 1979), representing a middle-class and environmentally conscious involvement rather than a radical fringe, as had first been expected.

Public participation experience on both sides of the Atlantic indicates the process is predominantly issue-oriented and is able to operate most effectively when these issues are local and can be approached at an early stage in the planning process, before commitments are made and battle lines drawn (Murphy 1978). The Skeffington Committee Report (Skeffington 1969) argued persuasively for wider public participation in British planning and many of its recommendations were subsequently adopted in the structure planning process of the late 1970s. In the United States, the wave of citizen participation has spread from the Model City Program of the inner cities to include interest group participation in the preparation of environmental impact statements, as outlined in the National Environmental Policy Act of

Planning and management

1969. In Canada, public participation has been made obligatory in neighborhood improvement programs and became the cornerstone of Justice Berger's MacKenzie Valley Pipeline Inquiry; but the most active arena for tourism-related public participation has been in response to various national park planning proposals (Herrero 1978; Sloan 1978; Hoole 1978; MacFarlane 1979a; Davidson 1979).

Public participation as a form of political action has modified existing institutions and planning procedures to affect social change and environmental preservation, so its extension to tourism (an activity so interwoven with community life) becomes inevitable. Tourism development is a local issue because that is the level where the action takes place. It possesses high visibility and impact so many are aware of its existence and many have experienced some ramifications, be they employment, congestion or new amenities (Easdale Holiday Village 1981). The question remains whether these same people are willing or able to become involved with tourism development decisions and how effective this is likely to be.

Perusal of the major tourism texts and planning guidelines indicates that in this activity, as in others, there is a slow retreat from large-scale technocratic plans toward a more humanistic and small-scale level of development. Gunn (1972), in his book *Vacationscape: Designing Tourist Regions*, reflected the view of the "expert planner" and traditional approach. The emphasis was on the economic and physical problems of tourism development with only two pages devoted to citizens' views. This concern was subtitled "citizen feedback" and as the title suggests, can be equated with a tokenism approach—allowing citizens to provide data and react to the proposals of experts, but not letting them become involved in setting priorities or participating in the decision making. In this book Gunn supported the standard planning process of periodic consultation with interested groups, noting that while "constructive local criticism is productive ... it is no substitute for professional responsibility and competence in carrying out the process" (Gunn 1972, 178).

His more recent work is similarly directed toward the physical and business concerns of tourism planning (Gunn 1979), but now contains an illuminating observation:

Early in all tourism planning it is essential to identify the *full range of actors*, those who have the ability to make changes in development and management of the tourism system. . . . The

decisions of many governmental and private organizations are important to tourism and maybe not all can actively participate in planning. Even so, it is the responsibility of the planner to be comprehensive in his assessment of tourism development actors. Lack of this has been a major *deterrent to implementation* of plans generally. (Gunn 1979, 202, author's italics)

Thus, there is now some recognition that more actors should become involved, those who are experts and those who are affected. Such interaction may reduce the frustrating delays of past confrontations and lead to more harmonious development.

In contrast to this traditional approach, Seekings (1980) suggests we bear in mind the whole community and think of "*pro bono publico*" (the public good), while Murphy (1980b) feels more consensus of opinion may exist between actor groups than is commonly supposed. Seekings considers that "tourism has become too important to be left to tourism experts" (1980, 253). He contends that individual entrepreneurs, various government agencies and multiple levels of administration have resulted in unsystematic and haphazard growth, where "the left hand not only cannot influence the right hand, it also does not know what the right hand is doing" (Seekings 1980, 256). Consequently, he calls for more coordination at all levels, including participation by the public:

The affairs of the industry should be deliberately subjected to public scrutiny and debate. In particular, all major policy proposals should be thoroughly ventilated in public before becoming officially adopted as policy. (Seekings 1980, 257)

The main concern of planners and government officials is whether such "ventilation" can lead to constructive proposals or strategies. Murphy's work suggests that if the public and private groups are given the chance to participate at an early stage there is sufficient consensus of opinion to permit broadly based planning objectives. Murphy was struck by

the willingness of the residents to participate and their ability to develop rational and practical options. This confirms that tourism planning need not remain the realm of the expert alone; given the chance, the public can provide a useful input into the decision-making process. (Murphy 1980b, 366)

In the case of those tourist centers examined, the residents wished to diversify their individual tourism sectors within a more balanced economy. They did not want to become over-dependent on a seasonal activity but were willing to see tourism develop as an additional economic base.

Systems planning

What are the implications of setting ecological community goals, such as community survival and evolution to a climax stage, for tourism planning? If these goals represent yet another elusive holy grail an ecological community approach will offer no real advance over tourism's current economic emphasis and growing environmental awareness. But this approach offers more substance than goals because it can be integrated into the current planning system and permits the crucial extension from planning to management.

An ecological community approach can be put into operation using the systems theory and analysis which is now widely used in urban and regional planning circles (Chapin 1965; McLoughlin 1970; Chadwick 1971; Hall 1974). Systems theory is mainly concerned with "*complicated* systems where components exhibit a high degree of *interdependence*. The behavior of the whole system is then usually something very much more than the sum of the parts," according to Wilson (1981, 3). The system under study can be hypothetical or real, and can vary in size and complexity, which makes this approach ideally suited to the study and planning of the multi-dimensional tourism industry within a community framework.

Systems analysis in planning considers four basic components. These include *human activities*, especially those which occur at specific locations and times, and consequently have a regular pattern; *communications* within the system which are recurrent and spatially clustered, such as media markets, information fields and transportation; the *space* within which these activities and communications take place; and a *time factor*, because to control any dynamic system one must know how it evolves and what outcomes various strategies are likely to have on its development.

Tourism activity relates as closely to this analytical approach as it did with the community ecology setting. The *human activity* patterns would include the seasonal and destination preferences of visitors, and planning for this influx would include strategies to disperse or concentrate the activity within a system. *Communication* is relevant in terms of information flows and the movement of visitors to and around the system. Communication in the form of a destination's "tourist image" is a vital first step used to inform potential visitors what to expect. Then, once they arrive, visitors must be

aided in finding the various attractions and directed away from congested or ecologically delicate areas. The *spatial size* of the system will depend on the type of community under consideration and problems to be considered. It can vary from a major physiographic region such as a watershed, where the emphasis will be on vegetation protection and pollution control, to an inner city district where heritage conservation and new uses for old buildings may be the major concern. The *time factor* will be the community's position on the evolutionary cycle of development, for a system's options will vary depending on whether it is at the "exploration" stage or "stagnation" stage of Butler's model.

A systems approach to the planning of tourism offers two advantages which fit in well with the ecological community model. First, its flexibility enables it to be applied at various levels with a different emphasis at each level. Second, the concept of continuous monitoring ties together the twin objectives of planning and management. McLoughlin (1970, 79), an advocate of systems planning, notes a "keypoint to remember is that a system is not the real world but a way of looking at it," therefore a systems approach is ideal for meeting the variety of goals outlined in Figure 42. As Rickson has observed:

Tourism is clearly not a closely-integrated or centralized industry and this makes it rather difficult to come to grips with and to manage and develop by central direction. Such an approach would, in fact, be unworkable. (Rickson 1973, 270)

Implementation of national directives must be pursued at regional and local levels. The main concern at the regional level is to integrate tourism into a viable regional product, which complements existing economic activities and protects the environment. As Krippendorf's proposals indicate, there is a close link between the systems approach and the ecological community concept; but use of the systems approach enables planning to extend downward to the municipal level that was not covered by Krippendorf. At the local level the emphasis switches from the economic and environmental strategies of general plans to community concerns about physical and social carrying capacities of projected development sites and their neighborhood effect on land-use plans.

Any ecosystem, involving as it does the interactions between users and the environment, requires constant monitoring to observe when areas or people are coming under stress. This monitoring is the first step toward total management, which either attempts to prevent the stress or steer the system to recovery. The link between environmental and human management is illustrated by the English Tourist Board's (1981a, 82) recommendations that: "The effective management of tourism will involve a range of techniques including marketing and publicity, information and interpretation as well as planning controls and traffic management measures." To provide such comprehensive direction and control for the industry within an ecosystem perspective requires the flexibility and continuous feedback of a systems planning approach.

The move toward some form of systems planning is already underway in several areas of tourism planning, most notably in the national park systems of North America and Britain, but there is no logical reason why the ecological community perspective and systems approach cannot be extended to more multiple land-use settings. The opportunity for a systems approach involving ecological goals is most apparent in non-urban settings where the visitor has come to use and admire the natural environment. Wall and Wright (1977) have developed a schematic concept which illustrates the need for all natural resource-based tourism to balance visitor volumes and types with environmental capacity considerations. Their four-fold impact scenario examines the potential visitor impact on soil, vegetation, wildlife, and water; but, as Simmons has pointed out, while the "types of ecosystem which people like to be in for their outdoor recreation are very varied … certain preferences emerge. Overriding them all is the attraction of water" (Simmons 1981, 95). Therefore, one of the greatest needs for systems planning in a tourism context is in areas where water is the major attraction and source of conflict over use.

Coastal zone management is a good example of systems planning based on ecological foundations, and is one where the tourism component is beginning to play a role. A systems approach is invaluable in a situation where there is a wide variety of physical features, a large range of capabilities and a multitude of land-use options—as is the case in these narrow coastal stretches of land. The significance of visitor access and contribution of tourism toward the conservation and prosperity of the coastal zone is becoming more apparent. For example, access to a coastal area and then to the beach attractions within it is a major planning concern for the Gower Peninsula in Wales. The "words of an old Welsh rugby song, 'If you want to go to Gower,

you can get there in an hour,' sum up the promise and threat to Gower and West Glamorgan," according to its County Planning Officer (King 1982). The new motorway mobility has brought this scenic, and hitherto isolated area, within easy driving range of the English Midlands and other major tourist-generating areas. Examples of conservation and tourism combining forces can be seen in the land-use planning of Les Mielles in the Channel Island of Jersey, where a balance has been struck "between recreation, tourism, conservation, agriculture and sand excavation" (Romeril 1983). In the Studland Heath National Nature Reserve in the county of Dorset, England, the coexistence of tourism/recreation and a fragile duneland has been achieved via controlled access and visitor education. Tourism-aided revitalization of declining harbor areas can be seen in the rebirth of St Katharine's Dock in London and the renovation of several other waterfront areas. Finally, the lure of the seaside continues to bring employment and revenue to many coastal resorts, despite the attraction of far and exotic lands in this age of jet travel.

Systems planning with ecological goals need not be restricted to wilderness or rural areas, for this form of planning can be applied to complex and dynamic human settlements like urban regions. Bourne (1982) has illustrated the link between a systems approach and urban analysis and planning. For a summary see Table 29, to which has been added a column extending the link to the ecological community of a destination area. The destination's *nucleus* is formed by the tourist resources which attracted visitors in the first place, be it climate, history, landscape, or a combination of all three. *Geometric area* is a function of the natural ecosystem and scale of planning jurisdiction most pertinent to the destination area. The *elements* are those numerous industrial components which are needed to develop and augment the original resources into a viable tourist product. The *organizational principle* or energy of the system is competition. Competition in the tourism market place is continuous for all destinations, for few possess truly unique attractions and, therefore, tourists have a multitude of options open to them. Competition is involved also in the use of community resources, although in this case economic considerations may be supplanted by social and conservation principles at the community level. The *behavior* of tourism is seasonal, especially in the higher latitudes where the weather is a prime con-

Table 29 Systems components in urban spatial structure and a destination area

System components	Corresponding elements in	
	Urban areas	Destination area
1. Nucleus: the point of system origin and locus of control	1. The initial settlement (e.g. a harbor and central business district)	1. Destination area (initial attractions, which are usually natural attractions)
2. Geometric area and boundaries of the system	2. Geographic extent and limits of urban area	2. Geographic extent and limits of destination area
3. Elements: the parts, units, or bits which form membership of the system	3. Social groups, land uses, activities, interactions, and institutions	3. Supply and demand sides of tourist market, including accommodation, additional facilities, infrastructure, visitor demands and preferences
4. Organizational principles: what ties the system together and allocates activities to areas; what "energy" drives the system?	4. Underlying logic or principles of urban structure (e.g. land market) and the determinants of growth	4. Underlying logic or principles of destination area development (e.g. market competition, relative accessibility, consumer demand), resource competition, resource management
5. Behavior: how the system acts over time; its routine and non-routine actions	5. The way the city works; its activity patterns and growth performance	5. Seasonality of activity, routine events (festivals), and non-routine (weather)
6. An environment: the "external" context that influences that system	6. Sources and types of external determinants of urban structure	6. International economic conditions, relative national position, and consumer preferences
7. Time path: a trend of evolution and change	7. A development sequence: historical profile of building cycles and transport eras	7. Development sequence: growth of leisure, transport eras, and evolution of destination area

Source: Based on Bourne (1982, 32)

sideration. Numerous cities are attempting to extend their tourist seasons and make better use of under-utilized capital by developing a conference/convention trade. *External* factors influencing the destination area generally affect its competitive position, as in the case of changing economic conditions in tourist-generating regions, relative accessibility influenced by changes in transport schedules and routes, and changes in consumer tastes. All growth and development takes place within a *time path* and the destination area is constantly changing and aging. When a destination evolves and becomes well known the type of visitor and tourist image will change, as well as its visitor volumes.

The systems link within urban destinations in terms of its ecological setting has been appreciated, and is beginning to be utilized in small-scale projects, but its relevance to tourism planning on a large scale has yet to be fully realized. Detwyler (1972) has illustrated the two-way process between a city and its surrounding environment, noting how urban outputs can transform not only the city's hinterland but also the environments of distant locations. Unfortunately, many of these outputs, such as heat, waste, and garbage, are hazardous to the long-term stability of receiving environments. Appreciation of these environmental externalities has led to increased environmental awareness and planning in delicate areas such as coastal areas and the rural–urban fringe (Mattyasovsky 1975; Great Britain 1975; Chasis 1980).

Such localized planning has benefited both the residents and the tourist image of those cities concerned. But while cities have strived to preserve visually prominent landscapes and heritage they have often ignored the condition of less obvious and longer-term environmental assets. Nowhere is this problem more acute than in the Mediterranean basin. Because of its climate and cultural heritage this area is a tourist Mecca, yet unrestricted industrial development and dumping has contaminated the sea and badly damaged the area's tourist image. According to the United

Planning and management

Nations Environment Program:

as a result of man's activities, 120 tons of mineral oils, 60 tons of detergents, 100 tons of mercury, 3,800 tons of lead, 2,400 tons of chromium, 21,000 tons of zinc, 90 tons of pesticides, 1,120 tons of nitrogen and phosphorus, and 2,500 curies of radio-nuclides enter the Mediterranean annually. A price of some five billion dollars has been estimated as the cost of putting into effect a protocol that would limit the annual discharge of these substances from land-based sources. (Brown 1981, 22–3)

Without more of the inter-sector and inter-regional cooperation outlined in the systems approach to ecological planning, the tourism plans and investments of destination developments like Languedoc–Roussillon could be nullified by independent events and decisions in surrounding communities.

Summary

This section has presented the community concept in its ecological and systems forms as a means by which to develop and assess the tourism industry. Although none of the ideas or techniques suggested are original in themselves, their combination and orientation toward a tourism goal is new and reflects the growing impor-tance of environmental and political decision making. The industry's attitude toward the environment needs to progress from economic exploitation to one of steward-ship if attractive landscapes and amenities are to be preserved or developed. Public opinion and political power must be courted and won if the industry is to continue to rely on government support and community assets for its survival and success. By stressing the community and systems aspects of tourism it becomes apparent that this activity is now interwoven into the social, economic, and environmental aspects of all communities, whether or not they are major des-tinations. Under these circumstances, tourism can be integrated into the general planning procedures of all communities and become coordinated with facility developments in the physical and social fabric of destination areas.

The economic problems of the late 1970s and early 1980s have led many communities to consider embracing this growth industry of the post-industrial era. To do so, however, without careful analysis and consideration of the consequences can lead these same communities into a quicksand of false expectations. This book has attempted to pull together the various threads of modern tourism, to reveal its interrelated nature, and two-edged capabilities, so that communities and individuals may approach the industry in a more judicious manner. One suggestion for a more sensitive and cautious approach to development is the adoption of an ecological community approach in conjunction with systems planning. In this way, existing or new destinations may create more community control over the pace and style of their tourism development; enabling them to become individually recognizable components of the tourism market mosaic.

Afterword

Participation in action

The author was recently given an opportunity to put some of these ideas into practice when the tourism industry of Greater Victoria, British Columbia, invited him to help reassess its structure and direction. With sponsorship from the local chamber of commerce, a workshop was convened to initiate ideas from within the community that could later be brought before a larger forum for deliberation. Forty delegates were invited to the workshop, representing six major interest groups: attractions and festivals, community groups, economic support, government, hospitality, and transportation and in-bound travel. Several of these groups had a very broad base, for example the attractions and festivals included representatives of local arts and sports groups because of their growing interest in organizing festivals and events that could also appeal to the visitor as well as the resident; while the transportation and in-bound travel group included local transport companies and island representatives as well as members of the local visitors' bureau.

The workshop was an intense work session, using a group approach to problem solving to identify community goals and strategies for the industry. The basis of the session was the Delbecq technique which has the advantages of being "simple to run, interesting for participants and very productive for a short time and energy investment" (Runyan 1977, 128–9). It also has the advantage of producing documented recommendations (ballots) which are useful references and guides for subsequent meetings and decision making. The result of this workshop was to lead a diverse group of individuals and interests toward a few short- and long-term strategies, the overriding one being to restructure the industry so that it would have a broader base – making it more representative of the community at large and more responsible to that same community.

The workshop went a long way in isolating key issues and suggesting possible remedies, but it was only the first step. The ideas of this small group were intended to ease and guide the deliberations of larger and more representative assemblies at a later date. The striking of a task force committee from among the workshop participants, plus the deliberations of two later and much larger meetings produced a single umbrella organization to coordinate the tourist industry of the Greater Victoria region (*Times-Colonist* 1985).

The new structure for Victoria's tourism industry (Figure 43) is designed not only to facilitate greater coordination between the numerous groups involved in the local industry, it also recognizes the symbiotic link between tourism and its host community. Within its overall marketing focus it intends to create more local involvement, through festivals and events sponsored by residents, data collection and research, via post-secondary institutions, and invited participation from various business and interest groups. It intends to develop a local theme for the tourism product, one that is representative of the area and acceptable to the community. One suggestion has been a heritage theme "From Colony to Confederation," for Victoria is the oldest European settlement in the northwest. It will identify weaknesses and gaps in the local tourism product and in consultation with local authorities and residents seek ways to remedy such deficiencies. Finally, it will develop annual statements so that its public "shareholders," the local residents, will know how it is performing and what it has contributed to the local economy.

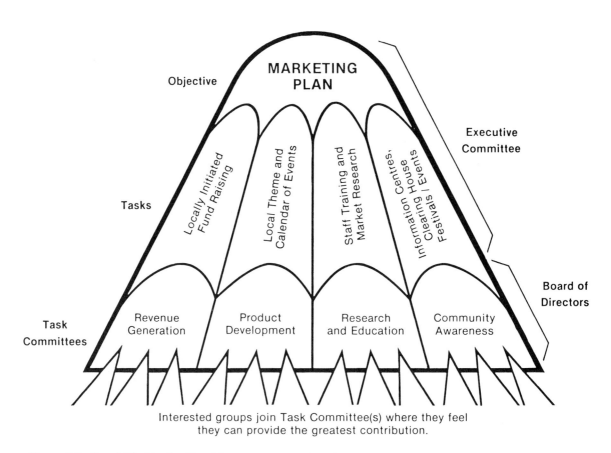

Figure 43 Task model for "Tourism Victoria"

References

Anderson, P. and Colberg, R. T. (1973) "Multivariate analysis in travel research: a tool for travel package design and market segmentation," *Proceedings of the Travel Research Association Fourth Annual Conference*, Sun Valley, Idaho, 225–40.

Appleyard, D. (ed.) (1979) *The Conservation of European Cities*, Cambridge, Mass., MIT Press.

Appleyard, D., Lynch, K., and Meyer, J. R. (1964) *The View from the Road*, Cambridge, Mass., MIT Press.

Archer, B. (1973) *The Impact of Domestic Tourism*, Bangor Occasional Papers in Economics, 2, Bangor, University of Wales.

Archer, B. H. (1976) "The uses and abuses of multipliers," in Gearing, C. E., Swart, W. W. and Var, T. (eds) *Planning for Tourism Development: Quantitative Approaches*, New York, Praeger, 115–33.

Archer, B. H. and Owen, C. B. (1971) "Towards a tourist regional multiplier," *Regional Studies*, 5, 289–94.

Ardagh, J. (1977) "Approaches to tourism development at the provincial level," *Tourism Development Approaches for the Future*, Proceedings of the Travel Research Association, Canadian Chapter, Ottawa, 1–13.

Arnstein, S. (1969) "A ladder of citizen participation," *Journal of American Institute of Planners*, 35, 216–24.

Baker, W. M. (1973) *The Nature and Extent of Vacation Home Data Sources and Research in Canada*, Ottawa, Statistics Canada.

Barkham, J. P. (1973) "Recreational carrying capacity: a problem of perception," *Area*, 5, 218–22.

Baud-Bovy, M. and Lawson, F. (1976) *Tourism Master Plan*, Toronto, Management Development Institute, Ryerson Polytechnical Institute.

Baud-Bovy, M. and Lawson, F. (1977) *Tourism and Recreation Development*, Boston, CBI.

Bayfield, N. G. (1971) "Some effects of walking and skiing on vegetation at Cairngorm," in Duffey, E. and Watt, A. S. (eds), *The Scientific Management of Animal and Plant Communities for Conservation*, Oxford, Blackwell, 469–85.

Beioley, S. (1981) *Tourism and Urban Regeneration: Some Lessons from American Cities*, London, English Tourist Board.

Bell, K. L. and Bliss, L. C. (1973) "Alpine disturbance studies: Olympic National Park, USA," *Biological Conservation*, 5, 25–32.

Best, G. M. (1972) *The Ulster and Delaware Railroad*, San Marion, Calif., Golden West Books.

Bielckus, C. L. (1977) "Second homes in Scandinavia," in Coppock, J. T. (ed.) *Second Homes: Curse or Blessing?*, Oxford, Pergamon, 35–46.

Binneweis, R. (1984) "Management strategies: Yosemite National Park experience," paper presented at the Symposium on Parks in British Columbia, Vancouver, February.

Blake, P. (1972) "Walt Disney World," *Architectural Forum*, June, 24–41.

Boissevain, J. (1979) "Impact of tourism on a dependent island: Gozo, Malta," *Annals of Tourism Research*, 6, 76–90.

Boorstin, D. J. (1975) *The Image: A Guide to Pseudo-Events in America*, New York, Atheneum.

Bourne, L. S. (1982) "Urban spatial structure," in Bourne, L. S. (ed.) *Internal Structure of the City*, Oxford, Oxford University Press, 28–45.

Brancher, D. M. (1972) "The minor road in Devon—a study of visitors' attitudes," *Regional Studies*, 6, 49–58.

British Columbia (1979) *Executive Summary of the Province of British Columbia Tourism Development Strategy*, Victoria, BC, Ministry of Tourism.

British Tourist Authority (1975) *Is There "Welcome" on the Mat?*, London, British Tourist Authority.

British Tourist Authority (1981) *The Economic Significance of Tourism within the European Community*, London, British Tourist Authority.

References

Brown, N. J. (1981) "International tourism: dynamics at destination," *Destination Dynamics: Tourism Research Planning and Information Implications.* Proceedings of The Travel and Tourism Research Association of Canada Conference, Vancouver, 1–35.

Brownrigg, M. and Greig, M. A. (1976) *Tourism and Regional Development*, Fraser of Allander Institute Speculative Papers, 5, Glasgow, Fraser of Allander Institute.

Bryan, A. (1973) *Much Is Taken, Much Remains*, North Scituate, Mass., Duxbury Press.

Bryan, W. R. (1981) "Improved mileage, discretionary income, and travel for pleasure," *Journal of Travel Research*, 20, 28–9.

Bryden, J. M. (1973) *Tourism and Development*, Cambridge, Cambridge University Press.

Buck, R. C. (1977) "Making good business better: a second look at staged tourist attractions," *Journal of Travel Research*, 15, 3, 30–2.

Buck, R. C. and Alleman, T. (1979) "Tourist enterprise concentration and old order Amish survival: explorations in productive coexistence," *Journal of Travel Research*, 13, 1, 15–20.

Budowski, G. (1977) "Tourism and conservation: conflict, coexistence and symbiosis," *Parks*, 1, 3–6.

Burde, J. H. and Lenzini, J. (1980) "Timber harvest and aesthetic quality: can they coexist?," in Hawkins, D. E., Shafer, E. L., and Rovelstad, J. M. (eds) *Tourism Planning and Development Issues*, Washington, DC, George Washington University Press, 121–32.

Burkart, A. J. and Medlik, S. (1974) *Tourism: Past, Present and Future*, London, Heinemann.

Burt, J. and MacKinnon, W. C. (1977) "Convention centres—their development and outlook," *Tourism Development: Approaches for the Future*, Proceedings of The Travel Research Association, Canadian Chapter, Ottawa, 137–55.

Burton, T. L. (1971) *Experiments in Recreational Research*, London, Allen & Unwin.

Burton, T. L. (1979) "A review and analysis of Canadian case studies in public participation," *Plan Canada*, 19, 1, 13–22.

Butler, R. W. (1975) "Tourism as an agent of social change," *Tourism as a Factor in National and Regional Development*, Occasional Paper 4, Peterborough, Ontario, Department of Geography, Trent University, 85–90.

Butler, R. W. (1980) "The concept of a tourism area cycle of evolution: implications for management of resources," *Canadian Geographer*, 24, 5–12.

Canada (1980) *Parks Canada Policy*, Ottawa, Ministry of the Environment.

Canadian Heritage **(1982)** "Heritage and tourism: a mixed blessing," May, 25–7.

Carr, S. and Schissler, D. (1969) "The city as a trip," *Environment and Behavior*, 1, 1, 7–35.

CGOT (1982) *Tourism Is Important to All of Us*, Ottawa. Canadian Government Office of Tourism.

Chadwick, G. (1971) *A Systems View of Planning*, London, Pergamon.

Chadwick, R. A. (1981) "Some notes on the geography of tourism: a comment," *Canadian Geographer*, 25, 191–7.

Chapin, F. S. (1965) *Urban Land Use Planning*, 2nd edn, Urbana, Ill., University of Illinois Press.

Chasis, S. (1980) "The coastal zone management act," *Journal of American Planning Association*, 46, 145–53.

Chau, P. (1973) "The economics of travel by Canadians in Canada," *Research for Changing Travel Patterns: Interpretations and Utilizations*, Fourth Annual Conference Proceedings of The Travel Research Association, Sun Valley, Idaho, 79–90.

Chau, P. (1977) "Unification of tourism measurement criteria," paper presented at World Tourism Organization Seminar on Tourism Statistics, Caracas, Venezuela.

Cheng, J. R. (1980) "Tourism: how much is too much? Lessons for Canmore from Banff," *Canadian Geographer*, 24, 72–80.

Christaller, W. (1964) "Some considerations of tourism location in Europe," *Papers and Proceedings of Regional Science Association*, 12, 95–105.

City of Westminster (1978) *City of Westminster District Plan*, London, City of Westminster.

Clark, R. N., Hendee, J. C., and Campbell, F. L. (1971) "Values, behavior and conflict in modern camping culture," *Journal of Leisure Research*, 3, 3, 143–59.

Clarke, A. (1981) "Coastal development in France: tourism as a tool for regional development," *Annals of Tourism Research*, 8, 447–61.

Clawson, M. and Knetsch, J. L. (1966) *Economics of Outdoor Recreation*, Baltimore, Johns Hopkins Press for Resources of the Future.

Clout, H. D. (1977) "Residences secondaires in France," in Coppock, J. T. (ed.) *Second Homes: Curse or Blessing?*, Oxford, Pergamon, 47–62.

Cohen, E. (1972) "Towards a sociology of international tourism," *Social Research*, 39, 164–82.

Cohen, E. (1974) "Who is a tourist?: a conceptual clarification," *Sociological Review*, 22, 527–55.

Cohen, E. (1979a) "A phenomenology of tourist experiences," *Sociology*, 13, 179–202.

Cohen, E. (1979b) "Rethinking the sociology of tourism," *Annals of Tourism Research*, 6, 18–35.

Cole, N. (1979) "Museums for the people," *Tourism in*

England, 28. London, English Tourist Board, 6–11.

Collins, L. R. (1978) "Review of hosts and guests: an anthropology of tourism," *Annals of Tourism Research*, 5, 278–80.

Commonwealth Geographical Bureau (1982) *Workshop on the Impact of Tourism on Small Developing Countries: Preliminary Report*, Suva, Fiji, School of Social and Economic Development, University of the South Pacific.

Cooper, M. J. (1976) *The Convention Industry and Sydney*, Armidale, NSW, Department of Geography, University of New England.

Coppock, J. T. (1977a) "Second homes in perspective," in Coppock, J. T. (ed.) *Second Homes: Curse or Blessing?*, Oxford, Pergamon, 1–15.

Coppock, J. T. (1977b) "Issues and conflicts," in Coppock, J. T. (ed.) *Second Homes: Curse or Blessing?*, Oxford, Pergamon, 195–215.

Coppock, J. T. and Rogers, A. W. (1975) "Too many Americans out in the wilderness," *Geographical Magazine*, 47, 8, 508–13.

Coppock, J. T. and Sewell, W. R. D. (eds) (1977) *Citizen Participation in Planning*, Chichester, Sussex, John Wiley.

Corsi, T. M. and Harvey, M. E. (1979) "Changes in vacation travel in response to motor fuel shortages and higher prices," *Journal of Travel Research*, 17, 4, 7–11.

Cosgrove, I. and Jackson, R. (1972) *The Geography of Recreation and Leisure*, London, Hutchinson.

Countryside Commission (1972) *The Goyt Valley Traffic Experiment*, London, Countryside Commission.

Countryside Commission (1974) *Farm Recreation and Tourism*, London, HMSO.

Countryside Commission (1976) *The Lake District Upland Management Experiment*, London, HMSO.

Cowan, G. (1977) "Cultural impact of tourism with particular reference to the Cook Islands," Finney, B. R. and Watson, K. A. (eds) *A New Kind of Sugar*, Santa Cruz, Calif., Center for South Pacific Studies, University of Santa Cruz, 79–85.

Cox, D. F. (1964) "Clues for advertising strategists," in Dexter, L. A. and White, D. M. (eds) *People, Society, and Mass Communications*, New York, Free Press, 359–94.

Cox, J. R. (1980) "The management of a heathland and sand dune landscape subject to heavy tourist and recreational pressures," in Romeril, M. and Hughes-Evans, D. (eds) *Tourism and the Environment*, London, Institute of Environmental Sciences, 57–61.

Cribier, F. (1983) "Retirement to tourist resorts on the French coast," *Leisure, Tourism and Social Change*, Proceedings of IGU Commission of the Geography

of Tourism and Leisure, Edinburgh, Tourism and Recreation Research Unit, Edinburgh University.

Crompton, J. L. (1979) "An assessment of the image of Mexico as a vacation destination and the influence of geographical location upon that image," *Journal of Travel Research*, 17, 4, 18–23.

Cutler, M. (1975) "Foreign use and Canadian control of our land and resources: are we alienating too much recreational land and too much of our best agricultural land?," *Canadian Geographical Journal*, 90, 5, 18–33.

Cybriwsky, R. A. (1970) "Patterns of mother tongue retention among several selected ethnic groups in western Canada," *Papers in Geography 5*, University Park, Penn., Department of Geography, Pennsylvania State University.

D'Amore, L. (1983) "Guidelines to planning harmony with the host community," in Murphy, P. E. (ed.) *Tourism in Canada: Selected Issues and Options*, Victoria, BC, University of Victoria, Western Geographical Series 21, 135–59.

Dann, G. (1976) "The holiday was simply fantastic," *Tourist Review*, 31, 3, 19–23.

Darlington, J. W. (1981) "Railroads and the evolution of the Catskill Mountain resort area, 1870–1920," *The Impact of Transport Technology on Tourism Landscapes* (Hugill, P. J., organizer), papers presented at the Annual Meeting of the Association of American Geographers, Los Angeles, 7–12.

Dartington Amenity Research Trust (1974) *Farm Recreation and Tourism in England and Wales*, Countryside Commission Paper 83, London, HMSO.

Dasmann, R. F. (1973) *Classification and Use of Protected Natural and Cultural Areas*, IUCN Occasional Paper 4.

Davidson, A. T. (1979) "Public participation in national park planning: reply," *Canadian Geographer*, 23, 176–9.

Davis, W. A. (1981) "The slipways are loaded with a new wave of ships," *Vancouver Sun*, October 24.

Dearden, P. (1983) "Tourism and the resource base," in Murphy, P. E. (ed.) *Tourism in Canada: Selected Issues and Options*, Victoria, BC, University of Victoria, Western Geographical Series 21, 75–93.

Deasy, G. F. and Griess, P. R. (1966) "Impacts of a tourist facility on its hinterland," *Annals of American Association of Geographers*, 56, 290–306.

de Kadt, E. (ed.) (1979) *Tourism: Passport to Development?*, Oxford, Oxford University Press.

Delaplane, S. (1983) "Kauai: loaded with spirits," *Times-Colonist*, April 9.

Dennier, D. A. (1978) "National park plans," *Town Planning Review*, 49, 175–83.

Dernoi, L. A. (1983) "Farm tourism in Europe," *Tourism*

References

Management, 4, 155–66.

de Vane, R. (1975) *Second Home Ownership*, Bangor Occasional Papers in Economics 6, Cardiff, University of Wales Press.

Diamond, J. (1977) "Tourism's role in economic development: the case re-examined," *Economic Development and Cultural Change*, 25, 539–53.

Dilsaver, L. M. (1979) "Some notes on the negative impacts of international tourism," *Association of Pacific Coast Geographers 1979 Yearbook*, 41, Corvallis, Oreg., Oregon State University Press, 109–18

Dower, M. (1975) "Tourism and conservation in Europe," *Ekistics*, 232, March, 192–5.

Downie, B. K. (1984) "Reflections on the National Park Zoning System," *The Operational Geographer*, 3, 15–19.

Downing, P. and Dower, M. (1973) *Second Homes in England and Wales*, Countryside Commission, London, HMSO.

Downs, R. M. and Stea, D. (1977) *Maps in Minds: Reflections on Cognitive Mapping*, New York, Harper & Row.

Doxey, G. V. (1975) "A causation theory of visitor–resident irritants, methodology, and research inferences," *The Impact of Tourism*, Sixth Annual Conference Proceedings of the Travel Research Association, San Diego, 195–8.

Doxey, G. V. (1983) "Leisure, tourism, and Canada's aging population," in Murphy, P. E. (ed.) *Tourism in Canada: Selected Issues and Options* , Victoria, BC, University of Victoria, Western Geographical Series 21, 57–72.

Duffield, B. S. and Long, J. (1981) "Tourism in the highlands and islands of Scotland: rewards and conflicts," *Annals of Tourism Research*, 8, 403–31.

Dunn, M. C. (1973) *Scenic Routes and Recreation Planning: The Teme Valley experiment, 1973*, Birmingham, Centre for Urban and Regional Studies, University of Birmingham.

Dunning, J. H. and McQueen, M. (1982) "Multinational corporations in the international hotel industry," *Annals of Tourism Research*, 9, 69–90.

Easdale Holiday Village (1981) "Conflict in tourism: the case of the Easdale Holiday Village development proposal," *Tourism Review*, 36, 3, 10–15.

Eastwood, D. A. and Carter, R. W. G. (1981) "The Irish dune consumer," *Journal of Leisure Research*, 13, 273–81.

Edgell, D. (1983) "US international tourism policy," *Annals of Tourism Research*, 10, 427–34.

Eidsvik, H. K. (1983) "Parks Canada, conservation and tourism: a review of the seventies—a preview of the eighties," *Tourism in Canada: Selected Issues and Options*, Victoria, BC, University of Victoria, Western Geographical Series 21, 241–69.

Elder, N. (1980) "Attraction development," *Resort of the Eighties*, Proceedings of Canada–British Columbia TIDSA Seminar, Vancouver, June.

England, R. (1980) "Architecture for tourists," *International Social Science Journal*, 32, 47–55.

English Tourist Board (1977) "A £5 billion industry," *Tourism in England*, 23, 4–5.

English Tourist Board (1978a) *Planning for Tourism in England*, London, ETB.

English Tourist Board (1978b) *Scarborough: A New Growth Point for Tourism*, London, ETB.

English Tourist Board (1978c) *Bude to Wadebridge: A New Growth Point for Tourism*, London, ETB.

English Tourist Board (1981a) *Tourism and the Inner City*, London, ETB.

English Tourist Board (1981b) *Planning for Tourism in England*, London, ETB.

English Tourist Board and Trades Union Congress (1976) *Holidays: The Social Need*, London, ETB.

Environment Canada (1979) *Canada's Special Resource Lands*, Ottawa, Lands Directorate, Environment Canada, 85–7.

Fairburn, A. N. (1951) "The grand tour," *Geographical Magazine*, 24, 3, 118–27.

Farrell, B. H. (1974) "The tourist ghettos of Hawaii," in Edgell, M. C. R. and Farrell, B. H. (eds) *Themes on Pacific Lands*, Victoria, BC, University of Victoria, Western Geographical Series 10, 181–221.

Farrell, B. H. (1982) *Hawaii, the Legend that Sells*, Honolulu, University Press of Hawaii.

Financial Post **(1985)** "Ottawa could be loser on Charlottetown Hotel," February 23, 37.

Finney, B. R. and Watson, K. A. (eds) (1977) *A New Kind of Sugar: Tourism in the Pacific*, Santa Cruz, Calif., Center for South Pacific Studies, University of Santa Cruz.

Forestry Commission (1970) *Conservation of the New Forest: Final Recommendations*, Lyndhurst, New Forest Joint Steering Committee, The Forestry Commission.

Forestry Commission (1976) *Progress Report on the Implementation of Conservation Measures 1971–76, and Proposals for Future Strategy*, Lyndhurst, New Forest Forestry Commission.

Forestry Commission (1981) *Management Plan 1982–91*, Lyndhurst, New Forest Forestry Commission.

Forward, C. N. (1982) "The importance of nonemployment sources of income in Canadian metropolitan areas," *Professional Geographer*, 34, 3, 289–96.

Frater, J. M. (1983) "Farm tourism in England: planning, funding, promotion and some lessons from Europe," *Tourism Management*, 4, 167–79.

Frechtling, D. C. (1977) "Travel in the 1980s: the demographic and economic climate," *The Travel Research Association 8th Annual Conference Proceedings*, Scottsdale, Ariz., 11–16

Galt, G. (1974) *Investing in the Past: A Report on the Profitability of Heritage Conservation*, Ottawa, Heritage Canada.

Gartner, W. C. and Holecek, D. F. (1983) "Economic impact of an annual tourism industry exposition," *Annals of Tourism Research*, 10, 199–212.

Georgulas, N. (1970) "Tourist destination features," *Journal of Town Planning Institute*, 56, 442–6.

Getz, D. (1982) *The Impact of Tourism in Badenoch and Strathspey*, Edinburgh, Highlands and Islands Development Board.

Getz, D. (1983) "A research agenda for municipal and community-based tourism in Canada," paper presented at The Travel and Tourism Research Association Conference, Banff.

Glamorgan (n.d.) *Gower Traffic Management Experiment, 1971–72*, Swansea, Glamorgan County Council.

Globe and Mail **(1982)** "Tourist boom takes toll on Banff," February 1.

Globe and Mail **(1984)** "Convention centers confident of success: deficits par for course in convention industry," November 19, B1 and B14.

Gonen, A. (1981) "Tourism and coastal settlement processes in the Mediterranean region," *Ekistics*, 290, 378–81.

Goodey, B. (1971) *Perception of the Environment*, occasional paper 17, Birmingham, Centre for Urban and Regional Studies, University of Birmingham.

Goodey, B. (1974) *Urban Walks and Town Trails*, Birmingham, Centre for Urban and Regional Studies, University of Birmingham.

Goodey, B. (1979) "Towards new perceptions on the environment: using the town trail," in Appleyard, D. (ed.) *The Conservation of European Cities*, Cambridge, Mass., MIT Press, 282–93.

Goodman, R. (1972) *After the Planners*, Harmondsworth, Penguin.

Gottmann, J. (1970) "Urban centrality and the interweaving of quaternary activities," *Ekistics*, 29, 174, 322–31.

Gould, P. and White, R. (1974) *Mental Maps*, Harmondsworth, Penguin.

Graburn, N. H. H. (ed.) (1976) *Ethnic and Tourist Arts: Cultural Expressions from the Fourth World*, Berkeley, University of California Press.

Graburn, N. H. H. (1984) "The evolution of tourist arts," *Annals of Tourism Research*, 11, 393–419.

Graham, R. (1979) "Yukon tourism development strategy: a tourism planning experience," *Tourism*

Strategies: Their Development and Implications, proceedings of The Travel Research Association (Canada Chapter), Banff, Alberta, October, 104–28.

Gravel, J.-P. (1979) "Tourism and recreational planning: a methodologic approach to the valuation and calibration of tourism activities," in Perks, W. T. and Robinson, I. M. (eds) *Urban and Regional Planning in a Federal State: The Canadian Experience*, Stroudsburg, Penn., Dowden, Hutchinson & Ross, 122–34.

Great Britain (1975) "Environmental planning," *Britain 1975*, London, Central Office of Information, 166–76.

Greater London Council (1974) *Tourism in London: A Plan for Management*, London, Joint Tourism Steering Group, Greater London Council.

Green, B. (1981) *Countryside Conservation*, London, Allen & Unwin.

Grosvenor, M. B. (1979) "A long history of new beginnings," *National Geographic*, 156, 1, 18–30.

Gulick, J. (1960) *Cherokees at the Crossroads*, Chapel Hill, NC, Institute for Research in Social Science, University of North Carolina.

Gunn, C. A. (1972) *Vacationscape: Designing Tourist Regions*, Austin, Texas, University of Texas, Bureau of Business Research.

Gunn, C. A. (1977) "Industry pragmatism vs tourism planning," *Leisure Sciences*, 1, 85–94.

Gunn, C. A. (1979) *Tourism Planning*, New York, Crane, Russak.

Hall, E. T. (1959) *The Silent Language*, Garden City, NY, Doubleday.

Hall, E. T. (1966) *The Hidden Dimension*, Garden City, NY, Doubleday.

Hall, G. D. (1982) *Slocan Valley Planning Program: Tourism Analysis*, Victoria, BC, Ministry of Municipal Affairs, Province of British Columbia.

Hall, P. (1970) *Theory and Practice of Regional Planning*, London, Pemberton Books.

Hall, P. (1974) *Urban and Regional Planning*, Harmondsworth, Penguin.

Hammond, J. S. and Andrus, C. D. (1979) "Sharing Alaska—how much for parks?," *National Geographic*, 156, 1, 60–5.

Hampshire County Council (1980) *South West Hampshire Structure Plan: Topic Reports*, Winchester, Hampshire County Council.

Hanna, M. (1976) *Tourism Multipliers in Britain*, London, ETB.

Hartmann, R. (1981) "Tourism, travel, and timing," paper presented at the Annual Meeting of the Association of American Geographers, Los Angeles.

Haulot, A. (1981) "Social tourism: current dimensions and future developments," *Tourism Management*, 2, 207–12.

References

Heeley, J. (1980) "Tourism and local government with special reference to the county of Norfolk" (2 vols), unpublished Ph.D. dissertation, University of East Anglia, Norwich.

Heeley, J. (1981) "Planning for tourism in Britain," *Town Planning Review*, 52, 61–79.

Heenan, D. A. (1978) "Tourism and the community, a drama in three acts," *Journal of Travel Research*, 16, 4, 30–2.

Helleiner, F. (1981) "The regionalization of a waterway: a study of recreational boat traffic," *Canadian Geographer*, 25, 1, 60–74.

Hendee, J. C. and Harris, R. W. (1970) "Foresters' perception of wilderness-user attitudes and preferences," *Journal of Forestry*, 68, 12, 759–62.

Hendee, J. C., Stankey, G. H., and Lucas, R. C. (1978) *Wilderness Management*, Washington, DC, Forest Service, US Department of Agriculture.

Henderson, F. M. and Voiland, M. P., Jr. (1975) "Information sources, attitudes and vacation area preferences: a comment," *Proceedings of the Association of American Geographers Conference*, 7, 88–91.

Henshall, J. D. (1977) "Second homes in the Caribbean," in Coppock, J. T. (ed.) *Second Homes: Curse or Blessing?*, Oxford, Pergamon, 75–84.

Herrero, S. (1978) "Parks Canada and public participation: the case of Village Lake Louise and Sunshine Village," in Sadler, B. (ed.) *Involvement and Environment: Proceedings of the Canadian Conference on Public Participation*, Edmonton, Environment Council of Alberta, 254–65.

Hills, T. L. and Lundgren, J. (1977) *The Impact of Tourism in the Caribbean—A Methodological Study*, Montreal, Department of Geography, McGill University.

Hookway, R. J. S. and Davidson, J. (1970) *Leisure: Problems and Prospects for the Environment*, London, Countryside Commission.

Hoole, A. F. (1978) "Public participation in park planning: the Riding Mountain case," *Canadian Geographer*, 22, 41–50.

Hoole, A. F. and Downie, B. K. (1978) *Zoning in National Parks*, Winnipeg, Parks Canada, Prairie Region.

Hovinen, G. R. (1982) "Visitor cycles: outlook for tourism in Lancaster County," *Annals of Tourism Research*, 9, 565–83.

Hudman, L. E. (1980) *Tourism: A Shrinking World*, Columbus, Ohio, Grid Inc.

Inglis, W. (1975) "Our industrial heritage," *Tourism in England*, 16, London, ETB, 22–6.

Ingram, B. (1981) "Protecting what's left: prospects for managing ecological reserves in British Columbia,"

Park News, 17, 4, 10–13.

IUOTO (1968) *The Economic Review of World Tourism*, Geneva, International Union of Official Travel Organizations.

IUOTO (1970) *International Travel Statistics*, Geneva International Union of Official Travel Organizations.

Jackson, E. L. and Schinkel, D. R. (1981) "Recreational activity preferences of resident and tourist campers in the Yellowknife region," *Canadian Geographer*, 25, 350–64.

Jackson, E. L. and Wong, R. A. G. (1982) "Perceived conflict between urban cross-country skiers and snowmobilers in Alberta," *Journal of Leisure Research*, 14, 1, 47–62.

Jordan, J. W. (1980) "The summer people and the natives: some effects of tourism in a Vermont vacation village," *Annals of Tourism Research*, 7, 34–55.

Jordan, R. P. (1979) "Will success spoil our parks?," *National Geographic*, 156, 1, 31–59.

Kahn, H. (1979) "Leading futurologist traces next half century in travel," *Travel Trade News*, January 31, 1–8.

Kaiser, C., Jr. and Helber, L. E. (1978) *Tourism: Planning and Development*, Boston, Mass., CBI Publishing.

Karn, V. A. (1977) *Retiring to the Seaside*, London, Routledge & Kegan Paul.

Kasperson, R. E. (1978) "Citizen participation in environmental policy-making: the U.S.A. experience," in Sadler, B. (ed.) *Involvement and Environment: Proceedings of the Canadian Conference on Public Participation*, 1, Edmonton, Environment Council of Alberta, 128–38.

Kent, N. (1977) "A new kind of sugar," in Finney, B. R. and Watson, K. A. (eds) *A New Kind of Sugar: Tourism in the Pacific*, Santa Cruz, Calif., Center for South Pacific Studies, University of California, Santa Cruz, 169–98.

Keogh, B. (1980) "Motivations and the choice decisions of skiers," *Tourist Review*, 1, 18–22.

King, G. A. D. (1982) "The Gower Peninsula," *Trends in Tourism Planning and Development*, paper presented at the Surrey International Conference, September.

Klineberg, O. (1964) *The Human Dimension in International Relations*, New York, Holt, Rinehart & Winston.

Kotler, P. (1975) *Marketing for Non-profit Organizations*, Englewood Cliffs, NJ, Prentice-Hall.

Kreck, L. A. (1981) "When Mount St. Helens blew its top," *Journal of Travel Research*, 19, 4, 16–22.

Kreutzwiser, R. D. (1973) "A methodology for

estimating tourist spending in Ontario counties," unpublished MA thesis, University of Waterloo, Ontario.

Krippendorf, J. (1975) *Die Landschaftsfresser*, Bern, Hallwag Verlag.

Labeau, G. (1965) "La consommation touristique belge," *Cahiers Economiques de Bruxelles*, 19.

Lawson, F. R. (1980) "Congresses, conventions, and conferences: facility supply and demand," *Tourism Management*, 1, 184–8.

Lazarsfeld, P. F., Berelson, B., and Gaudet, M. (1944) *The People's Choice*, New York, Duell, Sloan, & Pearce.

LeFevre, T. (1977) "Tourism: who gets what from tourists?" in Finney, B. R. and Watson, K. A. (eds) A *New Kind of Sugar*, Santa Cruz, Calif., Center for South Pacific Studies, University of California, Santa Cruz, 101–9.

Lengyel, P. (1980) "The anatomy of tourism," *International Social Science Journal*, 32, 1–13.

Levathes, L. (1979) "Gateway: elbow room for the millions," *National Geographic*, 156, 1, 86–97.

Linder, B. (1970) *The Harried Leisure Class*, New York, Columbia University Press.

Loukissas, P. J. (1982) "Tourism's regional development impacts: a comparative analysis of the Greek islands," *Annals of Tourism Research*, 9, 523–41.

Lowenthal, D. (1962) "Not every prospect pleases: what is our criterion for scenic beauty?," *Landscape*, 12, 19–23.

Lowenthal, D. and Prince, H. C. (1965) "English landscape tastes", *Geographical Review*, 55, 186–222.

Lucas, R. C. (1964) "Wilderness perception and use: the example of the Boundary Waters Canoe Area," *Natural Resources Journal*, 3, 3, 394–411.

Lundberg, D. E. (1976) *The Tourist Business*, Boston, Mass., CBI Publishing.

Lundgren, J. (1980) "The land component in national recreational planning: the Swedish case and its Canadian implications," *Canadian Geographer*, 24, 22–31.

Lundgren, J. (1983) "Development patterns and lessons in the Montreal Laurentians," in Murphy, P. E. (ed.) *Tourism in Canada: Selected Issues and Options*, Victoria, BC, University of Victoria, Western Geographical Series, 21, 95–126.

Lynch, K. (1960) *The Image of the City*, Cambridge, Mass., MIT Press.

MacCannell, D. (1973) "Staged authenticity: arrangements of social space in tourist settings," *American Journal of Sociology*, 79, 589–603.

MacCannell, D. (1976) *The Tourist: A New Theory of the Leisure Class*, London, Macmillan.

McCaskey, T. C. (1971) "Conservation of historic areas—management techniques for tourism being used in the USA," in *Tourism and the Environment*, London, British Tourist Authority, 52–8.

McCool, S. F. (1976) "Implications of recreational activity aggregates for tourism development policies," *Journal of Travel Research*, 14, 4, 1–4.

McCool, S. F. (1978) "Recreational activity packages at water-based resources," *Leisure Sciences*, 1, 163–73.

MacFarlane, R. N. (1979a) "Public participation in national park planning," *Canadian Geographer*, 23, 173–6.

MacFarlane, R. N. (1979b) "A comparative analysis of resident–visitor contact and resident attitudes towards tourism," paper presented at the Canadian Association of Geographers Annual Meeting, University of Victoria, BC.

McHarg, I. L. (1969) *Design with Nature*. Garden City NY, Doubleday.

McIntosh, R. W. (1977) *Tourism: Principles, Practices, Philosophies*, Columbus, Ohio, Grid Inc.

McLoughlin, J. B. (1978) *Urban and Regional Planning: A Systems Approach*, London, Faber & Faber.

Marsh, J. (1983) "Canada's parks and tourism: a problematic relationship," in Murphy, P. E. (ed.) *Tourism in Canada: Selected Issues and Options*, Victoria, BC, University of Victoria, Western Geographical Series, 21, 271–307.

Maslow, A. H. (1954) *Motivation and Personality*, New York, Harper & Row.

Mattyasovsky, E. (1975) "Key principles in planning for environmental quality," *Plan Canada*, 15, 38–43.

Maude, B. (1971) "The conflict between environment and accessibility in areas of high attraction and the means of solving it," *Ekistics*, 184, 213–15.

Mawhinney, K. A. and Bagnall, G. (1976) "The integrated social, economic and environmental planning of tourism," *Administration*, 24, 383–93.

Mayo, E. J. (1973) "Regional images and regional travel behavior," *Proceedings of The Travel Research Association Fourth Annual Conference*, Sun Valley, Idaho, 211–17.

Merriam, L. C. and Smith, C. K. (1974) "Visitor impact on newly developed campsites in the Boundary Waters Canoe Area," *Journal of Forestry*, 72, 627–30.

Metelka, C. J. (1977) "Tourism and development: with friends like these, who needs enemies?," paper presented at the Fifth Pacific Regional Science Conference, Vancouver, August, 1–13.

Middleton, V. T. C. (1974) *Tourism Policy in Britain: A Case for a Radical Reappraisal*, London, The Economist Intelligence Unit.

References

Mieczkowski, Z. T. (1981) "Some notes on the Geography of Tourism: a comment," *Canadian Geographer*, 25, 186–91.

Mihovilovic, M. A. (1980) "Leisure and tourism in Europe," *International Social Science Journal*, 32, 99–113.

Miles, J. C. (1972) *The Goyt Valley Traffic Experiment*, London, Countryside Commission.

Milgram, S. (1970) "The experience of living in cities," *Science*, 167, 1461–8.

Mings, R. C. (1978) "Tourist industry development: at the crossroads," *Tourist Review*, 33, 3, 2–9.

Mings, R. C. (1980) "A review of public support for international tourism in New Zealand," *New Zealand Geographer*, 36, 20–9.

Mishan, E. J. (1972) *Elements of Cost–Benefit Analysis*, London, Allen & Unwin.

Mitchell, B. (1979) *Geography and Resource Analysis*, London, Longman.

Montgomery, G. (1981) *An Evaluation of the Tourism Potential of the Cruise Ship Industry of BC*, Victoria, BC, Ministry of Industry and Small Business Development.

Montgomery, G. and Murphy, P. E. (1983) "Government involvement in tourism development: a case study of TIDSA implementation in British Columbia," in Murphy, P. E. (ed.) *Tourism in Canada: Selected Issues and Options*, Victoria, BC, University of Victoria, Western Geographical Series, 21, 183–209.

Moulin, C. L. (1983) "Social tourism: development and prospects in Quebec," in Murphy, P. E. (ed.) *Tourism in Canada: Selected Issues and Options*, Victoria, BC, University of Victoria, Western Geographical Series, 21, 161–81.

Moyes, A. (1977) "Recreational transport in England and Wales: some recent developments," *Geography*, 62, 209–12.

Muir, F. and Brett, S. (1978) *Frank Muir Goes Into . . .*, London, Robson Books.

Murphy, P. E. (1975) "The role of attitude in the choice decisions of recreational boaters," *Journal of Leisure Research*, 7, 3, 216–24.

Murphy, P. E. (1978) "Preferences and perceptions of urban decision-making groups: congruence or conflict?," *Regional Studies*, 12, 749–59.

Murphy, P. E. (1979) "Development and potential of tourism," in Forward, C. N. (ed.) *Vancouver Island: Land of Contrasts*, Victoria, BC, University of Victoria, Western Geographical Series, 17, 289–307.

Murphy, P. E. (1980a) "Tourism management using land-use planning and landscape design: the Victoria experience," *Canadian Geographer*, 24, 60–71.

Murphy, P. E. (1980b) "Perceptions and preferences of decision-making groups in tourist centers: a guide to planning strategy?," in Hawkins, D. E., Shafer, E. L., and Rovelstad, J. M. (eds) *Tourism Planning and Development Issues*, Washington, DC, George Washington University Press, 355–67.

Murphy, P. E. (1981) "Community attitudes to tourism: a comparative analysis," *International Journal of Tourism Management*, 2, 3, 189–95.

Murphy, P. E. (1982) "Tourism planning in London: an exercise in spatial and seasonal management," *Tourist Review*, 37, 1, 19–23.

Murphy, P. E. (1983) "Perceptions and attitudes of decision-making groups in tourism centers," *Journal of Travel Research*, 21, 3, 8–12.

Murphy, P. E. and Rosenblood, L. (1974) "Tourism: an exercise in spatial search," *Canadian Geographer*, 18, 201–10.

Nash, D. (1979) "The rise and fall of an aristocratic tourist culture: Nice, 1763–1936," *Annals of Tourism Research*, 6, 61–75.

National Park Service (1983) *National Park Statistical Abstract, 1982*, Denver, Colo., United States Department of the Interior.

Native Brotherhood of British Columbia (1980) *The Development of Native Tourism in British Columbia*, Victoria, BC, Ministry of Tourism.

Naylon, J. (1967) "Tourism: Spain's most important industry," *Geography*, 52, 23–40.

Nelson, J. G. (1973) "Canada's national parks: past, present, future," *Canadian Geographical Journal*, 86, 3, 68–89.

Nelson, J. G., Cordes, L. D., and Masyk, J. (1972) "The proposed master plans for Banff National Park: some criticisms and an alternative," *Canadian Geographer*, 16, 29–49.

Newsweek **(1979)** "Guaranteed getaways," December 17, 104.

Newsweek **(1980)** "Where to moor the Nautilus?," January 14, 17.

Newsweek **(1981)** "The baby boomers come of age," March 30, 34–7.

Newsweek **(1982)** "Finding parking space for bears," June 14, 18.

Newsweek **(1983)** "Battle over the wilderness," July 25, 22–32.

Nunez, T. A. (1977) "Touristic studies in anthropological perspective," in Smith, V. L. (ed.) *Hosts and Guests: The Anthropology of Tourism*, Philadelphia, University of Pennsylvania Press, 207–16.

Odum, E. P. (1970) "The strategy of ecosystem development," *Science*, 164, 262–70.

OECD (1980) "International tourism: slowdown and

resurgence," *OECD Observer*, 106, 28–30.

OECD (1983) "Tourism holds up," *OECD Observer*, 124, 29–30.

O'Riordan, J. (1975) *Springbrook Project: An Approach to Evaluating Multiple Resource Use Alternatives*, Victoria, BC, Ministry of the Environment.

O'Riordan, T. (1969) "Planning to improve environmental capacity: a case study in Broadland," *Town Planning Review*, 40, 39–58.

O'Riordan, T. (1978) "Participation through objection: some thoughts on the UK experience," in Sadler, B. (ed.) *Involvement and Environment: Proceedings of the Canadian Conference on Public Participation*, 1, Edmonton, Environment Council of Alberta, 139–63.

O'Riordan, T. (1979) "Alarm call for the Broads: signs of disaster and a policy for survival," *Geographical Magazine*, 52, 10, 51–7.

Overton, J. (1980) "Tourism development, conservation and conflict: game laws for caribou protection in Newfoundland," *Canadian Geographer*, 24, 40–9.

Palmer, J. and Probert, G. (1980) "Planning at the county level: a case study of Gwent, South Wales," *International Journal of Tourism Management*, 1, 158–67.

Papson, S. (1979) "Tourism: world's biggest industry in the twenty-first century?," *The Futurist*, 12, 249–57.

Papson, S. (1981) "Spuriousness and tourism: politics of two Canadian provincial governments," *Annals of Tourism Research*, 8, 220–35.

Parsons, J. J. (1973) "Southward to the sun: the impact of mass tourism on the coast of Spain," *Association of Pacific Geographers Yearbook*, 35, 129–46.

Patmore, J. A. (1972) *Land and Leisure*, Harmondsworth, Penguin.

Pearce, D. (1981) *Tourist Development*, London, Longman.

Pearce, P. L. (1982) *The Social Psychology of Tourist Behaviour*, Oxford, Pergamon.

Peck, J. G. and Lepie, A. S. (1977) "Tourism and development in three North Carolina coastal towns," in Smith, V. L. (ed.) *Hosts and Guests: The Anthropology of Tourism*, Philadelphia, University of Pennsylvania Press, 159–72.

Perez, L. A. (1974) "Aspects of underdevelopment: tourism in the West Indies," *Science and Society*, 37, 473–80.

Peters, M. (1969) *International Tourism*, London, Hutchinson.

Peterson, G. L. (1974) "A comparison of the sentiments and perceptions of wilderness managers and canoeists in the Boundary Waters Canoe Area," *Journal of Leisure Research*, 6, 194–206.

Pigram, J. J. (1980) "Environmental implications of tourism development," *Annals of Tourism Research*, 7, 554–83.

Pi-Sunyer, O. (1977) "Through native eyes: tourists and tourism in a Catalan maritime community," in Smith, V. L. (ed.) *Hosts and Guests: The Anthropology of Tourism*, Philadelphia, University of Pennsylvania Press, 149–55.

Pizam, A. (1978) "Tourism's impacts: the social costs to the destination community as perceived by its residents," *Journal of Travel Research*, 16, 4, 8–12.

Pizam, A. and Pokela, J. (1980) "The vacation farm: a new form of tourism destination," in Hawkins, D. E., Shafer, E. L., and Rovelstad, J. M. (eds) *Tourism Marketing and Management Issues*, Washington, DC, George Washington University Press, 203–16.

Pizam, A. and Pokela, J. (1983) "The 1979 US gasoline shortage and its impact on the tourism industry," *Tourism Management*, 4, 94–101.

Plog, S. C. (1972) "Why destination areas rise and fall in popularity," paper presented at Southern California Chapter of The Travel Research Association.

Porteous, J. D. (1971) "Design with people: the quality of the urban environment," *Environment and Behavior*, 3, 155–78.

Powell, J. (Chairman) (1978) *The Canadian Tourism Industry: A Report by the Sector Task Force*, Ottawa.

Priddle, G. and Kreutzwiser, R. (1977) "Evaluating cottage environments in Ontario," in Coppock, J. T. (ed.) *Second Homes: Curse or Blessing?*, Oxford, Pergamon, 165–80.

Province of British Columbia (1981) *Forest Landscape Handbook*, Victoria, BC, Ministry of Forests.

Province of British Columbia (1982) *The Vancouver Island Tourism Region*, Victoria, BC, Ministry of Industry and Small Business Development.

Ragatz, R. L. (1970) "Vacation housing: a missing component in urban and regional theory," *Land Economics*, 46, 118–26.

Ragatz, R. L. (1977) "Vacation homes in rural areas: towards a model for predicting their distribution and occupancy patterns," in Coppock, J. T. (ed.) *Second Homes: Curse or Blessing?*, Oxford, Pergamon, 181–93.

Redman, M. B. (1983) "Economic impact of a short-term tourism industry exposition: a comment," *Annals of Tourism Research*, 10, 435–6.

Reiter, R. R. (1977) "The politics of tourism in a French alpine community," in Smith, V. L. (ed.) *Hosts and Guests: The Anthropology of Tourism*, Philadelphia, University of Pennsylvania Press, 149–55.

Richardson, E. and Donehower, E. (1979) "Hawaii Visitors Bureau: Travel research arm for Hawaii," *A Decade of Achievement*, 10th Annual Conference

References

Proceedings of The Travel Research Association, Salt Lake City, 69–75.

Richardson, H. W. (1971) *Urban Economics*, Harmondsworth, Penguin.

Rickson, I. (1973) "Planning and tourism," *Journal of Royal Town Planning Institute*, 59, 269–70.

Ritchie, J. R. and Zins, M. (1978) "Culture as a determinant of the attractiveness of a tourist region," *Annals of Tourism Research*, 5, 252–67.

Robinson, H. (1976) *A Geography of Tourism*, London, Macdonald & Evans.

Rogers, A. W. (1977) "Second homes in England and Wales: a spatial view," in Coppock, J. T. (ed.) *Second Homes: Curse or Blessing?*, Oxford, Pergamon, 85–102.

Romeril, M. (1983) "A balanced strategy for recreation, tourism and conservation—the case of Les Mielles, Jersey," *Tourism Management*, 4, 126–8.

Romeril, M. and Hughes-Evans, D. (eds) (1980) *Tourism and the Environment*, London, Institute of Environmental Sciences.

Rose, E. (1974) "Philosophy and purpose of planning," in Bruton, M. J. (ed.) *The Spirit and Purpose of Planning*, London, Hutchinson, 23–65.

Rosenow, J. E. and Pulsipher, G. L. (1979) *Tourism: The Good, the Bad, and the Ugly*, Lincoln, Neb., Century Three Press.

Rubenstein, C. (1980) "Vacations: expectations, satisfactions, frustrations, fantasies," *Psychology Today*, May, 62–76.

Rudney, R. (1980) "The development of tourism on the Côte d'Azure: an historical perspective," in Hawkins, D. E., Shafer, E. L., and Rovelstad, J. M. (eds) *Tourism Planning and Development Issues*, Washington, DC, George Washington University Press.

Runyan, D. (1977) "Tools for community-managed impact assessment," *Journal of American Institute of Planners*, vol. 43, 125–34.

Runyan, D. and Wu, C.-T. (1979) "Assessing tourism's more complex consequences," *Annals of Tourism Research*, 6, 448–63.

Saarinen, T. F. (1969) *Perception of Environment*, Washington, DC, Association of American Geographers, Resource Paper 5.

Sadler, B. (ed.) (1978) *Involvement and Environment: Proceedings of the Canadian Conference on Public Participation*, 1 & 2, Edmonton, Environment Council of Alberta.

Sadler, B. (1983) "Ski area development in the Canadian Rockies: past lessons, future prospects," in Murphy, P. E. (ed.) *Tourism in Canada: Selected Issues and Options*, Victoria, BC, University of Victoria, Western Geographical Series, 21.

Safavi, F. (1971) "A cost–benefit model for convention centers," *Annals of Regional Science*, 5, 17–37.

St Ives (n.d.) *A Joint Report on a Traffic Plan for St Ives*, St Ives, Cornwall, St Ives Borough Council.

Sarbin, H. B. (1978) "Today's travelers—how their attitudes have changed," *Travel and Tourism Consultants International*, New York.

Sax, J. L. (1980) *Mountains without Handrails: Reflections on the National Parks*, Ann Arbor, Mich., University of Michigan Press.

Scottish Tourist Board (1975) *The Economic Impact of Tourism: A Case Study in Greater Tayside*, Edinburgh, Tourism and Recreation Research Unit, University of Edinburgh.

Seekings, J. (1980) "Pro bono publico: the case for a systematic system," in Hawkins, D. E., Shafer, E. L., and Rovelstad, J. M. (eds) *Tourism Planning and Development Issues*, Washington, DC, George Washington University, 251–7.

Sewell, W. R. D. (1974) "Perceptions, attitudes and public participation in countryside management in Scotland," *Journal of Environmental Management*, 2, 235–57.

Simmonds, A. (1977) "Benefits from beaches: preserving the East Anglian coast," *Geographical Magazine*, 50, 1, 1–4.

Simmons, I. G. (1981) *The Ecology of Natural Resources*, London, Edward Arnold.

Skeffington, A. M. (1969) *People and Planning*, London, Department of the Environment, HMSO.

Sloan, R. W. (1978) "The Sunshine Village issue: 1001 mistakes or how Parks Canada mismanaged public participation," in Sadler, B. (ed.) *Involvement and Environment: Proceedings of the Canadian Conference on Public Participation*, 2, Edmonton, Environment Council of Alberta, 266–73.

Smith, V. L. (1977a) "Eskimo tourism: micro-models and marginal men," *Hosts and Guests: The Anthropology of Tourism*, Philadelphia, University of Pennsylvania Press, 51–70.

Smith, V. L. (ed.) (1977b) *Hosts and Guests: The Anthropology of Tourism*, Philadelphia, University of Pennsylvania Press.

Smith, V. L. (1980) "Anthropology and tourism: a science-industry evaluation," *Annals of Tourism Research*, 7, 13–33.

Snowdonia National Park Authority (1977) *Snowdonia National Park Plan*, Penrhyndeudraeth, Gwynedd, Gwynedd County Council.

Sochor, E. (1976) "No litter please on Everest," *Geographical Magazine*, 48, 388.

South West Economic Planning Council (1975) *Surveys of Second Homes in the South West*, London, HMSO.

Stankey, G. H. (1971) *The Perception of Wilderness Recreation Carrying Capacity: A Geographic Study in Natural Resources Management*, unpublished Ph.D. dissertation, East Lansing, Mich., Michigan State University.

Stankey, G. H. (1981) "Integrating wildlife recreation research into decision making: pitfalls and promises," *Recreation Research Review*, 9, 31–7.

Stanton, M. E. (1977) "The Polynesian Cultural Center: a multi-ethnic model of seven Pacific cultures," in Smith, V. L. (ed.) *Hosts and Guests: The Anthropology of Tourism*, Philadelphia, University of Pennsylvania Press, 193–206.

Statistics Canada (1981) *Travel, Tourism and Outdoor Recreation: A Statistical Digest, 1978 and 1979*, Ottawa, Statistics Canada.

Steinbeck, J. (1962) *Travels with Charley: In Search of America*, New York, Bantam.

Stroud, H. B. (1983) "Environmental problems associated with large recreational subdivisions," *Professional Geographer*, 35, 303–13.

Sullivan, L. R. (1983) "The evaluation of landscape aesthetics in tourism planning: A case study of the Drumheller/Dinosaur/Brooks Tourism Corridor Study" unpublished honors essay, Victoria, BC, Department of Geography, University of Victoria.

Taaffe, E. J. (1962) "The urban hierarchy: an air passenger definition," *Economic Geography*, 38, 1–14.

Tatzin, D. L. (1978) "A methodological approach to estimating the value of public services consumed by tourists," *Using Travel Research for Planning and Profits*, 9th Annual Conference Proceedings of The Travel Research Association, Ottawa, 58–60.

Taylor, G. D. (1983) "Canada's tourism trends for the 1980s," in Murphy, P. E. (ed.) *Tourism in Canada: Selected Issues and Options*, Victoria, BC, University of Victoria, Western Geographical Series, 21, 29–55.

Teuscher, H. (1983) "Social tourism for all: the Swiss Travel Savings Fund," *Tourism Management*, 4, 216–19.

Thomason, P., Crompton, J. L., and Kamp, B. D. (1979) "A study of the attitudes of impacted groups within a host community toward prolonged stay tourist visitors," *Journal of Travel Research*, 17, 3, 2–12.

Tideman, M. C. (1982) "Cost–benefit analysis of congress tourism," *Tourist Review*, 37, 4, 22–5.

Tiebout, C. M. (1962) *The Community Economic Base Study*, New York, Committee for Economic Development.

Time **(1978)** "The convening of America," December 18, 36–42.

Time **(1981)** "Eurovacations: longer and cheaper," July 13, 39.

Time **(1983)** "Americans everywhere: they're taking off in record numbers and Europe is the big bonanza," July 25, 36–43.

Times-Colonist (1985) "Single voice for 53 tourism groups," April 18, B1.

Todhunter, R. (1981) "Banff and the Canadian national park idea," *Landscape*, 25, 2, 33–9.

Toffler, A. (1971) *Future Shock*, London, Pan.

Toffler, A. (1981) *The Third Wave*, New York, Bantam.

Tourism and Recreation Research Unit (1972) *The Touring Caravan in Scotland: Supply–Demand Report*, Edinburgh, University of Edinburgh.

Tourism and Recreation Research Unit (1981) *The Economy of Rural Communities in the National Parks of England and Wales*, TRRU Research Report 47, Edinburgh, Tourism and Recreation Research Unit, University of Edinburgh.

Tozer, D. (1981) "The case of the neighbourhood improvement programme in James Bay, Victoria," unpublished M.A. thesis, Victoria, BC, Department of Geography, University of Victoria.

Tuan, Y.-F. (1974) *Topophilia: A Study of Environmental Perception, Attitudes and Values*, Englewood Cliffs, NJ, Prentice-Hall.

Tucker, A. (1970) "Research for survival," quoted in McLoughlin, J. B. *Urban and Regional Planning: A Systems Approach*, London, Faber & Faber, 23.

Turner, L. and Ash, J. (1975) *The Golden Hordes: International Tourism and the Pleasure Periphery*, London, Constable.

Ullman, E. L. (1956) "The role of transportation and the bases for interaction," in Thomas, W. L. (ed.) *Man's Role in Changing the Face of the Earth*, Chicago, University of Chicago Press, 862–80.

UNESCO (1977) "The effects of tourism on socio-cultural values," *Annals of Tourism Research*, 4, 74–105.

United Nations Environment Programme (1979) *The State of the Environment, 1979*, Nairobi, UNEP.

United Nations General Assembly (1981) *World Tourism Conference: Report of the Economic and Social Change*, New York, UN.

Vancouver Sun **(1982)** "Cheaper-for-Chinese policy draws tourist flak," February 6, E6.

van den Berghe, P. L. and Keyes, C. F. (1984) "Tourism and rec-created ethnicity," *Annals of Tourism Research*, 11, 343–52.

van Wagtendonk, J. W. (1980) "Visitor use patterns in Yosemite National Park," *Journal of Travel Research*, 19, 2, 12–71.

Varley, R. C. G. (1978) *Tourism in Fiji: Some Economic and Social Problems*, Bangor Occasional Papers in

References

Economics 12, Bangor, University of Wales Press.

Veal, A. J. (1975) *Towards a Strategy for Tourism in the Heart of England*, Birmingham, Centre for Urban and Regional Studies, University of Birmingham.

Wager, J. A. (1961) "The carrying capacity of wild lands for recreation," unpublished Ph.D. dissertation. Ann Arbor, Mich., University of Michigan.

Wahab, S. (1975) *Tourism Management*, London, Tourism International Press.

Wales Tourist Board (1974) *Farm Tourism in Wales: A Practical Guide for Welsh Farmers*, Cardiff, Wales Tourist Board.

Walker, G. (1979) "Conventions: future for Victoria?," paper presented at the Joint Tourism Symposium, sponsored by the Victoria Chamber of Commerce and Greater Victoria Visitor Information Center, November.

Wall, G. (1972) "Socio-economic variations in pleasure-trip patterns: the case of Hull car owners," *Transactions of the Institute of British Geographers*, 57, 45–58.

Wall, G. (1973) "Car owners and holidays: the case of Kingston-upon-Hull," *Town Planning Review*, 44, 117–30.

Wall, G. and Sinnott, J. (1980) "Urban recreational and cultural facilities as tourist attractions," *Canadian Geographer*, 24, 1, 50–9.

Wall, G. and Wright, C. (1977) *The Environmental Impact of Outdoor Recreation*, Waterloo, Ontario, University of Waterloo, Department of Geography Publication Series, 11.

Waters, S. R. (1978) *Travel 78–79: The Big Picture*, New York, ASTA Travel News.

Webster's Third New International Dictionary **(1961)** London, Bell & Sons, 2417.

Wellman, J. D., Dawson, M. S., and Roggenbuck, J. W. (1982) "Park managers' predictions of the motivations of visitors to two national park service areas," *Journal of Leisure Research*, 14, 1, 1–15.

White, P. E. (1974) *The Social Impact of Tourism on Host Communities: A Study of Language Change in Switzerland*, Research Paper 9, Oxford, School of Geography, Oxford University.

White, P., Wall, G., and Priddle, G. (1978) "Anti-social behavior in Ontario provincial parks," *Recreational Research Review*, 2, 2, 13–25.

Wilkes, B. (1979) "The myth of the non-consumptive user," *Park News*, 15, 1, 16–21.

Williams, A. V. and Zelinsky, W. (1970) "On some patterns in international tourist flows," *Economic Geographer*, 46, 4, 549–67.

Willis, F. R. (1977) "Tourism as an instrument of regional economic growth: the Languedoc littoral," *Growth and Change*, 8, 2, 43–7.

Wilson, A. G. (1981) *Geography and the Environment*, Chichester, Sussex, John Wiley.

Wolfe, R. I. (1966) "Recreational travel: the new migration," *Canadian Geographer*, 10, 1–14.

World Council of Churches (1970) *Leisure–Tourism: Threat and Promise*, Geneva, World Council of Churches.

Yankelovich, D. and Lefkowitz, B. (1980) "National growth: the question of the 80s," *Public Opinion*, January, 44–57.

Young, Sir G. (1973) *Tourism: Blessing or Blight?*, Harmondsworth, Penguin.

Zehnder, L. E. (1975) *Florida's Disney World: Promises and Problems*, Tallahassee, Fla., Peninsular Publishing.

Zimmerman, R. C. (1980) "European tourism," *Landscape*, 24, 31–2.

Name index

Alleman, T. 130
Anderson, P. 11
Andrus, C. D. 34
Appleyard, D. 12, 56, 70
Archer, B. H. 90, 92, 93, 94, 95
Ardagh, J. 163
Arnstein, S. 159
Ash, J. 30

Bagnall, G. 9
Baker, W. M. 110
Barkham, J. P. 64, 65
Baud-Bovy, M. 159–60, 161, 162, 163
Bayfield, N. G. 64
Beioley, S. 140
Bell, K. L. 65
Berelson, B. 11
Best, G. M. 18
Bielckus, C. L. 111
Binneweis, R. 62
Birch, J. C. 123
Blake, P. 169–70
Bliss, L. C. 65
Boissevain, J. 119
Boltvinik, J. 92
Boorstin, D. J. 127–8, 129–30, 145
Bourne, L. S. 174, 175
Brancher, D. M. 70
Brett, S. 53
British Columbia 163–4
British Tourist Authority, 4, 80, 120, 122, 123, 170
Brougham, J. E. 123
Brown, N. J. 176
Brownrigg, M. 30, 97
Bryan, A. 49
Bryan, W. R. 26
Bryden, J. M. 31, 92, 103

Buck, R. C. 130, 145, 146
Budowski, G. 60, 66
Burde, J. H. 68
Burkart, A. J. 19
Burt, J. 89, 105, 107
Burton, T. L. 7, 17
Butler, R. W. 86, 87, 125, 126, 151

Campbell, F. L. 48
Canada 51
Canadian Heritage 148
Carr, S. 70
Carter, R. W. G. 44
CGOT 4
Chadwick, G. 173
Chadwick, R. A. 9
Chapin, F. S. 173
Chasis, S. 175
Chau, P. 9, 95
Cheng, J. R. 42
Christaller, W. 31
City of Westminster 142
Clark, R. N. 48
Clarke, A. 34, 35, 95
Clawson, M. 8, 54
Clout, H. D. 111
Cohen, E. 5, 6, 7, 86, 117, 128
Colberg, R. T. 11
Cole, N. 146
Collins, L. R. 149
Commonwealth Geographical Bureau 131
Cooper, M. J. 89, 106, 107
Coppock, J. T. 14, 41, 60, 112, 115, 132, 171
Cordes, L. D. 64
Corsi, T. M. 26
Cosgrove, J. 18
Countryside Commission 73, 110
Cowan, G. 144

Name index

Cox, D. F. 11
Cox, J. R. 44–5
Cribier, F. 114
Crompton, J. L. 11, 123, 125
Cutler, M. 112
Cybriwsky, R. A. 132

D'Amore, L. 134, 135, 137, 138, 139, 159
Dann, G. 10–11
Darlington, J. W. 18, 19
Dartington Amenity Research Trust 109
Dasmann, R. F. 62
Davidson, A. T. 172
Davidson, J. 61
Davis, W. A. 52
Dawson, M. S. 48
Dearden, P. 45–6, 69, 157
Deasy, G. F. 53
de Kadt, E. 30, 119, 120, 155
Delaplane, S. 84
Dennier, D. A. 62–3
Dernoi, L. A. 108
Detwyler, T. R. 175
de Vane, R. 111
Diamond, J. 97
Dilsaver, L. M. 32
Donehower, E. 90
Dower, M. 110, 111, 148
Downie, B. K. 62, 63
Downing, P. 110, 111
Downs, R. M. 56
Doxey, G. V. 27, 123, 124, 125, 126, 151, 169
Duffield, B. S. 95, 96
Dunn, M. C. 70
Dunning, J. H. 132

Easdale Holiday Village 172
Eastwood, D. A. 44
Edgell, D. 33, 157
Eidsvik, H. K. 50, 60, 61
Elder, N. 159, 163
England, R. 135, 148, 149
English Tourist Board 4, 140, 156, 163
English Tourist Board and Trades Union Congress 23

Fairburn, A. N. 17
Farrell, B. H. 14, 86, 111, 132, 135
Financial Post 105
Finney, B. R. 95
Forestry Commission 67, 68
Forward, C. N. 156
Frater, J. M. 109, 110

Frechtling, D. C. 27

Galt, G. 148
Gartner, W. C. 104
Gaudet, M. 11
Georgulas, N. 7
Getz, D. 137, 138, 144
Glamorgan 75
Globe and Mail 42, 105, 107
Gonen, A. 45
Goodey, B. 56, 70, 71
Goodman, R. 171
Gottmann, J. 104
Gould, P. 11, 56, 56–7, 57, 59
Graburn, N. H. H. 30
Graham, R. 159
Gravel, J.-P. 159, 160
Great Britain 175
Greater London Council 79, 142
Green, B. 62
Greig, M. A. 30, 97
Griess, P. R. 53
Grosvenor, M. B. 51
Gulick, J. 135
Gunn, C. A. 34, 157, 169, 172

Hall, E. T. 56
Hall, G. D. 156
Hall, P. 156, 173
Hammond, J. S. 34
Hampshire County Council 68
Hanna, M. 92, 95
Harris, R. W. 48, 48–9, 65
Hartmann, R. 8
Harvey, M. E. 26
Haulot, A. 24
Heart of England Tourist Board 80
Heeley, J. 100, 101, 102, 156, 163, 165
Heenan, D. A. 130
Helber, L. E. 9, 30, 33
Helleiner, F. 52
Hendee, J. C. 48, 48–9, 64, 65
Henderson, F. M. 11
Henshall, J. D. 111
Herrero, S. 172
Hills, T. L. 31
Holecek, D. F. 104
Hookway, R. J. S. 61
Hoole, A. F. 62, 172
Hovinen, G. R. 130
Hudman, L. E. 127
Hughes-Evans, D. 170

Inglis, W. 129
Ingram, B. 34, 61, 68
IUOTO 3, 5

Jackson, E. L. 46, 47–8
Jackson, R. 18
Jordan, J. W. 149, 150, 151
Jordan, R. P. 43, 47

Kahn, H. 19, 20, 27–8
Kaiser, C., Jr. 9, 30, 33
Kamp, B. D. 123, 125
Karn, V. A. 111, 156
Kasperson, R. E. 171
Kent, N. 30, 86, 119, 120
Keogh, B. 65
Keyes, C. F. 30
King, G. A. D. 174
Klineberg, O. 57
Knetsch, J. L. 8, 54
Kotler, P. 11
Kreck, L. A. 84
Kreutzwiser, R. D. 91, 114
Krippendorf, J. 171, 173

Lawson, F. R. 106, 159–60, 161, 162, 163
Lazarsfeld, P. F. 11
LeFevre, T. 144
Lefkowitz, B. 21–2, 155
Lenzini, J. 68
Lepie, A. S. 145
Levathes, L. 61
Lichty, R. W. 92
Linder, B. 79
Liu, J. 92
Long, J. 95, 96
Loukissas, P. J. 98–9, 108, 171
Lowenthal, D. 57
Lucas, R. C. 46, 64, 65, 134
Lundberg, D. E. 3, 9, 14, 23, 61, 91, 92, 99
Lundgren, J. 9, 18, 31, 51, 88, 89, 115, 156
Lynch, K. 40, 56, 70

MacCannell, D. 128, 130–1, 145, 165
McCaskey, T. C. 128
McCool, S. F. 47
MacFarlane, R. N. 81, 120, 122, 123, 172
McHarg, I. L. 44

McIntosh, R. W. 9, 157
MacKinnon, W. C. 89, 105, 107
McLoughlin, J. D. 173
McQueen, L. 132
Maine Vacation Travel Analysis Committee 90
Marsh, J. 43, 51
Masyk, J. 64
Mattyasovsky, E. 175
Maude, B. 71, 73
Mawhinney, K. A. 9
Mayo, E. J. 11
Medlik, S. 19
Merriam, L. C. 65
Metelka, C. J. 11–12
Meyer, J. R. 56, 70
Middleton, V. T. C. 33, 84
Mieczkowski, Z. T. 9
Mihovilovic, M. A. 33
Miles, J. C. 73
Milgram, S. 81
Mings, R. C. 36, 38, 134
Mishan, E. J. 103
Mitchell, B. 65
Montgomery, G. 52, 95, 97, 158
Moulin, C. L. 24, 110
Moyes, A. 71, 73
Muir, F. 53
Murphy, P. E. 10, 46, 54, 76, 95, 97, 109, 121–2, 123, 126, 127, 140, 142, 158, 171, 172

Nash, D. 87
National Park Service 41, 50
Native Brotherhood of British Columbia 137
Naylon, J. 33
Nelson, J. G. 32, 64
Newsweek 14, 25, 27, 34, 41, 163
Nunez, T. A. 131

Odum, E. P. 166
OECD 3, 4, 155
O'Riordan, J. 68
O'Riordan, T. 45, 66, 171
Overton, J. 49, 137
Owen, C. B. 92

Palmer, J. 163
Papson, S. 28–9, 131
Parsons, J. J. 33
Patmore, J. A. 21, 43, 66
Pearce, P. L. 23, 35
Peck, J. G. 145

Name index

Perez, L. A. 31
Peters, M. 8, 13
Peterson, G. L. 48, 65
Pigram, J. J. 66, 67
Pi-Sunyer, O. 131
Pizam, A. 4, 26, 108, 109, 120, 123
Plog, S. C. 6, 7, 86
Pokela, J. 4, 26, 108, 109
Porteous, J. D. 40
Powell, J. 4, 30, 165
Priddle, G. 46–7, 114
Prince, H. C. 57
Probert, G. 163
Province of British Columbia, 69, 144
Pulsipher, G. L. 155, 165

Quayson, J. 92

Ragatz, R. L. 110, 111
Redman, M. B. 104
Reiter, R. R. 30, 131
Richardson, E. 90
Richardson, H. W. 80
Rickson, I. 173
Ritchie, J. R. 127, 148
Robinson, H. 3, 18, 109
Rogers, A. W. 14, 41, 60, 111
Roggenbuck, J. W. 48
Romeril, M. 170, 174
Rose, E. 90, 170
Rosenblood, L. 54
Rosenow, J. E. 155, 165
Rubenstein, C. 22
Rudney, R. 14, 87
Runyan, D. 171, 177

Saarinen, T. F. 56
Sadler, B. 49, 171
Safavi, F. 107
St Ives 76
Sarbin, H. D. 22
Sax, J. L. 41, 50, 51, 60
Schinkel, D. R. 47–8
Schissler, D. 70
Scottish Tourist Board 90, 95
Seekings, J. 172
Sewell, W. R. D. 48, 171
Simmonds, A. 44
Simmons, J. G. 174
Sinnott, J. 156
Skeffington, A. M. 171

Sloan, R. W. 2
Smith, C. K. 65
Smith, V. L. 5, 6, 30, 120, 121, 137, 140
Snowdonia National Park Authority 69, 157
Sochor, E. 32
South West Economic Planning Council 92, 111
Stankey, G. H. 64, 65, 134
Stanton, M. E. 146
Stea, D. 56
Steinbeck, J. 53
Steinnes, D. N. 92
Stroud, H. B. 114–15
Sullivan, L. R. 70

Taaffe, E. J. 52
Tatzin, D. L. 106, 107
Taylor, G. D. 21, 23
Teuscher, H. 23
Thomason, P. 123, 125
Tideman, M. C. 107
Tiebout, C. M. 89
Time 23, 84, 104–5
Times-Colonist 177
Todhunter, R. 42
Toffler, A. 3–4
Tourism and Recreation Research Unit 69, 85, 98, 109
Tozer, D. 171
Tuan, Y.-F. 56, 57
Tucker, A. 167
Turner, L. 30

Ullman, E. L. 52
UNESCO 117
United Nations Environment Programme 32, 66
United Nations General Assembly 4

Vancouver Sun 129, 169
van den Berghe, P. L. 30
van Wagtendonk, J. W., 41, 71
Var, T. 92
Varley, R. C. G. 131
Veal, A. J. 163
Voiland, M.P. Jr. 11

Wager, J. A. 65
Wahab, S. 9, 145
Wales Tourist Board 109
Walker, G. 105, 107
Wall, G. 8, 46–7, 53, 156, 174
Waters, S. R. 3

Watson, K. L. 95
Wellman, J. D. 48
White, P. 46–7
White, P. E. 132–3
White, R. 11, 56, 56–7, 57, 59
Wilkes, B. 51, 60
Williams, A. V. 53, 54
Willis, F. R. 34
Wilson, A. G. 173
Wolfe, R. I. 3
Wong, R. A. G. 46
World Council of Churches 31

Wright, C. 174
Wu, C.-T. 171

Yankelovich, D. 21–2, 155
Young, Sir G. 122, 124, 134, 155

Zehnder, L. E. 52, 99
Zelinsky, W. 53, 54
Zimmerman, R. C. 170
Zins, M. 127, 148

Subject index

ability to travel, factors affecting 24–5
accessibility of destinations, factors affecting: perceived 53–6; physical 51–2, 60, 70–6
accommodation type, influence on: expenditure 89, 90; fire incidence 100; multiplier factors 93; revenue-expenditure ratio 107
acculturation 131–3, 146, 148
Afan Argoed Country Park (Wales) 61
air travel: development 19, 25–6; forecast 28
airline network development 52, 70
Albuquerque (N. Mex.) 114–15
Aloha Week 130
Amish culture 130, 145–6
Anglesey (Wales) 90, 93, 94
architecture 148
Arizona recreational subdivisions 114
Arkansas recreational subdivisions 114
Australia: convention numbers 105; international resort development 66–7
Austria farm tourism 108, 109
automobiles: forecast numbers 28; role in tourism 21, 25, 26
Aviemore (Scotland) 87, 138, 144

Badlands National Park 50
Bahamas: multiplier factor 92; tourist numbers 134
Baltimore (Md.) 140, 141
Banff National Park 41–2, 50, 64
Barbados Island 125
Barbican Centre, London 108
Bath (NC) 145
Beamish (England) 129, 146
Beaulieu (England) 148
Blue Ridge Parkway 41
Boundary Waters Canoe Area (Minn.) 46, 65
Brighton (England) 84, 87
Britain: national parks 60, 69; second homes 111

British Columbia: environment management 157; Indian culture exploitation 137; TIDSA program 95–6, 97, 158
Bude (England) 156
bus services 71, 76
business travel 5, 9

Cairngorms National Park 64
California recreational subdivisions 114
camping and campsites 25, 65
Canada: multiplier factor 92; second homes 110, 111, 112; tourism surveys 123; tourist numbers 85, 134
Canadian national parks, 41, 49, 50, 60, 68
Canadian Tourism Sector Task Force 165
canal redevelopment 52
Cape Cod (Mass.) tourism survey 121, 123
capital investment, role in tourism of 10, 13
Capricorn Coast (Australia) 66–7
caravans 114
Caribbean area: multiplier factors 92, 103; tourist numbers 85
Carlsbad Caverns National Park 50
carrying capacity: physical 64–7; social 134–9
Catskill Mountains 18, 19
Cedar Point (Ohio) 84
Central America tourist numbers 85
chalet summer homes 110
China 169
circular notes 19
circular routes 54
Clwyd Country Park (Wales) 61
coastal erosion 44
coastal zone management 174
cognitive–normative tourist models 6, 7
Colorado recreational subdivisions 114
community–tourist interaction: attitudes to tourist 120–4; improvement 135–9; planning 37–8, 165, 171–2; tolerance thresholds 124–6

complementarity concept 52
condominiums 110
consolidation stage of resort evolution 86
conventions: growth 104–6; requirements 106;
    revenue–expenditure ratio 106–8
Cook Islands 144
Cornwall (England) tourist attractions and resulting pressures
    47, 75–6, 111, 137
Corpus Christi (Tex.) tourism survey 123, 125
cost–benefit ratio 103
cost of travel, changes in 20
country parks 61
Countryside Act (1968) 69
covert tourist space 128, 130
Crater Lake National Park 50
Cromer (England) tourist revenue 44
Crown Jewels display 76
cruise ships 52
cultural attractions authentic and stage-managed 149–51;
    preservation 145–6; protection 137
cultural drift theory 149–51
cultural motivators 10
currency fluctuation 84
cycles of demand: long-term 84–9; medium-term 81–4;
    short-term 79–81

day-tripper 5
decline stage of resort evolution 86
demand for tourism: cyclical pattern, long-term 84–9, medium-
    term 81–4, short-term 79–81; factors affecting 10–11
demographic effects 27, 81
demonstration effect 119, 133
destination area defined 7–8
destination image defined 11–12
Detroit Boat Show 104
Development of Tourism Act (1969) 33
development stage of resort evolution 86
development zones 163
Devon (England) 111, 156
Disney World 52, 99, 169–70
Disneyland 142, 159, 163
domestic tourism 3, 8
dune management 44–5

East Anglia (England) multiplier factor 92
Eastbourne (England) 84
ecological models in tourism: planning 166–71, 172–3; practice
    173–6
Ecological Reserves Act (BC; 1971) 61
economic effects; benefits 32, 89–90, 95; costs 32, 99–102;
    measurement, multiplier concept 90–3; input–output model
    93–5

Ely (Mont.) multiplier factor 92
employment 4, 95–9
England: farm tourism 108; multiplier factor for southwest 92;
    tourism surveys 123
environmental degradation 32, 43, 44–5, 64–7
environmental perception, analysis of 55–9
Europe tourist numbers 85
Everest, Mount 32
Everglades National Park 50
evolutionary cycles of resorts 86–9
excursionist 5
Exmoor National Park 98
expenditure levels compared 89–90
exploration stage of resort evolution 86
export incomes from tourism 4

facilities for tourist: concentration policy 140–2; dispersion
    policy 142–4
fantasy motivators 10–11
farm tourism 108–10
Federal Republic of Germany farm tourism 108
festivals 104
Finland farm tourism 108
fire incidents, tourist related 100
Florida recreational subdivisions 114, 115
Florillan National Park 50
forestry-tourism management, 50, 63–4
Fort Steele (BC) 146, 147
France: farm tourism 108, 109; second homes 111; examples of
    farm tourism 23
Fundy National Park 50

Galveston (Tex.) 90
Gateway National Recreation Area 61
Gatlinburg (Tenn.) 41
Glacier National Park 50
goals in tourism planning: ecological analogy 166–71;
    identification 156–9; implementation 159–63
governmental role 33–6, 163
Gower Peninsula (Wales) 61, 73–4, 174
Goyt Valley (England) traffic scheme 73
Gozo 119
Grand Canyon National Park 49, 50
Grand Tour 17
Grasslands National Park 51
Great Smoky Mountains National Park 41, 50, 135
Great Yarmouth (England) 44, 100, 102
Greater Tayside 90, 92
Greece 92
Grenoble (France) 65
Gros Morne National Park 50
growth of tourism, factors affecting: ability 24–5; mobility 25–6;
    motivation 21–4; past growth 3, 17–21; predicted growth
    26–9

Subject index

Gwynedd (Wales) 92, 111

Hampton Court Palace 142, 143
Harkers Island (NC) 145
Harrogate (England) 86
Hatfield (England) 142, 143
Hawaii tourism: economic effects 84, 92, 99; social effects 119–20, 130
Hawaii Volcanoes National Park 50
Hazelton (BC) 137
Heathrow airport 106, 142
Heber Valley (Utah) 165
heritage trails and parks 70–1, 140
Herriot's country 148
historic buildings 148
holiday flats 110
honeypot distractions 61, 67
hotel industry 28, 132

income leakage 31, 90, 91
infrastructure requirements 13, 81, 100–2
input–output economic model 93–5
interactional tourist model 5, 6
International Bureau of Social Tourism (BITS) 24
international tourist numbers 3, 85
intervening opportunity region 52
investment return effects 169
involvement stage of resort evolution 86
Ireland: farm tourism 108; multiplier factor 92
Ironbridge (England) 129
irridex model 124–5
irritations to community: analysis 122, 124–6; identification 120–2, 123
Isle of Man 18

Jasper National Park 50
Jersey 174
jet-age travel 19, 25–6
journeys compared 20

Kampgrounds of America (KOA) 25
Kimberley (BC) 130, 138, 139
Kluane National Park 50, 51, 71
Knebworth Country Park (England) 62
Kootenay National Park 50

La Mauricie National Park 50

La Rochelle (France) 131
Laie Polynesian Cultural Center 146
Lake District (England) 109–10, 123
Lancaster County (Pa.) 130, 145–6
Land Between the Lakes (Tenn.) 68
Land's End (England) 47
language preservation 132–3
Languedoc–Roussillon project 34, 35, 87, 176
leisure activities 5, 9
Les Mielles (Channel Islands) 174
Llanberis Country Park (Wales) 61
Llandudno (Wales) 18
load factors 80
Local Government Act (1972) 69
London (England) attractions 76, 108, 140, 142, 143, 174; tourist numbers 79, 80
Long Beach (Calif.) 142
Lowell (Mass.) 140
Lowestoft (England) 44

Maine 90
Mammoth Cave National Park 50
management planning 163
Manitoba TIDSA agreement 158
Margate (England) 18
master plans, strengths and weaknesses of 159–60, 161, 162
Mediterranean, the 34, 35, 175–6
memorabilia 55
Mexico 85, 92
Miami Beach (Fla.) 52, 86
Missouri recreational subdivisions 114
mobility factors, 20, 22, 25–6
monuments 148
motivations for tourism 10–11, 21–4
Mount McKinley National Park 73
multiple resource management 68–70
multiplier coefficients 95
multiplier concept: description 90–2; measurement 92–3

Nanaimo (BC) 130
National Military Park 47
National Motor Museum 148
national parks classification 60–2
National Parks Policies Review Committee 34
National Tourism Policy Act (1981) 33, 156
natural environment zone 62
New Brighton (England) 18
New Brunswick TIDSA agreement 158
New Forest (England) 66–8
New Hampshire multiplier factor 92
New Mexico recreational subdivisions 114